*New Beacon Bible Commentary

1 CORINTHIANS
A Commentary in the Wesleyan Tradition

Alex R. G. Deasley

BEACON HILL PRESS
OF KANSAS CITY

Copyright 2021
by Beacon Hill Press of Kansas City

Beacon Hill Press of Kansas City
PO Box 419527
Kansas City, MO 64141
www.BeaconHillBooks.com

ISBN 978-0-8341-3940-4

All rights reserved. No part of this publication may be reproduced, stored in a retrieval system, or transmitted in any form or by any means—for example, electronic, photocopy, recording—without the prior written permission of the publisher. The only exception is brief quotations in printed reviews.

Cover Design: J.R. Caines
Interior Design: Sharon Page

Unless otherwise indicated, all Scripture quotations are from the Holy Bible, New International Version® (NIV®). Copyright © 1973, 1978, 1984, 2011 by Biblica, Inc.™ Used by permission of Zondervan. All rights reserved worldwide. www.zondervan.com. *Emphasis indicated by underlining in boldface quotations and italic in lightface quotations.*

The following version of Scripture is in the public domain:
King James Version (KJV)

The following copyrighted versions of Scripture are used by permission:

THE MESSAGE (MSG), copyright © 1993, 2002, 2018 by Eugene H. Peterson. Used by permission of NavPress. All rights reserved. Represented by Tyndale House Publishers, a Division of Tyndale House Ministries.

The New American Standard Bible® (NASB®), copyright © 1960, 1962, 1963, 1968, 1971, 1972, 1973, 1975, 1977, 1995 by The Lockman Foundation. www.Lockman.org.

The New English Bible (NEB), copyright © Cambridge University Press and Oxford University Press 1961, 1970. All rights reserved.

The New Jerusalem Bible (NJB), copyright © 1985 by Darton, Longman & Todd, Ltd. and Doubleday, a division of Random House, Inc. Reprinted by permission.

The New Revised Standard Version Bible (NRSV), copyright © 1989 National Council of the Churches of Christ in the United States of America. All rights reserved. *Emphasis indicated by italic.*

The Revised English Bible (REB), copyright © Cambridge University Press and Oxford University Press 1989. All rights reserved.

The Revised Standard Version (RSV) of the Bible, copyright © 1946, 1952, and 1971 by the Division of Christian Education of the National Council of the Churches of Christ in the United States of America. All rights reserved worldwide.

Library of Congress Cataloging-in-Publication Data

Names: Deasley, Alex R. G., author.
Title: 1 Corinthians / Alex R.G. Deasley.
Description: Kansas City, MO : Beacon Hill Press of Kansas City, [2021] | Series: New Beacon Bible commentary | Includes bibliographical references.
Identifiers: LCCN 2020038694 (print) | LCCN 2020038695 (ebook) | ISBN 9780834139404 (paperback) | ISBN 9780834139411 (ebook)
Subjects: LCSH: Bible. Corinthians, 1st—Commentaries.
Classification: LCC BS2675.3 .D43 2021 (print) | LCC BS2675.53 (ebook) | DDC 227/.207—dc23
LC record available at https://lccn.loc.gov/2020038694
LC ebook record available at https://lccn.loc.gov/2020038695

The Internet addresses, email addresses, and phone numbers in this book are accurate at the time of publication. They are provided as a resource. Beacon Hill Press of Kansas City does not endorse them or vouch for their content or permanence.

DEDICATION

To the Memory of My Father,
Robert Gibson Deasley (1900-1975),
A Minister of the Word
"He was a good man, full of the Holy Spirit and faith" (Acts 11:24).

COMMENTARY EDITORS

General Editors

Alex Varughese
    Ph.D., Drew University
    Professor Emeritus of Biblical
        Literature
    Mount Vernon Nazarene University
    Mount Vernon, Ohio

George Lyons
    Ph.D., Emory University
    Professor Emeritus of New Testament
    Northwest Nazarene University
    Nampa, Idaho

Section Editors

Robert Branson
    Ph.D., Boston University
    Professor Emeritus of Biblical
        Literature
    Olivet Nazarene University
    Bourbonnais, Illinois

Alex Varughese
    Ph.D., Drew University
    Professor Emeritus of Biblical
        Literature
    Mount Vernon Nazarene University
    Mount Vernon, Ohio

Kent Brower
    Ph.D., The University of Manchester
    Vice Principal
    Senior Lecturer in Biblical Studies
    Nazarene Theological College
    Manchester, England

George Lyons
    Ph.D., Emory University
    Professor Emeritus of New Testament
    Northwest Nazarene University
    Nampa, Idaho

CONTENTS

General Editors' Preface	9
Special Acknowledgments	13
Acknowledgments	15
Abbreviations	17
Bibliography	21
Table of Sidebars	30

INTRODUCTION — 31
    Prologue — 31
    A. The Corinthian Setting — 32
    B. The Occasion of the Letter — 33
    C. The Literary Character of the Letter — 33
    D. The Structure of the Letter — 35
    E. The Theological Focus of the Letter — 39

COMMENTARY — 43
    I. LETTER INTRODUCTION: I CORINTHIANS 1:1-9 — 43
        A. The Greeting (1:1-3) — 43
        B. The Thanksgiving (1:4-9) — 47
    II. THE GOSPEL AND DIVISIONS IN THE CHURCH:
    THE MESSAGE OF THE WISDOM OF THE CROSS:
    I CORINTHIANS 1:10—4:21 — 51
        A. The Problem of Divisions in the Corinthian Church (1:10-17) — 52
        B. The Gospel versus Wisdom (1:18—2:5) — 56
            1. The Message of the Cross as the True Wisdom (1:18-25) — 57
            2. The Composition of the Corinthian Church as Confirmation of the True Wisdom (1:26-31) — 61
            3. Paul's Ministry in Corinth as an Example of the True Wisdom (2:1-5) — 64
        C. Worldly Wisdom versus the Wisdom Revealed by the Spirit (2:6—3:4) — 66
            1. Wisdom: The False and the True (2:6-16) — 67
            2. Perfection: The False and the True (3:1-4) — 71
        D. The Folly of the Corinthians' Wisdom (3:5-23) — 74

1. The Folly of the Corinthians' "Wisdom" Demonstrated by the Subsidiary Role of Paul and Apollos as Servants of God (3:5-9) — 74
2. The Folly of the Corinthians' "Wisdom" Shown by the Security of the Foundation, Which Is Christ Alone (3:10-15) — 76
3. The Folly of the Corinthians' "Wisdom" Shown by the Danger It Poses to the Temple of God (3:16-17) — 77
4. The Folly of the Corinthians' "Wisdom" Shown by the Deceitfulness of Worldly Wisdom (3:18-23) — 78
- E. Paul's Apostleship as Exemplifying True Wisdom (4:1-21) — 80
  1. God's Verdict as the Verdict That Counts (4:1-5) — 81
  2. The Folly of Judging by Appearances (4:6-13) — 83
  3. Paul's Fatherly Affection for the Corinthians (4:14-17) — 86
  4. Paul's Forthcoming Visit to Corinth (4:18-21) — 87

III. THE GOSPEL AND MORAL FAILURE IN THE CHURCH: THE SUMMONS TO HOLINESS OF LIFE: I CORINTHIANS 5:1—6:20 — 91
- A. The Problem of Fornication (5:1-13) — 93
  1. Corinthian Toleration of Fornication Denounced (5:1-5) — 93
  2. The Danger to the Church (5:6-8) — 95
  3. A Clarification and a Command (5:9-13) — 97
- B. The Problem of Lawsuits (6:1-11) — 100
- C. The Problem of Sexual Immorality (6:12-20) — 105

IV. THE GOSPEL AND HOLY LIVING IN A PAGAN SOCIETY: I CORINTHIANS 7:1—11:1 — 113
- A. Christian Married Life in a Non-Christian Culture (7:1-40) — 114
  1. Christian Married Relationships (7:1-16) — 118
     a. The Place of Sex within Christian Marriage (7:1-7) — 119
     b. Advice to Widowers and Widows (7:8-9) — 122
     c. Directions Regarding Divorce (7:10-11) — 122
     d. Instruction to Those Married to Non-Christians (7:12-16) — 124
  2. The Underlying Principle: Remain as You Are (7:17-24) — 127
  3. The Question of Those Engaged but Not Yet Married (7:25-38) — 132
     a. The Options Open to Betrothed Persons and Paul's Recommendation (7:25-28) — 134
     b. The Pressures of the Present Eschatological Situation (7:29-31) — 135
     c. The Claims of the Service of the Lord (7:32-35) — 137
     d. Further Advice to the Engaged (7:36-38) — 139
  4. The Question of Widows and Remarriage (7:39-40) — 140
- B. Christian Freedom and Meat Offered to Idols (8:1—11:1) — 142
  1. Meat Offered to Idols (8:1-13) — 146
     a. What the Corinthians Thought They Knew but Did Not Know (8:1-3) — 146

	b. What the Corinthians Knew and Thought Everyone Knew (8:4-7)	147
	c. What the Corinthians Did Not Know about the Effect of Their Knowledge on Others (8:8-13)	149
2.	Paul's Rights as an Apostle and His Freedom in Using Them (9:1-27)	152
	a. Paul's Right as an Apostle to Receive Support (9:1-14)	154
	b. Paul's Refusal to Use His Rights (9:15-18)	156
	c. How Paul Uses His Freedom (9:19-23)	158
	d. The Need for Self-Discipline in the Exercise of Freedom (9:24-27)	160
3.	Meat Offered to Idols and the Exercise of Christian Freedom (10:1—11:1)	163
	a. The Danger of Idolatry (10:1-22)	163
	(1) Warnings from Israel's History (10:1-13)	163
	(2) The Incompatibility of the Lord's Table and the Table of Idols (10:14-22)	168
	b. The Touchstones of Freedom: The Good of One's Neighbor and the Glory of God (10:23—11:1)	171

V. THE GOSPEL AND PROPRIETY IN CHRISTIAN WORSHIP: I CORINTHIANS 11:2—14:40 — 177

A. Covering the Head in Worship (11:2-16) — 178
B. Conduct at the Lord's Supper: Worship That Makes Things Worse (11:17-34) — 183
C. Spiritual Gifts and Their Place in Worship (12:1—14:40) — 188
  1. The Lordship of Christ as the Touchstone of the Gifts (12:1-3) — 189
  2. The Varied Gifts as Given by the One Spirit (12:4-11) — 189
     a. The Fundamental Principle (12:4-6) — 190
     b. Some Individual Gifts (12:7-11) — 190
  3. The Varied Gifts for the One Body (12:12-31) — 192
     a. Diversity and Unity in the Human Body and the Body of Christ (12:12-14) — 193
     b. The Need of the Body for a Variety of Members (12:15-20) — 195
     c. The Need of Each Member for All the Others (12:21-26) — 195
     d. The Varied Gifts and Their Various Recipients (12:27-31) — 196
  4. Love as the Controlling Principle of the Use of the Gifts (13:1-13) — 199
     a. The Worthlessness of the Gifts without Love (13:1-3) — 200
     b. How Love Acts and Does Not Act (13:4-7) — 201
     c. The Permanence of Love (13:8-13) — 202
  5. In Worship Intelligibility and Order Are Preferable to Unintelligibility and Disorder (14:1-40) — 205
     a. Prophecy as Being of Greater Value than Tongues (14:1-5) — 207
     b. Meaning as More Important than Mode of Delivery (14:6-12) — 208
     c. The Place of the Mind in Worship and Its Implications (14:13-25) — 209

	d. Practical Guidelines (14:26-35)	213
	(1) Regarding the Exercise of the Gift of Tongues (14:26-28)	213
	(2) Regarding the Exercise of the Gift of Prophecy (14:29-33)	214
	(3) Regarding the Conduct of Women in Worship (14:34-35)	215
	e. Summary Conclusions and Advices (14:36-40)	215

VI. THE GOSPEL AND THE CHRISTIAN FUTURE: THE MESSAGE OF THE RESURRECTION: I CORINTHIANS 15:1-58 — 221

    A. The Resurrection of Christ as Central to the Gospel (15:1-34) — 223
        1. The Resurrection as Central in the Apostolic Kerygma (15:1-11) — 223
        2. The Denial of the Resurrection as Fatal to the Gospel (15:12-19) — 228
        3. The Resurrection of the Dead as Fundamental to the Final Triumph of God (15:20-28) — 230
        4. Some Personal Implications of the Denial of the Resurrection (15:29-34) — 234
    B. The Nature of the Resurrection Body (15:35-58) — 237
        1. The Character of the Resurrection Body as Suggested by Nature (15:35-44) — 238
        2. The Character of the Resurrection Body as Indicated by the Contrast Between Adam and Christ (15:45-49) — 240
        3. The Necessity for the Transformation of the Earthly Body (15:50-58) — 241

VII. REMAINING ISSUES AND FINAL GREETINGS: I CORINTHIANS 16:1-24 — 247

    A. The Collection for the Church in Jerusalem (16:1-4) — 248
    B. Paul's Forthcoming Travel Plans (16:5-9) — 250
    C. Two Other Visitors to Corinth: Timothy and Apollos (16:10-12) — 250
    D. The Need for Stability in the Corinthian Church and the Role of Stephanas (16:13-18) — 251
    E. Final Greetings (16:19-24) — 253

GENERAL EDITORS' PREFACE

The purpose of the New Beacon Bible Commentary is to make available to pastors and students in the twenty-first century a biblical commentary that reflects the best scholarship in the Wesleyan theological tradition. The commentary project aims to make this scholarship accessible to a wider audience to assist them in their understanding and proclamation of Scripture as God's Word.

Writers of the volumes in this series not only are scholars within the Wesleyan theological tradition and experts in their field but also have special interest in the books assigned to them. Their task is to communicate clearly the critical consensus and the full range of other credible voices who have commented on the Scriptures. Though scholarship and scholarly contribution to the understanding of the Scriptures are key concerns of this series, it is not intended as an academic dialogue within the scholarly community. Commentators of this series constantly aim to demonstrate in their work the significance of the Bible as the church's book and the contemporary relevance and application of the biblical message. The project's overall goal is to make available to the church and for her service the fruits of the labors of scholars who are committed to their Christian faith.

The *New International Version* (NIV) is the reference version of the Bible used in this series; however, the focus of exegetical study and comments is the biblical text in its original language. When the commentary uses the NIV, it is printed in bold. The text printed in bold italics is the translation of the author. Commentators also refer to other translations where the text may be difficult or ambiguous.

The structure and organization of the commentaries in this series seeks to facilitate the study of the biblical text in a systematic and methodical way. Study of each biblical book begins with an **Introduction** section that gives an overview of authorship, date, provenance, audience, occasion, purpose, sociological/cultural issues, textual history, literary features, hermeneutical issues, and theological themes necessary to understand the book. This section also includes a brief outline of the book and a list of general works and standard commentaries.

The commentary section for each biblical book follows the outline of the book presented in the introduction. In some volumes, readers will find section ***overviews*** of large portions of scripture with general comments on their overall literary structure and other literary features. A consistent feature of the commentary is the paragraph-by-paragraph study of biblical texts. This section has three parts: **Behind the Text**, **In the Text**, and **From the Text**.

The goal of the **Behind the Text** section is to provide the reader with all the relevant information necessary to understand the text. This includes specific historical situations reflected in the text, the literary context of the text, sociological and cultural issues, and literary features of the text.

In the Text explores what the text says, following its verse-by-verse structure. This section includes a discussion of grammatical details, word studies, and the connectedness of the text to other biblical books/passages or other parts of the book being studied (the canonical relationship). This section provides transliterations of key words in Hebrew and Greek and their literal meanings. The goal here is to explain what the author would have meant and/or what the audience would have understood as the meaning of the text. This is the largest section of the commentary.

The **From the Text** section examines the text in relation to the following areas: theological significance, intertextuality, the history of interpretation, use of the Old Testament scriptures in the New Testament, interpretation in later church history, actualization, and application.

The commentary provides ***sidebars*** on topics of interest that are important but not necessarily part of an explanation of the biblical text. These topics are informational items and may cover archaeological, historical, literary, cultural, and theological matters that have relevance to the biblical text. Occasionally, longer detailed discussions of special topics are included as ***excursuses.***

We offer this series with our hope and prayer that readers will find it a valuable resource for their understanding of God's Word and an indispensable tool for their critical engagement with the biblical texts.

Roger Hahn, Centennial Initiative General Editor
Alex Varughese, General Editor (Old Testament)
George Lyons, General Editor (New Testament)

Paul may have been influenced this feature from the oratorical style / rhetoric of contemporary orators (Witherington 1995, 264-5). At the same time his argument with the Corinthians is continued. The chapter is not so much about the evaluation of

4. Love as the Controlling Principle of the Use of the Gifts 13:1-13

BEHIND THE TEXT

☐ spiritual gifts than a poem extolling love (Fee 2014, 604 n 291); however, it

☐ The primary purpose of the chapter is the evaluation of spiritual gifts, but it does this by extolling the surpassing value of love.

1. 1 Cor 13 stands out in chs 12-14 (and indeed, in the letter as a whole) as unsurpassed a penetrating and eloquent exposition of the meaning of Christian love for its literary eloquence and style. For this reason it has sometimes been regarded as an independent composition (a poem or encomium) written by Paul on another occasion but called into service here. However, the contents of the chapter fit the Corinthian situation so well: the prior place given to the gifts of tongues and prophecy (vv 1-2, 8), not to mention the overriding need for love, that it would be remarkable if a casual or occasional piece of writing could address the need so perfectly. The suggestion that if ch 13 was composed previously it was with the Corinthian situation in mind (Thiselton 2000, 1029) comes close to being a distinction without a difference. Paul had thought long and deeply about love before (1 Thess 1:3; Rom 3:?, 12). It would not strain his powers as a writer to express himself with the elevation and incisiveness exhibited here. Moreover, the argument

2. In keeping with the foregoing the aspect of love which is emphasized is the ethical. The contentiousness stirred by the exhibitionist exaggerated display of the gifts is to be eliminated by the sea solvent of love. Love is set forth as being intrinsically superior to the gifts (vv 1-3). In moral context it embodies every honorable quality, attitude and activity (vv 4-7). While the gifts carry within themselves the seeds of their own decay love will continue as belonging to the eternal sphere (vv 8-13). Without love the exercise of the gifts is empty exhibitionism. Love does not merely embody every positive moral quality; it enacts them in the pressures and stresses

SPECIAL ACKNOWLEDGMENTS

On the facing page, you will see the handwritten copy of the first few verses of 1 Corinthians 13, just as Dr. Alex Deasley submitted it. I can think of no more fitting representation of this final volume—indeed of the whole forty-seven-volume New Beacon Bible Commentary—than Dr. Deasley's labor of love as he painstakingly wrote in longhand the content of the entire commentary on 1 Corinthians.

The handwriting took Dr. Deasley thirteen years; 1 Corinthians was one of the first volumes to be assigned, when the NBBC was conceived. Dr. Deasley's faithfulness mirrors the efforts of many writers, editors, and administrators who we are privileged to recognize here.

The Centennial Textbook Initiative of the Church of the Nazarene was launched in 1999 by proclamation of the Board of General Superintendents. Four years later, Nazarene Publishing House released the first college text in the initiative, *Discovering the Old Testament*. Other texts quickly followed: *Discovering the New Testament*, *Discovering the Bible*, and ultimately a host of other titles.

In early 2000, the dream of an even more ambitious project began to surface: a new commentary for the Wesleyan-Holiness tradition. The original Beacon Bible Commentary was published in the 1960s—the first of ten volumes (Matthew, Mark, Luke) was copyrighted in 1964. In the ensuing years, the denomination had nearly given up on creating a replacement commentary set—leadership agreed that a theological consensus would just be too hard to reach. In 2001, the decision was made to resume a dialogue to determine whether such a challenging undertaking was possible.

By 2003, the decision was made to move forward. Five years later, in 2008, the first volume (*Romans 1-8*, by Dr. William Greathouse, with George Lyons) of the New Beacon Bible Commentary was released. In 2021, only thirteen years later, you hold in your hands the forty-seventh and final volume, *1 Corinthians*.

The release of the NBBC, an unprecedented accomplishment in the given time frame, was made possible by the leadership and commitment of a great tribe of passionate and accomplished persons who supported the writers of each volume.

Centennial Initiative and NBBC General Editor
  Alex Varughese, without whom the NBBC would not exist

Special Consultant
  Roger Hahn, who conceptualized the literary framework: Behind the Text, In the Text, and From the Text

Section Editors
  Alex Varughese: Pentateuch (Genesis, Exodus, Leviticus, Numbers, Deuteronomy), Prophets (Isaiah, Jeremiah, Ezekiel, Hosea-Micah, Nahum-Malachi), Daniel, Ecclesiastes-Lamentations, Ezra-Nehemiah, 1 and 2 Chronicles, and Ruth-Esther-Songs
  Robert Branson: Historical Books (Joshua, Judges, 1 and 2 Samuel, 1 and 2 Kings), Wisdom Books (Job, Proverbs), and Psalms
  Kent Brower: Gospels (Matthew, Mark, Luke) and Acts
  George Lyons: John, all the Letters of Paul except 1 Corinthians, all the General Letters, and Revelation

Beacon Hill Press Editors
  Richard Buckner, managing editor
  Kathy Baker, copy editor

Support Staff
  Lynda Mullins
  Rene McFarland
  Darl McCready
  Sharon Page, graphic designer

Administrative Leadership
  C. Hardy Weathers: NPH President (1998—2012)
  Mark D. Brown: NPH President (2014-present)

To those named here, and to all who support them in their lives and ministry, the Church of the Nazarene and the larger Wesleyan-Holiness tradition gives thanks.

May the work of your hands be a living and holy sacrifice, a fragrant aroma that is pleasing to our Lord and Savior, Jesus Christ.

Bonnie Perry
Editorial Director
The Foundry Publishing

ACKNOWLEDGMENTS

My first debt is to the editors of the New Beacon Bible Commentary for inviting me to write this commentary, and for all the ancillary help from Beacon Hill Press. George Lyons gave invaluable assistance during the early stages of the process. Bonnie Perry has been an accomplished, tireless, and patient guide throughout.

I owe a special debt to the library of the Nazarene Theological Seminary in Kansas City. In particular I am indebted to the librarian, Debbie Bradshaw, who not only secured books for me from far and wide but went many more miles than the second by frequently delivering these books to my door.

Limited facility on my part with the word processor has been more than compensated for by the expertise of others who have triumphed over the obscurities and individualisms of my handwriting. The earliest chapters were processed by my late wife, Joyce, who indeed had typed or processed everything I have ever published. Following her incapacitation Rene McFarland of Beacon Hill Press took up the task, succeeding to the point of being able to decipher hieroglyphics that defeated their creator. My son Richard was also a steady source of assistance, in some cases saving me from near disaster.

The book is dedicated to my father. Denied an advanced education himself, he determined that I should have what he never had. Some of the risks he took to ensure it can still make my hair stand on end.

My debts to scholars who have trodden these Corinthian paths are enormous; they are at least partially indicated in the bibliography. First Corinthians is a challenge to any exegete, and I readily forswear any claim to having unlocked all of its secrets. But I hope I have grasped something of "what makes it tick." I hope I have succeeded also in suggesting some of the ways in which the epistle speaks to the mission of the church today.

ABBREVIATIONS

With a few exceptions, these abbreviations follow those in *The SBL Handbook of Style* (Alexander 1999).

General

→	see the commentary at
AD	Anno Domini (precedes date) (equivalent to CE)
BC	before Christ (follows date) (equivalent to BCE)
ch(s)	chapter(s)
e.g.	for example
ET	English translation
etc.	et cetera, and the rest
f(f).	and the following one(s)
Gk.	Greek
Heb.	Hebrew
ibid.	*ibidem*, in the same place
i.e.	*id est.*, that is
Lat.	Latin
lit.	literally
LXX	Septuagint
mg.	margin
MT	Masoretic Text (of the OT)
n.	note
no.	number
NT	New Testament
OT	Old Testament
passim	here and there
repr.	reprint(ed)
s.v.	*sub verbo*, under the word
v(v)	verse(s)

Modern English Versions

KJV	King James Version
MSG	The Message: The Bible in Contemporary Language
NASB	New American Standard Bible
NEB	New English Bible
NIV	New International Version
NJB	New Jerusalem Bible
NRSV	New Revised Standard Version
REB	Revised English Bible
RSV	Revised Standard Version

Print Conventions for Translations

Bold font	NIV (bold without quotation marks in the text under study; elsewhere in the regular font, with quotation marks and no further identification)
Bold italic font	Author's translation (without quotation marks)

Behind the Text: Literary or historical background information average readers might not know from reading the biblical text alone

In the Text: Comments on the biblical text, words, phrases, grammar, and so forth

From the Text: The use of the text by later interpreters, contemporary relevance, theological and ethical implications of the text, with particular emphasis on Wesleyan concerns

Ancient Sources

Old Testament

Gen	Genesis	Dan	Daniel		
Exod	Exodus	Hos	Hosea		
Lev	Leviticus	Joel	Joel		
Num	Numbers	Amos	Amos		
Deut	Deuteronomy	Obad	Obadiah		
Josh	Joshua	Jonah	Jonah		
Judg	Judges	Mic	Micah		
Ruth	Ruth	Nah	Nahum		
1—2 Sam	1—2 Samuel	Hab	Habakkuk		
1—2 Kgs	1—2 Kings	Zeph	Zephaniah		
1—2 Chr	1—2 Chronicles	Hag	Haggai		
Ezra	Ezra	Zech	Zechariah		
Neh	Nehemiah	Mal	Malachi		
Esth	Esther				
Job	Job				
Ps/Pss	Psalm/Psalms				
Prov	Proverbs				
Eccl	Ecclesiastes				
Song	Song of Songs/Song of Solomon				
Isa	Isaiah				
Jer	Jeremiah				
Lam	Lamentations				
Ezek	Ezekiel				

(Note: Chapter and verse numbering in the MT and LXX often differ compared to those in English Bibles. To avoid confusion, all biblical references follow the chapter and verse numbering in English translations, even when the text in the MT and LXX is under discussion.)

New Testament

Matt	Matthew
Mark	Mark
Luke	Luke
John	John
Acts	Acts
Rom	Romans
1—2 Cor	1—2 Corinthians
Gal	Galatians
Eph	Ephesians
Phil	Philippians
Col	Colossians
1—2 Thess	1—2 Thessalonians
1—2 Tim	1—2 Timothy
Titus	Titus
Phlm	Philemon
Heb	Hebrews
Jas	James
1—2 Pet	1—2 Peter
1—2—3 John	1—2—3 John
Jude	Jude
Rev	Revelation

Apocrypha

Bar	Baruch
Add Dan	Additions to Daniel
Pr Azar	Prayer of Azariah
Bel	Bel and the Dragon
Sg Three	Song of the Three Young Men
Sus	Susanna
1—2 Esd	1—2 Esdras
Add Esth	Additions to Esther
Ep Jer	Epistle of Jeremiah
Jdt	Judith
1—2 Macc	1—2 Maccabees
3—4 Macc	3—4 Maccabees
Pr Man	Prayer of Manasseh
Ps 151	Psalm 151
Sir	Sirach/Ecclesiasticus
Tob	Tobit
Wis	Wisdom of Solomon

Old Testament Pseudepigrapha

1 En.	*1 Enoch*
2 En.	*2 Enoch*
T. Job	*Testament of Job*

Dead Sea Scrolls

1QS	*Serek Hayaḥad* or *Rule of the Community*
4Q400-407	*Songs of the Sabbath Sacrifice*

Aristotle

Rhet.	*Art of Rhetoric*

Cicero

Clu.	*Pro Cluentio*

Josephus

Ag. Ap.	*Against Apion*

Secondary Sources

ABD	*Anchor Bible Dictionary* (see Freedman)
ACCS	Ancient Christian Commentary on Scripture (see Bray)
ANTC	Abingdon New Testament Commentaries
AYB	Anchor Yale Bible
BAGD	*A Greek-English Lexicon of the New Testament and Other Early Christian Literature*, 2nd ed. (see Bauer, Arndt, Gingrich, and Danker)
BBR	*Bulletin for Biblical Research*
BDAG	*A Greek-English Lexicon of the New Testament and Other Early Christian Literature*, 3rd ed. (see Bauer, Danker, Arndt, and Gingrich)
BDF	*A Greek Grammar of the New Testament and Other Early Christian Literature* (see Blass, Debrunner, and Funk)
BECNT	Baker Exegetical Commentary on the New Testament
CCBI	*The Cambridge Companion to Biblical Interpretation* (see Barton)
DLNT	*Dictionary of the Later New Testament and Its Developments* (see Martin and Davids)
DPL	*Dictionary of Paul and His Letters* (see Gerald F. Hawthorne, et al.)
DThIB	*Dictionary for Theological Interpretation of the Bible* (see Vanhoozer)
EDNT	*Exegetical Dictionary of the New Testament* (see Balz and Schneider)
HNTC	Harpers New Testament Commentaries
IBC	Interpretation: A Bible Commentary for Teaching and Preaching (see Hays)
Int	*Interpretation*
JBL	*Journal of Biblical Literature*
JSNT	*Journal for the Study of the New Testament*
JSNTSup	Journal for the Study of the New Testament Supplement Series
MM	*The Vocabulary of the Greek Testament* (see Moulton and Milligan)
NBBC	New Beacon Bible Commentary
NCB	New Century Bible
NCBC	New Cambridge Bible Commentary
NDBT	*New Dictionary of Biblical Theology* (see Alexander and Rosner)
NICNT	New International Commentary on the New Testament
NIDB	*New Interpreter's Dictionary of the Bible* (see Sakenfeld)
NIDNTT	*New International Dictionary of New Testament Theology* (see Brown)
NIDNTTE	*New International Dictionary of New Testament Theology and Exegesis*, 2nd ed. (see Silva)
NIGTC	New International Greek Testament Commentary
NTS	*New Testament Studies*
SP	Sacra Pagina
TCGNT	*A Textual Commentary on the Greek New Testament* (see Metzger)
TDNT	*Theological Dictionary of the New Testament* (see Kittel and Friedrich)
UBS[4]	*The Greek New Testament*, United Bible Societies, 4th ed.
WBC	Word Biblical Commentary
WUNT	Wissenschlaftliche Untersuchungen zum Neuen Testament
ZECNT	Zondervan Exegetical Commentary on the New Testament

Greek Transliteration

Greek	Letter	English
α	alpha	a
β	bēta	b
γ	gamma	g
γ	gamma nasal	n (before γ, κ, ξ, χ)
δ	delta	d
ε	epsilon	e
ζ	zēta	z
η	ēta	ē
θ	thēta	th
ι	iōta	i
κ	kappa	k
λ	lambda	l
μ	mu	m
ν	nu	n
ξ	xi	x
ο	omicron	o
π	pi	p
ρ	rhō	r
ρ	initial rhō	rh
σ/ς	sigma	s
τ	tau	t
υ	upsilon	y
υ	upsilon	u (in diphthongs: au, eu, ēu, ou, ui)
φ	phi	ph
χ	chi	ch
ψ	psi	ps
ω	ōmega	ō
‛	rough breathing	h (before initial vowels or diphthongs)

Hebrew Consonant Transliteration

Hebrew/Aramaic	Letter	English
א	alef	ʼ
ב	bet	b
ג	gimel	g
ד	dalet	d
ה	he	h
ו	vav	v or w
ז	zayin	z
ח	khet	ḥ
ט	tet	ṭ
י	yod	y
כ/ך	kaf	k
ל	lamed	l
מ/ם	mem	m
נ/ן	nun	n
ס	samek	s
ע	ayin	ʽ
פ/ף	pe	p; f (spirant)
צ/ץ	tsade	ṣ
ק	qof	q
ר	resh	r
שׂ	sin	ś
שׁ	shin	š
ת	tav	t; th (spirant)

BIBLIOGRAPHY

Adewuya, J. Ayodeji. 2001. *Holiness and Community in 2 Cor. 6:14—7:1: Paul's View of Communal Holiness in the Corinthian Correspondence.* Studies in Biblical Literature 40. New York: Peter Lang.

Ahn, Yongnan Jeon. 2013. *Interpretation of Tongues and Prophecy in 1 Corinthians 12—14: With a Pentecostal Hermeneutics.* Journal of Pentecostal Theology Supplement Series 41. Blandford Forum, UK: Deo.

Alexander, T. Desmond, and Brian S. Rosner. 2000. *New Dictionary of Biblical Theology.* Downers Grove, IL: InterVarsity Press.

Aune, David E. 1989. *The New Testament and Its Literary Environment.* Philadelphia: Westminster.

Bailey, Kenneth E. 1983. The Structure of 1 Corinthians and Paul's Theological Method with Special Reference to 4:17. *Novum Testamentum* 25:37-58.

———. 2011. *Paul Through Mediterranean Eyes: Cultural Studies in 1 Corinthians.* Downers Grove, IL: IVP Academic.

Baker, J. Christian. 1984. *Paul the Apostle: The Triumph of God in Life and Thought.* Philadelphia: Fortress.

Balch, David. 1983. 1 Corinthians 7:32-35 and Stoic Debates about Marriage, Anxiety and Distraction. *Journal of Biblical Literature* 102, no. 3: 429-39.

Balz, H., and G. Schneider, eds. 1990-93. *Exegetical Dictionary of the New Testament.* ET, Grand Rapids: Eerdmans.

Barclay, John M. G. 2016. *Pauline Churches and Diaspora Jews.* Grand Rapids: Eerdmans.

Barclay, William. 2002. *The Letters to the Corinthians.* New Daily Study Bible. 3rd ed., fully revised and updated. Louisville, KY: Westminster John Knox Press.

Barnett, P. W. 1993. Apostle. Pages 45-51 in *Dictionary of Paul and His Letters.* Downers Grove, IL: InterVarsity Press.

Barrett, C. K. 1961. *New Testament Background: Selected Documents.* New York: Harper and Row.

———. 1968. *The First Epistle to the Corinthians.* Harpers New Testament Commentaries. New York: Harper and Row.

Barth, Karl. 1933. *The Resurrection of the Dead.* ET, London: Hodder and Stoughton.

Barton, John. 1998. *The Cambridge Companion to Biblical Interpretation.* Cambridge: Cambridge University Press.

Bauer, W., W. F. Arndt, F. W. Gingrich, and F. W. Danker. 1979. *A Greek-English Lexicon of the New Testament and Other Early Christian Literature.* 2nd ed. Chicago: University of Chicago Press.

Bauer, W., F. W. Danker, and W. F. Arndt, and F. W. Gingrich. 2000. *A Greek-English Lexicon of the New Testament and Other Early Christian Literature.* 3rd ed. Chicago: University of Chicago Press.

Beale, G. K., and D. A. Carson, eds. 2007. *Commentary on the New Testament Use of the Old Testament.* Grand Rapids: Baker Academic.

Bittlinger, Arnold. 1973. *Gifts and Graces: A Commentary on 1 Corinthians 12–14.* London: Hodder and Stoughton.

Blass, F., A. Debrunner, and R. W. Funk. 1961. *A Greek Grammar of the New Testament and Other Early Christian Literature.* Chicago: Chicago University Press.

Blue, B. 1993. Apollos. Pages 37-39 in *Dictionary of Paul and His Letters.* Downers Grove, IL: InterVarsity Press.

Bornkamm, Gunther. 1975. *Paul.* London: Hodder and Stoughton.

Bray, Gerald, ed. 1999. *1-2 Corinthians.* Vol. 7 of Ancient Christian Commentary on Scripture. Downers Grove, IL: InterVarsity Press.

Brookings, Timothy A., and Bruce W. Longenecker. 2016. *1 Corinthians 10–16: A Handbook on the Greek Text.* Waco, TX: Baylor University Press.

Brower, Kent. 2009. *Living as God's Holy People: Holiness and Community in Paul.* Milton Keynes, UK: Paternoster.

Brower, Kent E., and Andy Johnson, eds. 2007. *Holiness and Ecclesiology in the New Testament.* Grand Rapids: Eerdmans.

Brown, Colin, ed. 1976. *New International Dictionary of New Testament Theology.* 3 vols. Grand Rapids: Zondervan.

Bruce, F. F. 1965. *The Letters of Paul: An Expanded Paraphrase*. Grand Rapids: Eerdmans.
———. 1976. *1 & 2 Corinthians*. New Century Bible. Repr., Greenwood, SC: Attic Press.
———. 1977. *Paul, Apostle of the Heart Set Free*. Grand Rapids: Eerdmans.
———. 1982. *The Epistle to the Galatians*. New International Greek Testament Commentary. Grand Rapids: Eerdmans.
Calvin, John. 1960. *The First Epistle of Paul the Apostle to the Corinthians*. Translated by John W. Fraser. Grand Rapids: Eerdmans.
Carson, D. A. 1987. *Showing the Spirit: A Theological Exposition of 1 Corinthians 12-14*. Grand Rapids: Baker.
Cartledge, Mark, ed. 2006. *Speaking in Tongues: Multi-Disciplinary Perspectives*. Milton Keynes: Paternoster.
Carver, Frank G. 2009. *2 Corinthians*. New Beacon Bible Commentary. Kansas City: Beacon Hill Press of Kansas City.
Chadwick, Henry. 1955. "All Things to All Men" (1 Cor. ix. 22). *New Testament Studies* 1, no. 4: 261-75.
Chow, John K. 1992. *Patronage and Power: A Study of Social Networks in Corinth*. Library of New Testament Studies. Journal for the Study of the New Testament Supplement Series 75. Sheffield, UK: Sheffield Academic Press.
Ciampa, Roy E., and Brian S. Rosner. 2010. *The First Letter to the Corinthians*. Pillar New Testament Commentary. Grand Rapids: Eerdmans.
Clarke, Andrew D. 1993. *Secular and Christian Leadership in Corinth: A Socio-historical and Exegetical Study of 1 Corinthians 1-6*. Leiden: E. J. Brill.
Collins, Raymond F. 1999. *First Corinthians*. Vol. 7 of Sacra Pagina. Collegeville, MN: Liturgical Press.
Conzelmann, Hans. 1975. *1 Corinthians*. Hermeneia. ET, Philadelphia: Fortress Press.
Crossley, Hastings. 1968. *The Golden Sayings of Epictetus*. Harvard Classics. Edited by Charles W. Eliot. New York: P. F. Collier.
Danby, Herbert. 1938. *The Mishnah, Translated from the Hebrew with Introduction and Brief Explanatory Notes*. Oxford: Oxford University Press.
Deasley, Alex R. G. 2000a. *Marriage and Divorce in the Bible and the Church*. Kansas City: Beacon Hill Press of Kansas City.
———. 2000b. *The Shape of Qumran Theology*. Carlisle: Paternoster Press.
———. 2007. *Philippians in Galatians, Philippians, Colossians*. Wesleyan Bible Commentary Series. Indianapolis: Wesleyan Publishing House.
Deissmann, Adolf. 1978. *Light from the Ancient East*. Grand Rapids: Baker Book House.
DeMaris, Richard E. 1995. Corinthian Religion and Baptism for the Dead (1 Corinthians 15:29): Insights from Archaeology and Anthropology. *Journal of Biblical Literature* 114, no. 4: 661-82.
Deming, Will. 2004. *Paul on Marriage and Celibacy: The Hellenistic Background of 1 Corinthians 7*. 2nd ed. Grand Rapids: Eerdmans.
den Dulk, Matthijs. 2020. Aquila and Apollos: Acts 18 in Light of Ancient Ethnic Stereotypes. *Journal of Biblical Literature* 139, no. 1: 177-89.
Dodd, B. J. 1995. Paul's Paradigmatic "I" and 1 Corinthians 6:12. *Journal for the Study of the New Testament* 59:39-58.
Dodd, C. H. 1951. *The Apostolic Preaching and Its Developments*. London: Hodder and Stoughton.
Dunn, James D. G. 1970. *Baptism in the Holy Spirit*. London: SCM Press.
———. 1975. *Jesus and the Spirit*. Philadelphia: Westminster Press.
———. 1985. The Pauline Letters. Pages 276-89 in *Cambridge Companion to Biblical Interpretation*. Edited by John Barton. Cambridge: Cambridge University Press.
———. 1998. *The Theology of Paul the Apostle*. Grand Rapids: Eerdmans.
Ellis, E. E. 1974. Spiritual Gifts in the Pauline Community. *New Testament Studies* 20, no. 2: 122-44.
———. 1993. Co-Workers, Paul and His. Pages 183-89 in *Dictionary of Paul and His Letters*. Downers Grove, IL: InterVarsity Press.
Enns, Peter. 1996. The "Moveable Well" in 1 Corinthians 10:4: An Extra-Biblical Tradition in an Apostolic Text. *Bulletin for Biblical Research* 6:23-38.
Fee, Gordon D. 1994. *God's Empowering Presence: The Holy Spirit in the Letters of Paul*. Peabody, MA: Hendrickson.
———. 1995. *Paul's Letter to the Philippians*. New International Commentary on the New Testament. Grand Rapids: Eerdmans.
———. 2005. *Paul, the Spirit, and the People of God*. 6th printing. Peabody, MA: Hendrickson.

———. 2014. *The First Epistle to the Corinthians*. New International Commentary on the New Testament. Grand Rapids: Eerdmans.

Findlay, G. G. 1912. *The First Epistle of Paul to the Corinthians*. Vol. 2 of the Expositor's Greek Testament. Edited by W. Robertson Nicoll. London: Hodder & Stoughton.

Fiore, Benjamin. 1985. "Covert Allusion" in 1 Corinthians 1—4. *Catholic Biblical Quarterly* 47:85-102.

Fitzmyer, J. A. 2008. *First Corinthians: A New Translation with Introduction and Commentary*. Anchor Yale Bible. New Haven, CT: Yale University Press.

Flemming, Dean. 2009. *Philippians*. New Beacon Bible Commentary. Kansas City: Beacon Hill Press of Kansas City.

Forbes, Christopher. 1986. Comparison, Self-Praise and Irony: Paul's Boasting and the Conventions of Hellenistic Rhetoric. *New Testament Studies* 32, no. 1: 1-30.

———. 1997. *Prophecy and Inspired Speech in Early Christianity and Its Hellenistic Environment*. Peabody, MA: Hendrickson.

Freedman, D. N., ed. 1992. *Anchor Bible Dictionary*. 6 vols. New York: Doubleday.

Fung, Ronald Y. K. 1988. *The Epistle to the Galatians*. New International Commentary on the New Testament. Grand Rapids: Eerdmans.

Furnish, Victor Paul. 1978. *Theology and Ethics in Paul*. 4th printing. Nashville: Abingdon.

Gagnon, Robert A. J. 2001. *The Bible and Homosexual Practice: Texts and Hermeneutics*. Nashville: Abingdon Press.

———. 2005. Sexuality. Pages 739-48 in *Dictionary for Theological Interpretation of the Bible*. Edited by Kevin J. Vanhoozer, et al. Grand Rapids: Baker Academic.

Gardner, Paul. 2018. *1 Corinthians*. Zondervan Exegetical Commentary on the New Testament. Grand Rapids: Zondervan.

Garland, David E. 2003. *1 Corinthians*. Baker Exegetical Commentary on the New Testament. Grand Rapids: Baker Academic.

Gill, David. 1990. Head-Coverings in 1 Cor 11:2-16. *Tyndale Bulletin* 41, no. 2: 245-60.

———. 1993. In Search of the Social Elite in the Corinthian Church. *Tyndale Bulletin* 44, no. 2: 323-37.

Gillihan, Y. M. 2002. Jewish Laws on Illicit Marriage, the Defilement of Offspring and the Holiness of the Temple: A New Halakic Interpretation of 1 Corinthians 7:14. *Journal of Biblical Literature* 121, no. 4: 711-44.

Godet, Frederic Louis. 1889. *Commentary on First Corinthians*. Repr., 1977. Grand Rapids: Kregel.

Gorman, Michael J. 2001. *Cruciformity: Paul's Narrative Spirituality of the Cross*. Grand Rapids: Eerdmans.

———. 2017. *Apostle of the Crucified Lord: A Theological Introduction to Paul and His Letters*. 2nd ed. Grand Rapids: Eerdmans.

Goulder, M. D. 1991. Sophia in Corinthians. *New Testament Studies* 37, no. 4: 516-34.

Green, Joel B. 2008. *Body, Soul, and Human Life: The Nature of Humanity in the Bible*. Grand Rapids: Baker.

Grenz, Stanley J. 1998. *Welcoming but Not Affirming: An Evangelical Response to Homosexuality*. Louisville, KY: Westminster John Knox.

Guenther, Alan R. 2002. One Woman or Two? 1 Corinthians 7:34. *Bulletin for Biblical Research* 12, no. 1: 33-45.

Gundry-Volf, Judith. 1997. Gender and Creation in 1 Corinthians 11:2-16: A Study in Paul's Theological Method. Pages 151-71 in *Evangelium Schriftauslegung Kirche*. Edited by J. Adna, O. Hofius, S. Hafemann. Goettingen, DEU: Vandenhoeck and Ruprecht.

Hall, D. R. 1994. A Disguise for the Wise: METASCHEMATISMOS in 1 Corinthians 4:6. *New Testament Studies* 40:143-49.

Hansen, G.W. 1993. Rhetorical Criticism. Pages 822-26 in *Dictionary of Paul and His Letters*. Downers Grove, IL: IVP.

Harris, Murray. 2005. *The Second Epistle to the Corinthians*. New International Greek Testament Commentary. Grand Rapids: Eerdmans.

Hartley, John E. 1992. *Leviticus*. Vol. 4 in Word Biblical Commentary. Dallas: Word Books.

Hawthorne, Gerald F., Ralph P. Martin, and Daniel G. Reid. 1993. *Dictionary of Paul and His Letters*. Downers Grove, IL: InterVarsity Press.

Hays, Richard B. 1992. The Conversion of the Imagination: Scripture and Eschatology in 1 Corinthians. *New Testament Studies* 45, no. 3: 391-412.

---. 1996. *The Moral Vision of the New Testament: A Contemporary Introduction to New Testament Ethics*. New York: HarperCollins.

---. 1997. *First Corinthians*. Interpretation: A Bible Commentary for Teaching and Preaching. Louisville, KY: John Knox Press.

Hengel, Martin. 1991. *The Pre-Christian Paul*. Philadelphia: Trinity Press International.

Hill, C. E. 1988. Paul's Understanding of Christ's Kingdom in 1 Corinthians 15:20-28. *Novum Testamentum* 30, no. 4: 297-320.

Hock, Ronald. 1978. Paul's Tentmaking and the Problem of His Social Class. *Journal of Biblical Literature* 97, no. 4: 555-64.

---. 1980. *The Social Context of Paul's Ministry: Tentmaking and Apostleship*. Philadelphia: Fortress Press.

Hodgson, Robert, Jr. 1992. Holiness (NT). Pages 249-54 in vol. 3 of *Anchor Bible Dictionary*. New York: Doubleday.

Hollander, H. W., and J. Holleman. 1993. The Relationship of Death, Sin and Law in 1 Cor. 15:56. *Novum Testamentum* 35:270-91.

Hooker, Morna D. 1963. "Beyond the Things Which Are Written": An Examination of 1 Cor. IV.6. *New Testament Studies* 10:127-32.

Horrell, David G. 1997. "The Lord Commanded . . . but I Have Not Used . . ." Exegetical and Hermeneutical Reflections on 1 Cor 9:14-15. *New Testament Studies* 43, no. 4: 587-603.

Horsley, Richard A. 1980. Gnosis in Corinth: 1 Corinthians 8:1-6. *New Testament Studies* 27, no. 1: 32-51.

---. 1998. *1 Corinthians*. Abingdon New Testament Commentaries. Nashville: Abingdon Press.

Hurtado, Larry W. 1988. *One God, One Lord: Early Christian Devotion and Ancient Jewish Monotheism*. London: SCM Press.

Instone-Brewer, David. 2002. *Divorce and Remarriage in the Bible*. Grand Rapids: Eerdmans.

Johnson, Andy. 2003. On Removing a Trump Card: Flesh and Blood and the Reign of God. *Bulletin for Biblical Research* 13, no. 2: 175-92.

---. 2007. Holy, Holiness, NT. Pages 846-50 in vol. 2 of *New Interpreter's Dictionary of the Bible*. Nashville: Abingdon.

---. 2009. Sanctify, Sanctification. Pages 96-101 in vol. 5 of *New Interpreter's Dictionary of the Bible*. Nashville: Abingdon.

Johnson, Luke Timothy. 1992. Tongues, Gift of. Pages 596-600 in vol. 6 of *Anchor Bible Dictionary*. New York: Doubleday.

Judge, E. A. 1984. Cultural Conformity and Innovation in Paul: Some Clues from Contemporary Documents. *Tyndale Bulletin* 35:3-24.

---. 2008. *Social Distinctives of the Christians in the First Century*. Edited by David M. Scholer. Peabody, MA: Hendrickson.

Kearney, Peter J. 1980. He Appeared to 500 Brothers (1 Cor. XV 6). *Novum Testamentum* 22, no. 3: 248-63.

Keener, Craig S. 2000a. Kiss, Kissing. Pages 628-29 in *Dictionary of New Testament Background*. Downers Grove, IL: IVP.

---. 2000b. Marriage. Pages 684-85 in *Dictionary of New Testament Background*. Downers Grove, IL: IVP.

---. 2001. *Paul, Women, and Wives: Marriage and Women's Ministry in the Letters of Paul*. Peabody, MA: Hendrickson.

---. 2003. Gifts, Spiritual. Pages 155-61 in *The Westminster Theological Wordbook of the Bible*. Edited by Donald E. Gowan. Louisville, KY: Westminster John Knox.

---. 2005. *1-2 Corinthians*. New Cambridge Bible Commentary. Cambridge: Cambridge University Press.

---. 2012-15. *Acts: An Exegetical Commentary*, Vols. 1-4. Grand Rapids: Baker Academic.

---. 2016. *The Mind of the Spirit: Paul's Approach to Transformed Thinking*. Grand Rapids: Baker.

Kinman, Brent. 1997. "Appoint the Despised as Judges!" (1 Corinthians 6:4). *Tyndale Bulletin* 48, no. 2: 345-54.

Kittel, G., and G. Friedrich, eds. 1974-2018. *Theological Dictionary of the New Testament*. Translated by G. W. Bromiley. 10 vols. Grand Rapids: Eerdmans.

Kreitzer, L. J. 1993. Body. Pages 71-76 in *Dictionary of Paul and His Letters*. Downers Grove, IL: IVP.

Kuck, David W. 1992. *Judgment and Community Conflict: Paul's Use of Apocalyptic Judgment Language in 1 Corinthians 3:5-4:5*. Supplements to Novum Testamentum 66. Leiden: Brill.

Laansma, J. C. 1997. Lord's Day. Pages 679-80 in *Dictionary of the Later New Testament and Its Developments*. Downers Grove, IL: IVP.

Ladd, George Eldon. 1975. *I Believe in the Resurrection of Jesus*. Grand Rapids: Eerdmans.

———. 1993. *A Theology of the New Testament*. Rev. ed. Grand Rapids: Eerdmans.

Lampe, Peter. 1990. Theological Wisdom and the "Word About the Cross": The Rhetorical Scheme in 1 Corinthians 1-4. *Interpretation* 44/2:117-31.

Levison, John R. 2009a. *Filled with the Spirit*. Grand Rapids: Eerdmans.

———. 2009b. Tongues, Gift of. Pages 625-27 in vol. 5 of *New Interpreter's Dictionary of the Bible*. Nashville: Abingdon.

Lewis, C. S. 1980. *The Weight of Glory and Other Addresses*. New York: Macmillan.

Lightfoot, J. B. 1892. *Saint Paul's Epistles to the Colossians and to Philemon*. London: Macmillan.

———. 1895. *Notes on the Epistles of Paul*. London: Macmillan; repr. Winona Lake, IN: Alpha Publications, n.d.

Lim, Timothy H. 1987. "Not in persuasive words of wisdom, but in the demonstration of the Spirit and power" (1 Cor. 2:4). *Novum Testamentum* 29, no. 2: 137-49.

Lincoln, Andrew T. 1991. *Paradise Now and Not Yet, Studies in the Role of the Heavenly Dimension in Paul's Thought with Special Reference to His Eschatology*. Grand Rapids: Baker Book House.

Litfin, Duane. 1994. *St. Paul's Theology of Proclamation: 1 Corinthians 1-4 and Greco-Roman Rhetoric*. Cambridge/New York: Cambridge University Press.

Longenecker, Richard N. 1976. *Paul, Apostle of Liberty*. Grand Rapids: Baker.

———. 1990. *Galatians*. Vol. 41 in Word Biblical Commentary. Dallas: Word Books.

———. 1998a. Is There Development in Paul's Resurrection Thought? Ch 8 in *Life in the Face of Death*. Edited by R. N. Longenecker. Grand Rapids: Eerdmans.

———, ed. 1998b. *Life in the Face of Death: The Resurrection Message of the New Testament*. Grand Rapids: Eerdmans.

Lyons, George. 2012. *Galatians*. New Beacon Bible Commentary. Kansas City: Beacon Hill Press of Kansas City.

MacArthur, S. D. 1980. "Spirit" in Pauline Usage: 1 Corinthians 5:5. Pages 249-56 in *Studia Biblica 1978*. Edited by E. A. Livingstone. Journal for the Study of the New Testament: Supplement Series 3. Sheffield, UK: JSOT Press.

Macdonald, M. Y. 1990. Women Holy in Body and Spirit: The Social Setting of 1 Cor 7. *New Testament Studies* 36:161-81.

Malcolm, Matthew R. 2013. *The World of 1 Corinthians: An Exegetical Source Book of Literary and Visual Backgrounds*. Eugene, OR: Cascade Books.

Malina, Bruce J. 1993. *The New Testament World: Insights from Cultural Anthropology*. Rev. ed. Louisville, KY: John Knox Press.

Marshall, I. Howard. 1980. *Last Supper and Lord's Supper*. Exeter: Paternoster Press.

———. 1989. Church and Temple in the New Testament. *Tyndale Bulletin* 40, no. 2: 203-22.

———. 1993. *The Theology of the Shorter Pauline Letters*. Cambridge: Cambridge University Press.

———. 2004. *New Testament Theology: Many Witnesses, One Gospel*. Downers Grove, IL: InterVarsity Press.

Marshall, Peter. 1987. *Enmity in Corinth: Social Conventions in Paul's Relations with the Corinthians*. Wissenschaftliche Untersuchungen zum Neuen Testament II, no. 23. Tubingen: Mohr Siebeck.

Martin, Dale B. 1990. *Slavery as Salvation*. New Haven, CT: Yale University Press.

———. 1995. *The Corinthian Body*. New Haven, CT: Yale University Press.

Martin, Ralph P. 1984. *The Spirit and the Congregation: Studies in 1 Corinthians 12-15*. Grand Rapids: Eerdmans.

———. 2014. *2 Corinthians*. Vol. 40 in Word Biblical Commentary. 2nd ed. Grand Rapids: Zondervan.

Martin, Ralph P., and Peter H. Davids, eds. 1997. *Dictionary of the Later New Testament and Its Developments*. Downers Grove, IL: IVP Academic.

McGowan, A. T. B. 2017. Human Sexuality and Christian Anthropology. Pages 174-89 in *Marriage, Family and Relationships: Biblical, Doctrinal and Contemporary Perspectives*. Edited by T. A. Noble, S. K. Whittle, and P. S. Johnston. London: Apollos.

McKelvey, R. J. 2000. Temple. Pages 806-11 in *New Dictionary of Biblical Theology*. Downers Grove, IL: InterVarsity Press.

McKnight, S. 1993. Collection for the Saints. *Dictionary of Paul and His Letters*. Downers Grove, IL: InterVarsity Press.

McRae, Rachael M. 2011. Eating with Honor: The Corinthian Lord's Supper in Light of Voluntary Association Meal Practices. *Journal of Biblical Literature* 130, no. 1: 165-81.

Meeks, Wayne A. 1983. *The First Urban Christians: The Social World of the Apostle Paul.* New Haven, CT: Yale University Press.

Metzger, Bruce M., ed. 1994. *Theological Dictionary of the New Testament.* 2nd ed. Stuttgart: Deutsche Bibelgesellschaft.

———. 2007. *A Textual Commentary on the Greek New Testament.* 2nd ed. Stuttgart: German Bible Society.

Mills, Watson E. 1972. *Understanding Speaking in Tongues.* Grand Rapids: Eerdmans.

Mitchell, Margaret M. 1989. Concerning *Peri de* in 1 Corinthians. *Novum Testamentum* 31 (July 1989): 229-56.

———. 1992. *Paul and the Rhetoric of Reconciliation: An Investigation of the Language and Composition of 1 Corinthians.* Louisville, KY: Westminster/John Knox Press.

———. 2005. "Paul's Letters to Corinth: The Interpretive Intertwining of the Literary and Historical Intertwining" in Daniel N. Schowalter and Steven J. Friesen, *Urban Religion in Roman Corinth: Interdisciplinary Approaches.* Cambridge, MA: Harvard University Press.

Montague, George. 2011. *First Corinthians.* Catholic Commentary on Sacred Scripture. Grand Rapids: Baker.

Morris, L. Redemption. 1993. Pages 784-86 in *Dictionary of Paul and His Letters.* Downers Grove, IL: IVP.

Moule, C. F. D. 1953. *An Idiom Book of New Testament Greek.* Cambridge: Cambridge University Press.

Moulton, J. H., and G. Milligan. 1952. *The Vocabulary of the Greek Testament.* London: Hodder and Stoughton.

Murphy-O'Connor, Jerome. 1983. *St. Paul's Corinth: Texts and Archaeology.* Wilmington, DE: Michael Glazier.

———. 1996. *Paul: A Critical Life.* Oxford: Oxford University Press.

———. 2009. *Keys to First Corinthians.* Oxford: Oxford University Press.

Nash, Robert Scott. 2009. *1 Corinthians.* Smyth & Helwys Bible Commentary. Macon, GA: Smyth & Helwys.

Noble, Thomas A., Sarah K. Whittle, and Philip S. Johnston, eds. 2017. *Marriage, Family and Relationships: Biblical, Doctrinal and Contemporary Perspectives.* London: Apollos.

Oster, Richard E. 1988. When Men Wore Veils to Worship: The Historical Context of 1 Cor 11:4. *New Testament Studies* 34, no. 4: 481-505.

Paige, Terence. 2002. The Social Matrix of Women's Speech at Corinth: The Context and Meaning of the Command to Silence in 1 Corinthians 14:33b-36. *Bulletin for Biblical Research* 12, no. 2: 217-42.

———. 2017. *1 & 2 Thessalonians.* New Beacon Bible Commentary. Kansas City: Beacon Hill Press of Kansas City.

Parsons, Michael. 1988. Being Precedes Act: Indicative and Imperative in Paul's Writing. *Evangelical Quarterly* 88, no. 2: 99-127. Reprinted in *Understanding Paul's Ethics.* Edited by B. S. Rosner. Grand Rapids: Eerdmans, 1995, 217-47.

Perkins, Pheme. 2012. *First Corinthians.* Paideia Commentaries on the New Testament. Grand Rapids: Baker.

Perriman, A. C. 1994. The Head of a Woman: The Meaning of Kephale in 1 Cor 11:3. *Journal of Theological Studies* 45:602-22.

Phipps, W. E. 1983. Is Paul's Attitude toward Sexual Relations Contained in 1 Cor. 7.1? *New Testament Studies* 28, no. 1: 125-31.

Pickup, Martin. 2013. "On the Third Day": The Time Frame of Jesus' Death and Resurrection. *Journal of the Evangelical Theological Society* 56/3:511-42.

Porter, Stanley E. 1993. Holiness, Sanctification. Page 401 in *Dictionary of Paul and His Letters.* Downers Grove, IL: IVP.

———. 2016. *The Apostle Paul: His Life, Thought, and Letters.* Grand Rapids: Eerdmans.

Raditsa, L. F. 1980. Augustus' Legislation Concerning Marriage, Procreation, Love Affairs and Adultery. *Aufstieg und Niedergang der römischen Welt: Geschichte und Kultur Roms im Spiegel der neueren Forschung* 2, no. 13: 278-339.

Ramelli, Ilaria L. E. 2011. Spiritual Weakness, Illness and Death in 1 Corinthians 11:30. *Journal of Biblical Literature* 130, no. 1: 145-63.

Reid, D. G. 1993. Principalities and Powers. Pages 746-52 in *Dictionary of Paul and His Letters*. Downers Grove, IL: IVP.
Richardson, Peter. 1983. Judgment in Sexual Matters in 1 Corinthians 6:1-11. *Novum Testamentum* 25:37-58.
Ridderbos, Hermann. 1975. *Paul: An Outline of His Theology*. Grand Rapids: Eerdmans.
Robeck, C. M. 1993. Tongues. Pages 939-43 in *Dictionary of Paul and His Letters*. Downers Grove, IL: IVP.
Robertson, A., and A. Plummer. 1914. *A Critical and Exegetical Commentary on the First Epistle of St. Paul to the Corinthians*. International Critical Commentary. 2nd ed. Edinburgh: T&T Clark.
Rosner, Brian S. 1991. Temple and Holiness in 1 Corinthians 5. *Tyndale Bulletin* 42, no. 1: 137-45.
———. 1994. *Paul, Scripture and Ethics: A Study of 1 Corinthians 5-7*. Leiden/New York/Köln: E. J. Brill.
———. 1998. Temple Prostitution in 1 Corinthians 6:12-20. *Novum Testamentum* 40, no. 4: 336-51.
Sakenfeld, Katharine Doob, ed. 2006-2009. *New Interpreter's Dictionary of the Bible*. 5 vols. Nashville: Abingdon.
Sampley, J. Paul. 2002. *The First Letter to the Corinthians*. Vol. 10 of the New Interpreter's Bible. Edited by Leander E. Keck. Nashville: Abingdon.
Sanders, E. P. 1992. *Judaism: Practice and Belief 63 BCE—66 CE*. London: SCM Press.
Schenck, Kenneth. 2006. *1 and 2 Corinthians*. Wesleyan Bible Commentary Series. Indianapolis: Wesleyan Publishing House.
Schmidt, Thomas E. 1996a. Homosexuality. Pages 351-55 in *Evangelical Dictionary of Biblical Theology*. Edited by Walter Elwell. Grand Rapids: Baker.
———. 1996b. *Straight or Narrow: Compassion and Clarity in the Homosexual Debate*. Downers Grove, IL: IVP.
Schnelle, Udo. 2005. *Apostle Paul: His Life and Theology*. Translated by M. E. Boring. Grand Rapids: Baker Academic.
Scholer, David M., ed. 2008. *Social Distinctives of the Christians in the First Century: Pivotal Essays by E. A. Judge*. Peabody, MA: Hendrickson Publishers.
Schowalter, Daniel N., and Steven J. Friesen, eds. 2005. Urban Religion in Roman Corinth: Interdisciplinary Approaches. Harvard Theological Studies 53. Cambridge, MA: Harvard University Press for Harvard Theological Studies, Harvard Divinity School.
Schreiner, Thomas R. 2001. *Paul, Apostle of God's Glory in Christ: A Pauline Theology*. Downers Grove, IL: InterVarsity Press.
———. 2008. *New Testament Theology: Magnifying God in Christ*. Grand Rapids: Baker.
———. 2018. *Spiritual Gifts: What They Are and Why They Matter*. Nashville: B&H Publishing Group.
Scott, J. J. 1993. Immortality. Pages 431-33 in *Dictionary of Paul and His Letters*. Downers Grove, IL: IVP.
Sider, R. J. 1975. The Pauline Conception of the Resurrection Body in 1 Corinthians XV:35-54. *New Testament Studies* 21, no. 3: 428-39.
Sigountos, James G. 1994. The Genre of 1 Corinthians 13. *New Testament Studies* 40, no. 2: 246-60.
Silva, Moisés, ed. 2014. *New International Dictionary of New Testament Theology and Exegesis*. 5 vols. 2nd ed. Grand Rapids: Zondervan.
Smit, J. F. M. 1993. Two Puzzles: 1 Corinthians 12:31 and 13:3: A Rhetorical Solution. *New Testament Studies* 39, no. 2: 246-64.
Soards, Marion L. 1999. *1 Corinthians*. New International Biblical Commentary. Peabody, MA: Hendrickson.
South, James T. 1993. A Critique of the "Curse/Death" Interpretation of 1 Corinthians 5:1-8. *New Testament Studies* 39:539-61.
Spawforth, Anthony J. S. 1995. The Achaean Federal Imperial Cult I: Pseudo-Julian, Letters 198. *Tyndale Bulletin* 46, no. 1: 151-68.
Stamps, D. L. 2000. Rhetoric. Pages 953-59 in *Dictionary of New Testament Background*. Downers Grove, IL: InterVarsity Press.
Stowers, Stanley K. 1986. *Letter Writing in Greco-Roman Antiquity*. Philadelphia: Westminster Press.
———. 1992. Diatribe. Pages 190-93 in vol. 2 of *Anchor Bible Dictionary*. New York: Doubleday.
Theissen, Gerd. 1982. *The Social Setting of Pauline Christianity: Essays on Corinth*. English translation by John Schultz. Philadelphia: Fortress Press.
Thiselton, Anthony C. 1978. Realized Eschatology at Corinth. *New Testament Studies* 24:510-26.
———. 2000a. 1 Corinthians. Pages 297-306 in *New Dictionary of Biblical Theology*. Edited by T. D. Alexander and B. S. Rosner. Downers Grove, IL: IVP.

———. 2000b. *The First Epistle to the Corinthians: A Commentary on the Greek Text*. New International Greek Testament Commentary. Grand Rapids: Eerdmans.

Thompson, G. L. 2000. Roman Military. Pages 993-94 in *Dictionary of New Testament Background*. Downers Grove, IL: InterVarsity Press.

Turner, Max. 1996. *The Holy Spirit and Spiritual Gifts, Then and Now*. Carlisle: Paternoster Press.

Vanhoozer, Kevin J., et al. 2005. *Dictionary for Theological Interpretation of the Bible*. Grand Rapids: Baker Academic.

Wagner, J. Ross. 1998. "Not beyond the Things which Are Written": A Call to Boast Only in the Lord (1 Cor 4:6). *New Testament Studies* 44:279-87.

Wan, Sze-Kar. 2009. Mind. Pages 90-91 in vol. 4 of *New Interpreter's Dictionary of the Bible*. Nashville: Abingdon.

Ward, R. B. 1990. Musonius and Paul on Marriage. *New Testament Studies* 36, no. 2: 281-89.

Watson, Duane F. 1989. 1 Corinthians 10:23—11:1 in the Light of Greco-Roman Rhetoric. *Journal of Biblical Literature* 108, no. 2: 301-18.

Webb, William J. 2005. Slavery. Pages 751-53 in *Dictionary for Theological Interpretation of the Bible*. Edited by K. J. Vanhoozer. Grand Rapids: Baker Academic.

Weiss, Johannes. 1910. *Der erste Korintherbrief*. Goettingen: Vandenhoeck & Ruprecht.

Wenham, Gordon J. 1979. *The Book of Leviticus*. New International Commentary on the Old Testament. Grand Rapids: Eerdmans.

Wesley, John. 1978. *The Works of John Wesley*. 3rd ed. Kansas City: Beacon Hill Press of Kansas City.

Westerholm, Stephen. 2004. *Perspectives Old and New on Paul*. Grand Rapids: Eerdmans.

White, Joel R. 1997. "Baptized on Account of the Dead": The Meaning of 1 Corinthians 15:29 in Its Context. *Journal of Biblical Literature* 116, no. 3: 487-99.

Willis, Wendel Lee. 1985. *Idol Meat in Corinth: The Pauline Argument in 1 Corinthians 8 and 10*. SBL International Series 68. Chico, CA: Scholars Press.

Wink, Walter. 1984. *Naming the Powers: The Language of Power in the New Testament*. Philadelphia: Fortress Press.

Winter, Bruce W. 1989. Secular and Christian Responses to Corinthian Famines. *Tyndale Bulletin* 40:86-106.

———. 1990. Theological and Ethical Responses to Religious Pluralism: 1 Corinthians 8-10. *Tyndale Bulletin* 41, no. 2: 209-26.

———. 1991. Civil Litigation in Secular Corinth and the Church: The Forensic Background to 1 Corinthians 6:1-8. *New Testament Studies* 37, no. 4: 559-72.

———. 1993. Rhetoric. Pages 820-22 in *Dictionary of Paul and His Letters*. Downers Grove, IL: InterVarsity Press.

———. 1994. *Seek the Welfare of the City: Christians as Benefactors and Citizens*. Grand Rapids: Eerdmans.

———. 1995. The Achaean Federal Imperial Cult II: The Corinthian Church. *Tyndale Bulletin* 46, no. 1: 169-78.

———. 1997. 1 Corinthians 7:6-7: A Caveat and a Framework for the "Sayings" in 7:8-24. *Tyndale Bulletin* 48, no. 1: 57-66.

———. 1998. Puberty or Passion? The Referent of the *Hyperakmos* in 1 Cor 7:26. *Tyndale Bulletin* 49, no. 1: 71-89.

———. 2001. *After Paul Left Corinth: The Influence of Secular Ethics and Social Change*. Grand Rapids/Cambridge: Eerdmans.

———. 2003. The "Underlays" of Conflict and Compromise in 1 Corinthians. Pages 140-49 in *Paul and the Corinthians: Studies in a Community in Conflict: Essays in Honour of Margaret Thrall*. Edited by T. J. Burke and J. K. Elliott. Leiden: Brill.

———. 2005. Revelation versus Rhetoric: Paul and the First-Century Fad. Pages 135-50 in *Translating Truth: The Case for Essentially Literal Bible Translation*. Wheaton, IL: Crossway Books.

———. 2007. Carnal Conduct and Sanctification in 1 Corinthians: *Simul sanctus et peccator?* Pages 184-200 in *Holiness and Ecclesiology in the New Testament*. Edited by K. E. Brower and A. Johnson. Grand Rapids: Eerdmans.

Wise, Michael, Martin Abegg Jr., and Edward Cook. 1996. *The Dead Sea Scrolls: A New Translation*. San Francisco: HarperSanFrancisco.

Wiseman, James R. 1979. Corinth and Rome I: 228 BC—AD 267. Pages 438-548 in II.7.1 of *Aufstieg und Niedergang der Römischen Welt*. Edited by H. Temporini and W. Haase. Berlin: Walter de Gruyter.

Witherington, Ben, III. 1993. Not So Idle Thoughts About *Eidolothuton*. *Tyndale Bulletin* 44, no. 2: 237-54.
———. 1994. *Jesus the Sage: The Pilgrimage of Wisdom*. Minneapolis: Augsburg Fortress.
———. 1995. *Conflict and Community in Corinth: A Socio-Rhetorical Commentary on 1 & 2 Corinthians*. Grand Rapids: Eerdmans.
Wright, D. F. 1993. Homosexuality. Pages 413-15 in *Dictionary of Paul and His Letters*. Downers Grove, IL: InterVarsity Press.
Wright, N. T. 1993. *The Climax of the Covenant: Christ and the Law in Pauline Theology*. Minneapolis: Fortress Press.
———. 1996. *Jesus and the Victory of God*. Vol. 2 of Christian Origins and the Question of God Series. Minneapolis: Fortress Press.
———. 2002. *The Letter to the Romans*. Vol. 10 of the New Interpreter's Bible. Edited by Leander E. Keck. Nashville: Abingdon.
———. 2003. *The Resurrection of the Son of God*. Minneapolis: Fortress Press.
———. 2004. *Paul for Everyone: 1 Corinthians*. Louisville, KY: Westminster John Knox Press.
———. 2013. *Paul and the Faithfulness of God*, Book II, Parts III and IV. Minneapolis: Fortress Press.
Wu, J. L. 1993. Liturgical Elements. Pages 557-60 in *Dictionary of Paul and His Letters*. Downers Grove, IL: InterVarsity Press.
Young, Norman H. 1987. *Paidagogos*: The Social Setting of a Pauline Metaphor. *Novum Testamentum* 29, no. 2: 150-76.
Zaas, Peter S. 1984. Cast the Evil Man from Your Midst. *Journal of Biblical Literature* 103:259-61.
———. 1988. Catalogues and Context: 1 Corinthians 5 and 6. *New Testament Studies* 34:622-29.
Ziesler, J. A. 1972. *The Meaning of Righteousness in Paul: A Linguistic and Theological Enquiry*. Cambridge, UK: Cambridge University Press.

TABLE OF SIDEBARS

Title	Location
The Greek Letter in Paul's Day	Introduction
"The Rulers of This Age" in 1 Corinthians	2:6
The Significance of the Plural in 1 Cor 2:6-16	2:16
Pauline Perfection versus Corinthian Perfection	3:4
Paul's Rhetorical Strategy in 1:18—3:23	3:21-23
Eschatology and the Corinthians	4:12b-13
Paul as a Servant-Leader	From the Text for 4:1-21
The Significance of the Indicative and the Imperative	5:8
Holiness as Corporate and Individual	5:12-13
Paul, the Corinthians, and Homosexuality	6:9-11
The Holiness of Unbelievers and Children	7:14
Paul's Teaching on Marriage and Divorce	7:16
Slavery in the Roman World and Paul's Attitude to It	7:24
Paul's Use of the Image of the Body to Refer to the Church	12:11
The Gift of Tongues at Corinth	From the Text for 14:1-40
The Gift of Prophecy in 1 Corinthians	From the Text for 14:1-40
Paul's Understanding of the Resurrection Body	From the Text for 15:35-58

INTRODUCTION

Prologue

At first sight 1 Corinthians may seem strangely removed from the world of today. It may appear to consist of a collection of rebukes and corrections addressed to an argumentative group of Christians about matters that have little to do with the world as we know it. What interest have we in disagreements about who had the best command of rhetorical technique; about the evils of submitting disputes among Christians to the judgment of pagan courts; about the pros and cons of eating idol meat in pagan temples; about overeating (and overdrinking) at the Lord's Supper?

Such features have sometimes led to 1 Corinthians being labeled as "practical" (in a derogatory sense) rather than "theological," as well as to being somewhat disjointed and difficult to follow. An earlier generation of scholars (not altogether extinct), of whom the German scholar Johannes Weiss was perhaps the most influential, concluded that 1 Corinthians was a collection of pieces of different Pauline writings, patched together with varying degrees of continuity (1910, xl-xliii). But if it is possible to trace connections between the successive parts of the letter, as most scholars believe, there is little reason for questioning its integrity.

In many respects, the various topics treated in the letter gather around the single theme of the church: more specifically, how to be the church. If the letter has anything to say about that to the church in the twenty-first century, then the church and its members should be all ears.

A. The Corinthian Setting

As much as any Pauline letter, if not more, it appears that the issues that created tensions between Paul and his Corinthian readers arose from the distinctive background and character of Corinth.

1. The Geographical and Historical Setting: Corinth Old and New

The geographical situation of Corinth guaranteed the city's significance. On a North-South axis it stood at the south end of the landbridge between mainland Greece and the Peloponnese. On an East-West axis it formed a ready link between the Aegean and Adriatic Seas, having a port on each side of the landbridge: Lechaeum on the west and Cenchreae on the east. The two were connected by a track—the Diolkos—on which ships' cargoes could be dragged, thereby avoiding a risky voyage around the Peloponnese. Corinth was thus well-placed to become a center of trade and travel. Its history confirms this. In classical times it flourished until it joined other Greek cities in opposing the rising power of Rome in 146 BC, as a result of which it was mostly destroyed. It was rebuilt as a Roman colony by Julius Caesar in 44 BC, becoming capital of the Roman province of Achaia. This meant its inhabitants enjoyed the status of Roman citizens.

2. The Social Setting

The city overthrown by the Romans, if not wholly demolished, had ceased to be a functioning entity. The population was largely slaughtered or enslaved. Its most distinctive institutions, including the Temple of Aphrodite with its thousand cult prostitutes, were destroyed (J. Wiseman 1979, 438-548). The new city was fundamentally Roman, by virtue of being a Roman colony. Still more, a significant portion of the population consisted of Caesar's veterans who had been rewarded for their years of military service by grants of land. At the same time Greek influence was by no means absent. As the largest city in Greece it inevitably attracted the surrounding population, while its prospects as a setting for trade and travel brought aspiring hopefuls from the eastern Mediterranean. This mix was capable of producing opposite outcomes. On the one hand it could produce wealth for some while leaving many in poverty. This in turn could create social divisions (Gill 1993; Clarke 1993, chs 2-3). One way in which these found expression was in a system of patronage and benefaction that brought with it the demand for recognition and approval. Religiously, it was a setting of "gods many, and lords many" (8:5 KJV) and with it the idol worship and immorality that polytheism brings. "To live like a Corinthian" (*korinthiazesthai*) was an accepted term for loose living; and idol feasts were scenes where that was not unknown. It is therefore probable that many of the problems in the Corinthian church had their roots in the society in which its adherents lived (Garland 2003, 5-6).

B. The Occasion of the Letter

Why was 1 Corinthians written? What triggered its writing? We do not have to look far or deeply for the answer to these questions. Paul had already been in communication with the Corinthians in a letter now lost to us (5:9). However, he says enough to show that at least one particular subject of that letter (if not the only one) was how to be the church in the world, with specific reference to the admission of the sexually immoral into the fellowship of the church (5:10-13). The Corinthians had misunderstood his teaching, and he is now writing to correct their misunderstanding (5:11). He also refers to a letter they had written to him (7:1), and sets out to address the issues they had raised there.

In addition to these written communications Paul had also received verbal reports. Some of these were from members of the household of Chloe (1:11), who was probably a businesswoman whose business interests extended as far as Ephesus (where 1 Corinthians was written [16:8]). From these Paul learned that divisions had surfaced in the church in Corinth (1:11). Reference is also made to unattributed reports of "sexual immorality among you" (5:1). These may have been conveyed by Stephanas, Fortunatus, and Achaicus, who had recently arrived in Ephesus from Corinth (16:17-18).

We need not go farther at this point to see how Paul was prompted to write to the Corinthian Christians. The survival of the church as authentically Christian was at stake. It was this that prompted Paul to take up his pen.

C. The Literary Character of the Letter

Paul was writing in the Greek-speaking world where the shape of the letter did not change much from 300 BC to AD 300. The typical letter began with a greeting constructed on the formula "A (name of sender) to B (name of recipient), greeting." A wish-prayer might follow this. Next came the message, followed by a health wish and, last of all, a word of farewell. Thousands of papyrus letters of this kind have been discovered. They consist essentially of private, personal correspondence.

The Greek Letter in Paul's Day

The following is a fairly standard example in which one party, about to pay a visit to Thebes, tries to arrange a meeting with a friend there. It dates from the early second century AD in Egypt.

> Claudius Agathas Daimon to most beloved Sarapion, Greetings. Since I am going to Thebes, I salute you dearest, sweetest Sarapion and I exhort you also to do the same thing. If you need anything from Thebes, I encourage you to write to me, dearest, and it shall be done. I pray for your health continually together with that of your children. Farewell. (Cited in Stowers 1986, 61)

However, letters were also used for official or public purposes. In the case of literary letters, something of a line was crossed from written, personal conversation to public persuasion and argument. Moreover, letters were not read *by* the recipients but *to* them (since few could read or write, or found reading and writing tedious). The door was thereby opened for the use of the whole range of rhetorical devices employed by orators who were highly esteemed in the Greco-Roman world. Indeed, letter writing was taught in the schools of rhetoric.

There was thus an interweaving of the tools of rhetoric with the form of the letter. Letters would typically consist of the elements noted above, often with the addition of the statement of the theme of the letter (*propositio*), following the greeting; then a description of the events prompting the writing of the letter (*narratio*). After this would come the argument proving the theme (*probatio*); and finally the concluding summary (*peroratio*).

Rhetorically, letters would be categorized into one of three types. These were distinguished in handbooks on the subject dating from the fourth century BC Greek of Aristotle to Paul's first century AD Latin contemporary Quintilian.

- Forensic rhetoric was the rhetoric of the law court and was essentially concerned to establish what had happened in the past.
- Deliberative rhetoric was designed to lead hearers to a new course of action in the future.
- Demonstrative rhetoric focused on the present and was intended to convey either praise or blame.

It is maintained by numbers of scholars that Paul's letters in general reflect the influence of this type of rhetoric. First Corinthians in particular is held to belong to the deliberative category (e.g., Mitchell 1992, chs II and IV; Witherington 1995, 75-77; Collins 1999, 1-31).

A very different perspective is advocated by those who underline Paul's Jewish roots as "a Hebrew of Hebrews." Kenneth Bailey has long argued that the rhetorical character of 1 Corinthians owes more to the Hebrew prophetic tradition than to Greek rhetoric (1983, 159, 167, 179-84). Thus the form of Paul's arguments is not simply to state each problem and reply to it. Rather, he follows a pattern of argument akin to that of the prophets, in which he (1) recalls some teaching he has given them; (2) states the practical problem; (3) defines the fundamental theological issue; (4) restates the practical problem in the light of the theological teaching; and (5) affirms his own personal conclusion. This pattern, first found in 1 Cor 1:17—2:2, Bailey regards as borrowed from such prophetic passages as Isa 24:14-18 and 50:5-11 (2011, 72-76, 89-90; see 38-40).

A view that is kindred in principle though not in form is that of Ciampa and Rosner, who contend that it is better to take OT and Jewish frames of reference as the primary lenses through which to read the form and contents of 1 Corinthians than the categories of Greek rhetoric (2010, 20). In their view the letter is primarily concerned to correct ethical behaviors that were prevalent throughout the Gentile world—namely, sexual immorality and idolatry (ibid., 21-22).

It is questionable whether any one view should be taken as the controlling literary key to 1 Corinthians. There can be no doubt that Paul was familiar with the standard form of the Greek letter noted earlier. However, it seems something of a stretch to say that labeling 1:18—16:12 as the probatio of the letter adds significantly to the understanding of the content. Again, Paul's familiarity with the forms of prophetic composition can hardly be gainsaid. But that he followed them with unwavering uniformity is difficult to demonstrate.

To read the letter from a largely ethical perspective is too narrow a gauge for a letter that presupposes and alludes to such a wide range of Christian doctrines, and contains lengthy treatments of the cross and the resurrection.

James Dunn is closer to the mark when he says that Paul took the standard forms of his day and transformed them to fit his own purposes. Paul's guideline in both substance and sequence is the logic of his own thought and the situation addressed (Barton 1998, 278-300).

D. The Structure of the Letter

Discernible structure is a most helpful clue in tracing the argument of any document. In the history of the interpretation of 1 Corinthians opinions have ranged widely. F. L. Godet, a nineteenth-century commentator, found four natural groups that show a "rational gradation" from ecclesiastical questions (1:10—4:21), to moral questions (chs 5—10), to liturgical questions (chs

11—14), to doctrinal questions (ch 15) (repr. 1977, 27-31). A recent commentator at the opposite pole, J. Murphy-O'Connor declares that "the salient feature of 1 Corinthians is the absence of any detectable logic in the arrangement of its contents" (1996, 253).

Several features offer guidance in defining the leading themes of the letter. These may serve as pointers to the structure and the logic behind it.

1. The contents of the greeting (1:1-2) and the thanksgiving (vv 4-10). It is well known that the greeting could be expanded beyond the bare-bones form found in the letter quoted in section C above. Indeed, the greetings in Paul's letters show a significant degree of adaptation to meet the situation he is addressing. For example, the greeting in Romans, which begins with an affirmation of his apostleship and dedication to the gospel (Rom 1:1) is promptly followed by a summary of the gospel (vv 2-4) widely regarded as a form used by the church in Rome. Galatians begins with an expanded—and vigorous—assertion of Paul's apostolic vocation (Gal 1:1-2) followed by a gospel summary stressing the redemptive work of Christ (vv 3-5). Philippians makes no mention at all of Paul's apostleship, describing himself and Timothy simply as "servants of Christ Jesus" (Phil 1:1).

When we turn to the greeting in 1 Corinthians, four ideas stand out: (1) Paul's status as "an apostle of Christ Jesus by the will of God" (1:1); (2) the status of the Corinthian believers as "the church of God in Corinth" (v 2a): an emphatic declaration of their unity; (3) a description of the spiritual status and calling of the Corinthian believers: "sanctified in Christ Jesus and called to be . . . holy" (v 2b); and (4) an affirmation that the Corinthians are not the only believers on earth, but share the faith "with all those everywhere who call on the name of our Lord Jesus Christ—their Lord and ours" (v 2c). God's church is bigger than the church in Corinth, and the gospel is not their private property to be shaped in keeping with their own tastes.

If we now move forward into the thanksgiving (vv 4-9), we may expect to find foreshadowings of the central concerns of the letter. This was one of the functions of the thanksgiving (→ vv 4-9). Several features are referred to as characterizing the Corinthian believers: (1) enrichment in speech (v 5); (2) enrichment in knowledge (v 5); (3) abundance of spiritual gifts (v 7); (4) eager expectation of the return of the Lord Jesus (v 7b); and (5) the assurance that they will be blameless when he comes (vv 8-9).

Allowing that the thanksgiving typically gives advance notice of the main topics to be discussed in the letter, it is easy to see that the problem of eloquent speech is the controlling theme of chs 1—4; that knowledge (or the lack of it) surfaces again and again in chs 5—11; that spiritual gifts are clearly the subject in chs 12—14; and that questions (and answers) of various kinds regarding the resurrection constitute the heart of ch 15.

This does not mean that the ideas floated in 1:1-2 are forgotten. On the contrary, they serve as early warning signals of the themes that will be spelled out more concretely in the thanksgiving and later in the body of the letter. Paul's apostleship, the unity of the church, the call to holiness, and the eager expectation of the return of Christ are all ideas that will be picked up in due course. They are set out from the start, so that they will not be overlooked.

2. A second feature that has been appealed to frequently as a guide in determining the structure of the letter are the reports that Paul has received regarding the state of affairs in the Corinthian church. Chief among these are the report he has received from the household of Chloe (1:11), and one from an unnamed source (5:1). Allied with these is a letter that Paul has received from the Corinthians (7:1), as well (presumably) as information brought by messengers from Corinth (11:18; 16:17). It is suggested that the order in which Paul treats the various topics is the order in which the reports came to him (Fitzmyer 2008, 55).

There can be no doubt that much of the goings-on in Corinth since Paul left came to him by report. It could hardly be otherwise. He most probably learned the criticisms of himself (9:1-6) from some third party. But the greeting and the thanksgiving give too much evidence that he knew where he was going when he first began to dictate the letter for it to be credible that he struck out in a new direction with the arrival of the postman or visitors from Corinth.

3. A third feature taken as a guide to the structure of the letter consists of indications of topical progression. In a way, this simply draws out the implications of the evidence of the greeting and the thanksgiving, though it also goes beyond it. According to this, Paul treats a series of recognizably defined issues in the letter. Chapters 1—4 are concerned with divisions in the Corinthian church, and chs 5 and 6 with ethical problems. The issues become especially clear when Paul takes up "the matters you wrote about" (7:1). These are introduced by the phrase "now about" (*peri de*), which first appears in 7:1 and reappears in 7:25, 8:1, 12:1, and 16:1, 12. At each of these points, there is a significant change of topic.

There can be little doubt that the expression "now about" marks the beginning of a new topic (Mitchell 1989, 233-34, 256). However, it does not indicate whether the topics it introduces are raised *in the order* in which they stood in the Corinthians' letter to Paul. Furthermore, it seems probable that there are other topics that lack this introductory formula. First Corinthians

11:2, 11:17, and 15:1 seem clearly to introduce independent topics, but the formula "now about" is conspicuously absent.

Some scholars attempt to solve the problem by combining the evidence of the reports with that of the progression of topics (Fee 2014, viii-xi; Fitzmyer 2008, 57-58). However, this merely adds the problems of one view to those of the other. Indeed, Fee qualifies his position by observing that in 7:1—16:12 "there is a certain logic to the whole presentation and the present sequencing is probably Paul's own" (Fee 2014, 295; similarly Ciampa and Rosner 2010, 272). But this leaves the question unanswered: on what principle did Paul organize his material?

4. There is a certain "natural chronology" (if one may use the expression) marking the movement in the successive blocks of material. Paul's ministry in Corinth began with "the message of the cross" (1:18; 2:1-2), giving rise to the dispute about true wisdom (1:17—4:21). But conversion to the Christian way leads to the question of how the Christian life is to be lived, that is, to ethics (5:1—7:40). Also arising are the challenges of living a Christian life in a non-Christian society (8:1-11). But accompanying this are tensions that arise within the Christian community itself (11:2—14:40). Chapter 15 has been characterized in opposite ways. On the one hand it has been said to mark "an abrupt change of subject matter" (Fee 2014, 793). On the other hand it has been seen as "not only the close and crown of the whole epistle, but also . . . the clue to its meaning, from which place light is shed on the whole" (Barth 1933, 11).

The resurrection is undoubtedly the coping stone of the gospel. In 15:2-4 Paul speaks of it as part of the gospel by which they were saved. He has already referred to it in 6:14 in similar terms: "By his power God raised the Lord from the dead, and he will raise us also." It had evidently become the subject of questioning among the Corinthians. Paul appears to be intent on drawing out its significance for a wide range of issues troubling the Corinthian church. This may account for its position at the end of the letter.

These considerations suggest that a macro plan is at work throughout the letter, and that it arises and follows from the inherent progress of Christianity in Corinth. In a broad sense it is not unlike the progress of Christianity anywhere. Nonetheless, at each step the uniqueness of the Corinthian setting stamps its character on the substance, but the order and content derive broadly from the unfolding life of a Christian church.

These features, taken singly or together, do not amount to a demonstration of why 1 Corinthians is organized as it is. They do suggest that the arrangement is not haphazard. It is uncertain whether the problems arose *in the order* in which Paul treats them. In some degree they could well have arisen simultaneously. But assuredly they are the *kinds of problems* that could readily arise in a setting such as Paul's Corinth. Corinth was a talking shop, a scene of party strife, not particular about its morals, ready to embrace (and overrate) the extraordinary in religion, and debate, dispute, and dismiss matters that did not fall within accepted parameters of thought. First Corinthians is not a ragbag of unrelated ideas, but their relatedness lies in the Corinthian situation rather than in logic. First Corinthians is credible as the writing of a Christian apostle to such a scene.

E. The Theological Focus of the Letter

A remarkable feature of 1 Corinthians is the range of doctrines referred to, alluded to, or implied. For example, Kenneth Bailey notes how Paul's argument against fornication in 6:12-20 appeals to the doctrines of the cross (v 20), the resurrection (v 14), the Trinity (vv 15, 19), and the church (v 15) (2011, 183). By way of contrast Romans—often regarded as the exposition of Paul's theology *par excellence*—never mentions the doctrines of the church, the Lord's Supper, and eschatology. In 1 Corinthians several theological themes recur with such frequency as to suggest that, together, they define the theological focus of the letter.

1. The first theme is that of the church. There is a remarkably heavy use of the term "church" (*ekklēsía*): twenty-two occurrences, as against nine in 2 Corinthians and five in Romans. Especially notable is Paul's use of the intensive expression "the church of God" (1 Cor 1:2; 10:32; 11:16, 22; 15:9). Every problem raised by the Corinthian situation he brings to the touchstone of what he teaches in every church (4:17; 7:17; 11:16; 14:33; 16:1).

Another term used by Paul to refer to the church is "the body" (*sōma*). Sometimes Paul uses the term in an individual sense with reference to the human person under various aspects (5:3; 6:13*b*-15; 7:4; 9:27). But he also uses it corporately or collectively. Partakers of the one loaf at the Lord's Supper are "one body" (10:16-17). The one body has many members (12:12-26) and "each one of you is a part of it" (12:27). Half of Paul's forty-one uses of the term in 1 Corinthians carry a corporate or collective sense and refer to the main problems convulsing the Corinthian church: divisions, immorality, and self-seeking.

2. A second, recurrent theme giving definition to the theological focus of the letter is the gospel (*to euangelion*). Particularly noteworthy are the repeated references to, and in some cases summaries of, the gospel message Paul preached in Corinth and everywhere else he preached. These he describes variously as "our testimony about Christ" (1:6); "my way of life in Christ Jesus, which agrees with what I teach everywhere in every church" (4:17); "yet for

us there is but one God, the Father . . . and . . . one Lord Jesus Christ" (8:6); "the traditions just as I passed them on to you" (11:2); "I want to remind you of the gospel I preached to you, which you received and on which you have taken your stand" (15:1; see vv 2-5). It is evident that the gospel is Paul's guiding light throughout the letter, and he does not need to do more than refer to it since his hearers already know it.

The foregoing appears to be confirmed by the occurrence of two terms in a density and intensity that is suggestive and significant. The first is the term "gospel," either in its noun form (*euangelion*) or verb form (*euangelizesthai*), "preach the gospel." These cognates appear more frequently in 1 Corinthians (fifteen times) than in any other of Paul's writings (next in order of frequency is Romans with twelve occurrences). It is striking how emphatically he uses the terms: "For Christ did not send me to baptize, but to preach the gospel" (1 Cor 1:17a). "In Christ Jesus I became your father through the gospel" (4:15b). "I want to remind you of the gospel I preached [lit. **the gospel I gospelled**] to you, which you received and on which you have taken your stand. By this gospel you are saved" (15:1-2a).

The second term confirming the centrality of the gospel in 1 Corinthians is the term "apostle" (*apóstolos*). Like "gospel" the term "apostle" appears more frequently in 1 Corinthians (ten times) than in any other of Paul's writings (no other has more than four). All but one (15:7) refer to himself individually or by inclusion. Again, Paul's usage is emphatic. "Paul, called to be an apostle of Christ Jesus by the will of God" (1:1). "Am I not an apostle? . . . You are the seal of my apostleship in the Lord" (9:1b, 2a). In ch 9 the correlative of Paul's refusal to claim his rights as an apostle is his overriding concern to do nothing to hinder the advance of the gospel (vv 12b-18).

Taken together, these considerations suggest that 1 Corinthians should be approached as "the gospel to the Corinthians" as much as "the correction of Corinthian misunderstandings." The problems of the Corinthians are the *occasion* of the letter. But the driving force behind it is the gospel. Paul's basic concern with the Corinthian church was that it was not a *gospel* church. It is not that the Corinthians had not been taught the gospel nor that they had not accepted it. Repeatedly Paul reminds them of both (2:1-5; 4:15-17; 9:2; 11:2; 15:1-5, 11). But they had failed in its *application*. First Corinthians is therefore to be viewed as an exercise in *applied gospel* (Conzelmann 1975, 9). It is in the apostolic gospel, and in the church as the creation of the gospel, that the letter finds its theological unity and its focus. The theme is not dealt with theoretically or comprehensively, but rather with how it applies to and is worked out (or not being worked out) in the specific case of the church in Corinth.

3. A third theme, implicit in the second, which brings the theological focus of the letter into more exact definition, is holiness. Michael Gorman goes so far as to say that "Paul himself is preoccupied with holiness" and that "holiness is . . . the focus of 1 Corinthians" (Brower and Johnson 2007, 149, 151). It seems fair to say that in 1 Corinthians holiness has three distinguishable aspects: commitment, character, and conduct. The church is constituted of "those sanctified in Christ Jesus" (1:2). They are set apart by their relationship to Christ. But they are also "called to be . . . holy." Holiness of commitment is to be accompanied by holiness of character. This is not an unrealizable ideal. On the contrary, Paul assures them that the Lord Jesus Christ will keep them so that they "will be blameless on the day of our Lord Jesus Christ" (1:8). This motif of realizing in character and conduct what they are in commitment recurs throughout the letter on both the corporate and individual levels. Paul moves freely from the one level to the other.

The conflict among the Corinthians regarding the true wisdom, entailing in turn differences about who was the best leader, was evidence of their lack of spirituality (*pneumatikòs* [2:12-15]) or perfection (*teleios* [2:6]), and of their immaturity and worldly-mindedness (3:1). Jealousy and quarreling could be evidence of nothing else (3:3). Together the Corinthian believers constituted the temple of God, but one of them could pose a threat to its purity (3:16-17). Sexual immorality must be banished from among them (chs 5—6) for each of them individually is a temple of the Holy Spirit (6:28-30).

If it be asked what is the distinguishing feature of the life of holiness, the answer is love. In many respects chs 8—16 are a sustained exhortation to the Corinthians to be governed by love as they exercise their Christian freedom. Love is the mark of knowing God (8:3). Therefore, whether in the matter of eating food offered to idols (8:4-13) or celebrating the Lord's Supper (11:17-22) or exercising the gifts of the Spirit in worship (chs 12, 14), the way of love is "the most excellent way" (12:31*b*—13:13). What this comes down to is that the way of holiness is the way of the cross: the crucifixion of self-interest even in matters not necessarily wrong in themselves, but having the capacity to be damaging to others. The life of holiness is the life of love (12:31—13:13). In a word, the holy life is the crucified life, or—to borrow Michael Gorman's preferred term—the life of cruciformity (Gorman 2001).

COMMENTARY

I. LETTER INTRODUCTION: I CORINTHIANS 1:1-9

A. The Greeting (1:1-3)

BEHIND THE TEXT

Paul founded the church in Corinth during his second missionary campaign, of which we have some account in Acts 16:1—18:21. By that account Paul's efforts were met with determined opposition from Jews (Acts 18:5-6) who tried to drive him out (vv 12-17). Nevertheless, Paul remained in Corinth for eighteen months (vv 11, 18), numbering among his converts Sosthenes, the synagogue leader (v 17; 1 Cor 1:1). However, after his departure splits and divisions emerged in the church (vv 10-11), prompting him to write this letter. We should therefore be alert to the possibility of finding them referred to from the start.

The pattern of the Hellenistic letter would lend itself to such references. (→ Introduction, part C above.) This is the pattern followed by Paul here: "Paul, . . . to the church of God in Corinth, . . . grace and peace" (vv 1-3). However, Paul has greatly expanded each of these elements, and the way in which he has done so tells us something about the state of affairs in the Corinthian church and the lines along which Paul addresses it.

It is instructive to compare the greeting in other of Paul's letters with that in 1 Corinthians. In Rom 1:1-7 the emphasis falls on the gospel message and Paul's divine appointment as apostle to the Gentiles. In Gal 1:1-3 Paul's divine commission as an apostle is described in almost explosive terms together with the reference to Christ's saving death (v 4). In Phil 1:1-2 there is no mention at all of his apostolic commission: he is simply a servant "of Christ Jesus." This shows that the greetings in Paul's letters were carefully composed to convey something of significance regarding the situation in the church to which he was writing.

IN THE TEXT

■ **1** Paul, as author of the letter, places his name first in keeping with current convention, but immediately directs attention to the role in which he writes to them—namely, as **an apostle**. An apostle was not merely one who was sent (as the underlying Greek term *apostello* might be taken to imply), but one who was invested with the authority of the sender (Rengstorf in *TDNT* 1:413-24, 437-43). Paul will appeal to this fact again and again in the letter (e.g., 9:1-2; 15:7-10). Not only so but he was **called to be an apostle of Christ Jesus by the will of God**: language that is doubly emphatic in that it affirms that he was **called** and did not take the task by his own choice; and that it was **by the will of God** that he was called. Paul includes in the greeting **our brother Sosthenes**, who is most naturally taken to be the converted leader of the synagogue, named in Acts 18:17. As one of themselves, now associated with Paul in his missionary endeavors, he reinforces Paul's linkage with the Corinthians.

■ **2** The letter is addressed **to the church of God in Corinth**. **Church** (*ekklēsia*) was primarily a political term in Corinth, denoting the citizens in conclave discussing civic affairs. Paul transfers the term to the assembly of believing Christians. Still more, he describes it as the church **of God**: an expression used only here and in 2 Cor 1:1, as if to say that the church is God's property, not that of any human leader. Just as he has characterized himself as one divinely called in 1 Cor 1:1, so he now characterizes the Corinthian Christians. They are **sanctified in Christ Jesus and called to be his holy people**. **Sanctified** and **holy** are derived from the same Greek root (*hagios*), but here denote different aspects of sanctification or holiness. **Sanctified** is a perfect passive participle denoting an act that took place in the past but whose effects continue in the present. Such sanctification takes place by being **in Christ Jesus**—that is, belonging to him or set apart to him. But those who belong to Christ are **called to be . . . holy** in character. Holiness of status is to be matched by holiness of heart and life.

Two further facets of Paul's understanding of the church emerge here. First, while the word **church** is singular, its members—those **sanctified . . . and called to be his holy people**—are referred to in the plural. In Paul's mind, while the church is a corporate entity, its members do not thereby forfeit their individual identity and moral responsibility. This is confirmed by the further aspect (also expressed in the plural) that the believers in Corinth are united to **all those everywhere who call on the name of our Lord Jesus Christ—their Lord and ours**. The Lord Jesus is not the private possession of the Corinthians as a whole or any faction of them. Thus, there is a double thrust in these words. The divisions among the Corinthians (to which Paul will come presently) imply not only that Christ is the property of one group of the Corinthian Christians rather than any other but also that Christ is the possession of the church in Corinth rather than the church anywhere else. Paul rebuts this notion by addressing his letter to believers everywhere. This does not mean that the letter is not fundamentally Corinth-specific. It does mean that the church of God is bigger than the church in Corinth.

To call on the name of the Lord Jesus is to repose one's trust in him, and so be saved (Rom 10:9). Strikingly, the multiple form **Lord Jesus Christ** and the simple form **Lord** are used side by side. In the Greek OT (the Septuagint or LXX) "Lord" is the standard translation for the various forms of the divine name (Yahweh [*adonai*]). Here Paul uses it in reference to Jesus.

■ **3** Once more the standard formula in the Greek letter is modified, indeed, Christianized. The conventional term "greeting" (*chairein*) becomes **grace** (*charis*). With this he combines the standard Hebrew form of greeting: **peace** (*shalom*). **Grace** denotes God's spontaneous, undeserved favor toward sinners. **Peace** flows from grace and denotes not merely the absence of inward stress but the cessation of hostility between God and the sinner (Rom 5:1). This distinctively Christian meaning is underlined by the statement that the grace and peace in question come **from God our Father and the Lord Jesus Christ**. God's fatherly love is seen most clearly in the life and death of the Lord Jesus Christ. The conjoining of the names of God the Father and the Lord Jesus Christ as the source of these blessings is a powerful attestation of their unity.

FROM THE TEXT

While it is easy to overinterpret a formal greeting, there are good grounds for seeing the following as particular points of emphasis bearing on the situation in the Corinthian church and indicating from the start Paul's message to it.

First, *the greeting says something about Paul; namely, that he is an apostle*. It is true that he makes the same claim in others of his letters (Rom 1:1; 2 Cor 1:1; Gal 1:1; Eph 1:1). It is also true that in some of his letters he makes no mention of it (Phil 1:1; 1 Thess 1:1; 2 Thess 1:1), being content to describe himself as a servant "of Christ Jesus" (as in Philippians), or with no self-description at all (as in 1 and 2 Thessalonians). The robustness of his self-description in 1 Cor 1:1 alerts us to look for debates about authority among the Corinthians, and we do not have to look far to find them (e.g., 1 Cor 1:12-15).

Second, *the greeting says something about Christ*. The frequency with which his name is used in the greeting is unequalled in any other of Paul's letters. Paul is "an apostle of Christ Jesus" (v 1); the church consists of those who are "sanctified in Christ Jesus" and "who call on the name of our Lord Jesus Christ" (v 2); the source of "grace and peace"—with "God our Father"—is "the Lord Jesus Christ" (v 3). This emphatic placing of Christ in the central role points again to the focal point of the agitation in the Corinthian church: an issue picked up immediately (v 12).

Third, *the greeting says something about the church*. Only in the Corinthian letters does the expression "the church of God" occur in the greeting. The closest parallel is in the Thessalonian letters where Paul uses the phrase "to the church of the Thessalonians in God the Father" (1 Thess 1:1; 2 Thess 1:1). The form of words in the Corinthian letters rules out any mistaken inference that the church might belong to the Corinthians. Also significant is the point (not unique to 1 and 2 Corinthians) that the prime mark of the church—both collectively and individually—is holiness. The contents of the letter will show what Paul meant by this. Suffice it to say at this point that it covers a wide range of meaning from the ethical (3:16-17) to the eschatological (6:1-3). Notable too is Paul's insistence that the Corinthians are not the only Christians on the earth but are part of the greater company of "all those everywhere who call on the name of our Lord Jesus Christ" (1:3). He is their Lord too. The church is bigger than Corinth.

Paul does not write these things to every church, or at least emphasize them as he does here. This suggests that they are framed as they are because in Paul's view they have a direct bearing on the problems he sees in the Corinthian church. We have been warned from the start what to look out for.

B. The Thanksgiving (1:4-9)

BEHIND THE TEXT

A common element in the introductory part of many Hellenistic letters was a section given over to thanksgiving. In a good many it consisted chiefly of an expression of gratitude or good wishes for the health of the recipient, and it tended to be relatively brief.

A thanksgiving section is found in almost all of Paul's letters (Galatians being a conspicuous exception). However, in Paul's hands it underwent a considerable development. For one thing, it became significantly longer. At least two factors seem to account for this. The first has to do with the contents of the epistle. Frequently, the thanksgiving section contains a foreshadowing if not an advance statement of the main themes to be dealt with in the rest of the letter. So "all kinds of speech and . . . all knowledge" (v 5) are dealt with primarily in 1:18—4:21. Being "blameless on the day of our Lord Jesus Christ" (1:8) is treated in 5:1—11:33. The reference to "any spiritual gift" (1:7) is picked up in chs 12—14. "Eagerly wait[ing] for our Lord Jesus Christ to be revealed" (1:7) anticipates ch 15; and "fellowship with his Son, Jesus Christ our Lord" (1:9) is a possible reference to the collection for the saints in Jerusalem in ch 16.

However, the thanksgiving section is significant not only because of its contents but also because of its tone. It must always be remembered that Paul's letters were not *written*; they were *spoken* by him and copied for him by an amanuensis. This means they are to be *heard* rather than *read*. Their rhetorical tone conveys as much of the message as the written words. They are *written speech*. Accordingly, one must always ask: In what tone of voice did Paul say this?

Inasmuch as a thanksgiving by definition gives thanks, it serves to establish an amicable mood between the writer and the readers, and thereby prepares the way for the acceptance of the message that follows. So it is not just a formality. At the same time, it may also be intended to create an openness on the part of the readers to what the author has to say in terms of further instruction or correction. Since this particular thanksgiving foreshadows in a very explicit way the main themes treated in the letter where Paul has much to say by way of further instruction, correction of misunderstanding, and toning down of exaggerated practice, 1:4-9 plays a critical role in creating the mood in which Paul wishes his message to be heard.

Overall, then, Paul appears to have taken a fairly standard component of the introduction (or exordium, as it is technically known) of the Greek letter and fashioned it to fulfill his own needs and purposes.

IN THE TEXT

■ **4** The thanksgiving is addressed to God, which implies that it bears the character of a prayer. The Corinthians are thus being permitted to overhear Paul's prayer for them. The prayer has a strongly personal note as being directed to <u>my</u> God. Paul's ministry was grounded in a deeply personal knowledge of God. Matching this is the Corinthians' relationship with God: **his grace given you in Christ Jesus**. The repetition of the word **grace** from v 3 is significant as is the channel of his grace **Christ Jesus**, already mentioned four times in 1:1-3. The heart of Paul's thanksgiving for the Corinthians is that they have come to know God's grace in Christ. It is significant that, despite the problems in Corinth, Paul strikes the note of thanksgiving from the start (contrast Gal 1:6).

■ **5** The particular forms of grace they have received are speaking (*logos*) and knowledge (*gnōsis*). The Greek is best translated *every kind of speaking and every kind of knowledge*. The measure of the grace they have received is expressed in emphatic language: **in him you have been enriched in every way**. The locus of this grace is **in Christ**. As to why Paul names **speech** and **knowledge** as the singular gifts they have received: it is evidently because these were not only greatly used but also greatly prized by the Corinthians. Both terms occur later in polemical contexts and appear to have carried a flavor commending itself to Corinthian tastes. Even so, Paul does not brush them aside, even if he will lay stress on other aspects of them than the Corinthians did.

■ **6** The riches received by the Corinthians have come directly from the gospel. The NIV's **our testimony about Christ** (where the Greek has "the testimony") shifts the focus from the gospel to Paul, from the message to the messenger. The intent is rather to underscore that the message Paul passed on to the Corinthians was not his own invention but was the tradition about Christ that he had received. He will refer to this again at crucial points in the letter (1 Cor 4:17; 8:6; 11:2; 15:1-4; Bailey 2011, 62, 155, 229, 296, 423ff.).

■ **7** The result of this is that **you do not lack any spiritual gift** (*charisma*). *Charisma* is a term used almost exclusively by Paul in the NT (sixteen of the seventeen instances, with 1 Pet 4:10 being the sole exception). Its meaning ranges from "eternal life" (Rom 6:23) and deliverance from danger (2 Cor 1:10) to "gifts of healings" (1 Cor 12:9, 28, 30). The word by itself does not denote **spiritual gift** so much as a concrete gift of grace, as its derivation from the word "grace" (*charis*) suggests. The double use of the word "grace" in this context (1:3, 4) points in this direction. However, the reference to "speech" and "knowledge" in v 5 with their probable overtones of Corinthian tendencies, together with the fact that their enrichment in these qualities (v 5) is advanced as explaining why **you do not lack any spiritual gift** (v 7) suggests that Paul is using the term in a deliberately comprehensive way. Again, the point of this will become clear later (chs 12—14).

Significantly, Paul now proceeds to provide the gifts of God's grace with a context. They are to be accepted and used **as you eagerly wait for our Lord Jesus Christ to be revealed**. They have, so to speak, an eschatological setting and, indeed, an eschatological horizon. As he will say, "prophecies . . . will cease," "tongues . . . will be stilled," "knowledge . . . will pass away" (13:8)—precisely those gifts to which he has referred in 1:5. They are not ends in themselves but are, rather, aids in preparing for the end.

■ 8 They are not left to their own resources in being prepared. The Lord Jesus Christ **will also keep you firm to the end, so that you will be blameless on the day of our Lord Jesus Christ**. Just as the gospel was confirmed in them (v 6), so Christ will continue that confirming work so that they stand without reproach when he returns. The word "blameless" is often taken to have a strictly declaratory or judicial sense (Grundmann in *TDNT* 1:357; Thiselton 2000b, 101-2). However, Paul uses it in harness with "holy" (*hagios*) and "without blemish" (*amōmos*) in Col 1:22; while in 1 Thess 3:13—a parallel context—he uses the same terminology in an ethical sense. The two senses though distinct are not to be clinically separated.

■ 9 Lest the Corinthians quail at this lofty expectation, Paul reassures them that its fulfillment is not their own doing but God's: **God is faithful**. In particular, he will be faithful to the call he has given them **to be participants in the life of his Son** (lit. "the fellowship of his Son"). Fellowship (*koinonia*) denotes primarily not fellow-feeling but communal sharing in the same reality—namely, Christ and the life he brings. This sets the stage for the topic Paul turns to immediately: the divisions rending the Corinthian church.

FROM THE TEXT

Several matters of abiding theological significance emerge from what looks like a strictly formal introduction to a letter.

The first is *the almost breathless gratitude for the lavish outpouring of the grace of God*. Paul himself had an overpowering awareness that God's grace alone had caused the great turnabout in his own life (15:9-10). Now he sees that same undeserved mercy showered upon the Corinthians, and he responds in thanksgiving. The only appropriate response to grace is gratitude. It is the power that turns the turbines of the spiritual life.

Related to this is *the repeated note that this grace has come to them* "in Christ Jesus" (1:4). The name of Jesus—in various forms—is mentioned five times in vv 4-9, maintaining the frequency of vv 1-3. It is remarkable that

Christ, rather than the Spirit (who is not mentioned at all), is named as the agent of the gifts. Lightfoot observes that, whenever God the Father and Christ are mentioned together, the Father is named as the source, Christ as the mediator of things physical as well as spiritual (he cites 8:6). He notes how interesting it is that at this early stage in Christian history the doctrine of the person of Christ was maintained with such exactness (1895, 150). Put together, these features suggest that it is easy to "overspiritize" the understanding of Christian faith.

A third notable feature of the thanksgiving is *the heavy stress upon the return of Christ* (1:7-9). While thankful for the grace that God has given to the Corinthians, with its accompanying gifts, Paul places them in the setting of Christ's return. This is the backdrop against which they are to be measured: do they prepare believers to face scrutiny before the final judge? Still more, what is needed is not a holiness that will be imparted to them at the end but one that "will . . . keep you firm to the end" (v 8). The gifts of God in their full range thus have an eschatological purpose, and that purpose is salvific: fitness leading to acceptance on the day of Christ.

II. THE GOSPEL AND DIVISIONS IN THE CHURCH: THE MESSAGE OF THE WISDOM OF THE CROSS: I CORINTHIANS 1:10—4:21

Overview

Several features suggest that 1:10—4:21 is a consciously defined unit. First, the whole is bound together by a common theme that may be expressed most broadly as the reversal of appearances. The cross looks like foolishness, weakness, and defeat measured by the yardstick of worldly wisdom, whereas by God's standard the reverse is true (1:17-25; 2:1-5). Worldly wisdom produces party spirit and divisions (1:11-13; 3:18-23), which are the marks of spiritual childishness and immaturity (3:1-4). The wisdom of the cross is the mark of the spiritually mature and bears the stamp of the mind of Christ (2:6-16). The inner substance of the reversal of appearances is the embracing of the crucified life as the apostles did (4:8-13). It is this that is the heart of their holy calling (1:3). This theme: that it is folly to judge things by how they look, finds its starting point and focus in the cross and is the thread that binds these chapters together.

Second, the conceptual unity of these chapters is confirmed by rhetorical markers. The phrases "I appeal to you" (1:10) and "I urge you" (4:16; *parakalō* in both cases) serves as something of an inclusion, as do Paul's references to preaching the gospel in 1:17 and 4:15. The repeated appeal to personal examples (2:1-5; 3:1-10; 4:9-13) is seen by some as typical of Hellenistic rhetoric (though the use of personal examples by the Hebrew prophets should not be overlooked; see Hos 1:2-9; Amos 7:10-15; Jer 18:1-11). Equally important is the function of the rhetoric in enjoining the readers to live in keeping with the message Paul proclaimed. The rhetoric is deliberative in character; that is, it urges the Corinthians to shape their lives after the pattern of the cross. They must replace their childish and sinful ways with the mind of Christ. In this way they will become God's holy temple (3:16-17) and will fulfill the call to holiness that was theirs from the start (1:3). The Christian life is the crucified life (4:8-13, 16), not the expansive life of self-indulgence and self-seeking.

Third, the whole is written under the umbrella of Paul's apostolic authority. This is affirmed forcefully in the first verse of the letter. It is repeated in the use of the verb in 1:17: "Christ did not send [*apostellō*] me to baptize, but to preach the gospel." Paul does not deny that he has fellow workers (3:5-9, 21-22). Still less does he deny that he views the Corinthians with fatherly affection: after all, he brought the gospel to them (4:14-16). But his apostolic role goes beyond this (→ 4:9-13, where "we" seems to have singular reference). It is for this reason that Timothy's task will be to remind them of "what I teach everywhere in every church" (4:17).

A. The Problem of Divisions in the Corinthian Church (1:10-17)

BEHIND THE TEXT

The Corinth in which Paul preached was fundamentally a Roman city, though remnants of the old Greek city and way of life remained and, indeed, eventually became dominant. This applied to religion, which found expression in three main forms: official Roman cults, cults with Greek roots, and fringe Greek cults. Another aspect of Corinthian culture derived from the heyday of Greek philosophy in the fifth and subsequent centuries BC. Acts 17:21 describes this aptly in reference to the Athens Paul visited before coming to Corinth by saying that the Athenians "spent their time doing nothing but talking about and listening to the latest ideas." The professional merchants of "the latest ideas" were known as sophists (*sophos*: "wise man"), who gave increasing importance to rhetoric: how they said it, rather than what they said.

Inevitably, one sophist would gain a greater popularity than another depending on his rhetorical style and eloquence.

This seems clearly to have been the background of 1 Cor 1—4, where Paul uses the terms "wise" (*sophos*) and "wisdom" (*sophia*) twenty-six times against nine times in all the rest of his writings. The first example occurs in 1:17.

If the foregoing is correct, the problems in the Corinthian church had a sociological rootage, though this is not to say that they did not have theological implications. Indeed, it is these that Paul addresses head-on right from the start.

IN THE TEXT

■ **10** The verse is important as expressing the first issue that Paul raises—namely, the presence of differences of opinion among the Corinthians. Precisely what these were will be made clearer in due course. Their existence was his primary concern. The language he uses covers a wide range of emotions. First, there is a note of appeal (*parakalō*). However, it is not merely a private appeal from Paul: it is one issued **in the name of our Lord Jesus Christ**—that is, with the authority of Christ. The verb is used in official Greek letters in the sense of "authoritative request." At the same time Paul addresses them affectionately as **brothers and sisters**. The substance of his request is **that all of you agree with one another** (lit. "that you all say the same thing"), thus putting an end to **divisions** (*schismata*). The nature of these divisions can only be determined by the evidence of 1 Corinthians. There is nothing in chs 1—4 to suggest that there were organized factions. There was no tension between Paul and Apollos, two of those with groups of followers (3:5-9, 21-23). Where *schismata* is again used (11:18) it seems to refer to distinctions between the wealthier and poorer members of the church (11:18-22). The third use of the noun in the epistle (12:25) speaks of the necessary contribution of all members of the body, thus ensuring equality. Doubtless there would be some kind of commonality among the followers of a favored preacher, but it is going too far to speak of parties. Paul urges the need for a common mind (*nous*) and viewpoint (*gnōmē*). The terms occur elsewhere in 1 Corinthians, the former six times, the latter three, and have the same basic meaning.

Verse 10 is seen by some scholars as the statement of the theme (*propositio*) of the whole epistle. But many topics arise (marriage, idol meat) that appear to have been subjects of confusion rather than contention. It seems more likely that divergences of opinion are treated first because Paul had just learned of them from Chloe's people and because he regarded them as the most serious threat to the gospel.

■ **11** Paul had received reports of the disagreements among the Corinthians from members of the household of Chloe. This is the only mention of Chloe in the NT. It makes the most sense if Chloe's house was the meeting place of one of the house churches in Corinth since she is referred to as one well known to Paul's readers. In that case the members of her household who reported to Paul were slaves carrying out her business in Ephesus (that such contacts were possible is shown by 1 Cor 1:16; 16:15-18). The substance of their report was that there were **quarrels** among the Corinthian believers. The Greek word *eris*, despite its use in Greek literature to refer to political or domestic discord, can also be used of argument for its own sake (as in Phil 1:15; 1 Tim 6:4; Titus 3:9; 2 Cor 12:29). Even so, Paul still addresses the Corinthians with the affectionate expression **my brothers and sisters**.

■ **12** Apparently, a preacher-popularity contest had broken out in Corinth. Its exact content is not easy to determine, given the degree of disparity among the individuals named. That Paul had his admirers is easy to understand, given that he founded the church (3:6, 10). Apollos nurtured the believers and evidently ministered in a style different from Paul's (4:6-7; see Acts 18:24-25, 28). There is no record that Peter (Cephas) visited Corinth, but Paul speaks of him in the same breath as Apollos and himself (1 Cor 3:22) and makes a passing reference that assumes that the Corinthians were familiar with his activities (9:5). His being the leader figure among the Twelve and an intimate of Jesus might well have given him favor with some of the Corinthians. Still more, his being a spokesman and representative of the Jewish Christianity that, while not insisting on circumcision for Gentile converts, required the observance of the ceremonial laws regarding food (see Acts 15:28-29; compare 1 Cor 8:1ff., 10:25ff.), would have commended him to the Christian converts from Judaism (Acts 18:1-8).

The parallel mention of Christ—as though he were a competitor with the other three—is odd. For this reason it has been suggested that it is Paul's affirmation of his own loyalty. However, in the original, its form is exactly parallel with the other three, and it makes better sense to see it as yet another way of carving Christ up, which is exactly what Paul proceeds to discuss in the next verse. Paul's later insistence in the context of a discussion of the Corinthians' claims to wisdom that "all things are yours, whether Paul or Apollos or Cephas... all are yours, and you are of Christ, and Christ is of God" (3:21-23) may imply that the Christ party were those laying claim to superior spirituality (3:1). (Bruce [1976, 33] follows T. W. Manson [1962, 207], for such a view. H. Koester holds a kindred position in Schowalter and Friesen [2005, 344-45].)

■ **13** Paul now unveils his underlying concern. Competing loyalties to human leaders destroy loyalty to Christ. The question **Is Christ divided?** is rhetorical, showing the absurdity of the Corinthians' behavior. Paul elaborates the absurdity in reference to himself. Significantly, his first question is whether he was crucified for them. Clearly, the cross stood at the forefront of Paul's understanding of the gospel. Equally absurd is the idea that they were **baptized in the name of Paul**. Christ was the reality into which they were baptized (compare Rom 6:3).

■ **14-16** Paul allows himself a personal aside expressing his relief that he baptized so few of the Corinthians, thereby diminishing the number of those who could say they were his followers. Crispus the ruler of the synagogue was one of Paul's first converts in Corinth (Acts 18:8). If Gaius is identical with Titius Justus (the three names in that order would make a complete Roman name) then he would be another early convert who opened his house for Christian worship when Paul was ejected from the synagogue (Acts 18:7). Paul recalls that he also baptized Stephanas and his household (1 Cor 16:17). He may also have baptized others though he does not remember any. The number who could claim to have been baptized into his name is very small (fifteen), thereby showing that that was not his mission.

■ **17** Paul draws a sharp distinction between the Corinthians' view of his apostolic mission and his own. **Christ did not send me to baptize, but to preach the gospel**. But there is a deeper issue at stake than the identity of the preacher by whom one was baptized. It is whether that individual was preferred on grounds that undermined the gospel message. Paul believed this to be the case in the Corinthian church. The telling phrase that gives expression to this is **not with wisdom and eloquence**. (He repeats the phrase at 2:1, 4, 13.) If the cross has to be proclaimed *cleverly*, then it is not the cross that saves but the cross plus human cleverness. The cross is thereby **emptied of its power**.

FROM THE TEXT

The first concern expressed by Paul in these verses is for unity. The language of 1:10-12 is replete with it: "agree with one another" (v 10), "no divisions among you," "be perfectly united in mind and thought." But it is not a superficial or sentimental unity in which Paul is interested. It is unity in the gospel. For the Corinthians to group themselves behind different leaders (v 12), each regarded as the true voice of Christ, is in effect to say that there is more than one gospel. But there is only one Christ and therefore there is only one gospel. Truth is the guarantee of unity.

Paul's second move is to place at the forefront *the heart of the gospel message: Christ crucified*. The reason why neither Paul nor anyone else can be their lodestar is that it was Christ who was crucified for them (v 13). It is the cross in all of its stark repugnance that takes center place, and no camouflage that obscures it can be tolerated (v 17).

A third notable feature in these verses is *the contrast Paul draws between preaching and baptism*. He is thankful that he baptized so few of them, "for Christ did not send me to baptize, but to preach the gospel." Paul is not disparaging baptism. He admits that he practices it. What he is deploring is the separation of the sacrament from the Word so that it becomes no more than admission into the charmed circle of the disciples of one particular guru. The message of the crucified Christ alone gives meaning to baptism into Christ.

B. The Gospel versus Wisdom (1:18—2:5)

BEHIND THE TEXT

This block of verses both stands together as a coherent unit, yet at the same time falls into three distinguishable parts. As to the former: the section is bracketed at both ends by words expressing the same idea, which may be paraphrased: "preaching not in human wisdom but in the power of the cross" (1:18; 2:5).

At the same time there are clear indications that the argument develops in three distinct stages. In 1:18-25 Paul deals with the theme of human versus divine understandings of wisdom and power, and the passage is bound together by summary statements of this idea (vv 18, 25). Verses 26-31 illustrate this same idea as it is exemplified in the social makeup of the Corinthian church and, indeed, in human history as a whole. In 2:1-5 Paul takes the further step of reminding them that this was the principle on which his own mission had been conducted. It was not with swelling words of eloquence that Paul preached in Corinth, but rather with the powerful simplicity of the message of the cross (vv 4, 5).

It is frequently observed that Paul does, in fact, make use of rhetorical devices in his writings, not least in 1 Corinthians. The development of his argument in the mounting steps of this passage—the abstract statement (1:18-25); the application to the Corinthians (vv 26-31); Paul's personal example (2:1-5)—exemplify the rising tide of argument. Rhetorical questions (1:20); comparison and contrast (vv 22-23, 27-28; 2:4); repetition (1:17; 2:5); are all weapons in Paul's armory. One might reply that the only way to preach is by use of words, and that the only choice is whether to use them badly or use them well. The point at issue for Paul and the Corinthians (not to mention preachers and hearers in every age) is whether the message proclaimed becomes lost in the nimbus of its presentation. If that point is reached "the cross of Christ is emptied of its power" (1:17).

The passage is marked out as a unit rhetorically by the shift in the dominating personal pronouns: from the first and second persons in 1:10-17 to the third in vv 18-25. To put it otherwise: from discussing the response of the Corinthians to the proclamation and his own involvement in it, Paul now takes up the *theme* of the cross.

There are numerous examples of rhetorical style in these verses. Rhetorical questions are fired machine-gun style in v 20; play on words: notably "wisdom" in v 21; and the use of paradox in v 25.

Paul refers to the non-Christian world in terms of the distinction between Jews and Greeks (vv 22, 24), and Jews and Gentiles (v 23). While some scholars hold that "Greeks" was the common way of referring to Gentiles (Winter 2001, 23ff.), it seems significant that he uses the former when he is discussing wisdom, the latter when the reference is more comprehensive. Paul refers to Gentiles forty-seven times in all the letters that bear his name, but only three times in 1 Corinthians (1:23; 5:1; 12:2). "Greeks" he uses much less often: thirteen times in all the epistles, but only four times in 1 Corinthians (1:22, 24; 10:32; 12:13).

IN THE TEXT

1. The Message of the Cross as the True Wisdom (1:18-25)

■ **18** The issue of dissension slips into the background, as Paul now highlights what demonstrates its folly. Paul's concern is to set forth **the message of the cross**. Paul speaks rarely of the cross of Christ: much more commonly of the death of Christ. While crucifixion was not uncommon in the Roman Empire, it was a fate reserved for outcasts. No Roman citizen could be crucified. The very mention of the word (Lat. *crux*) was offensive in polite society. Paul defies these cultured conventions by asserting bluntly that his message is **the message of the cross**. It may be that he used this language because the Corinthians found the idea of the crucified Christ repugnant. Certainly, it was **foolishness to those who are perishing**. The obverse of that is that **to us who are being saved it is the power of God**. The contrast implies that it was the weakness of the crucified Christ that the Corinthians found offensive. At issue was not the need for salvation but that it could be accomplished through one reduced to helplessness by this mode of execution. There were two classes of people in the world as Paul saw it: **those who are perishing** and those **who are being saved**. The present continuous participle is used of each. The former are on the *road to destruction*, the latter on the *road to salvation*. To the former the message of the cross is **foolishness**; to the latter **it is the power of God**. The latter expression adds a pragmatic dimension to Paul's understanding of wisdom. It is not merely a thing of the mind, but something at work in the life and the heart.

With the mention of **the message of the cross** Paul introduces a whole new standpoint from which, or yardstick by which, wisdom is seen and measured. The cross is the obverse of conventional wisdom and therefore in comparison is regarded as foolishness. In reality, the cross is the quintessential expression and demonstration of wisdom (v 24). Accordingly, the cross is the great dividing line both as an event in history and as a challenge in human experience by which human beings attach themselves to **those who are perishing**, or to those **who are being saved**. It is an event with eternal implications. It is an indication of the importance of this understanding of wisdom to Paul that of the seventeen occurrences of "wisdom" (*sophia*) in 1 Corinthians, sixteen are found in chs 1 to 3. (In the rest of Paul's writings the term occurs only eleven times.)

■ **19** Paul reinforces his argument with a quotation from Isa 29:14. The introductory verb **it is written** (*gegraptai*) is the standard formula indicating a biblical quotation, which means that the argument is beyond dispute. While the part of the passage that Paul quotes refers to **wisdom** by name, and so makes explicit the point that God **will destroy the wisdom of the wise**, the context in which it stands illustrates Paul's point even more pungently. This is not uncommon with Paul's use of the OT (not to mention NT writers generally). The quotation brings its context with it. The overall background is that in which Jerusalem's politicians sought to secure Israel's safety from the threat of Assyria by making an alliance with Egypt. This worldly-wise diplomacy merely enraged the Assyrians who besieged Jerusalem, till it was almost occupied, and was saved in the end only by a miracle (Isa 36—37). The oracle in Isa 29 alludes to those who think they understand better than God (vv 15-16). In time they will come to see their folly (v 24). Richard Hays thinks it is "reasonably sure" that the reference in v 13 to those who "come near to me with their mouth and honor me with their lips, but their hearts are far from me" is a sideswipe at the Corinthians' pride in their eloquent rhetoric as well as their ability to speak in tongues (1997, 28). Nevertheless, out of their overweening vanity and self-assurance, God will bring a new order in his own way, which they dismissed as foolish (vv 18, 22-24).

It is significant that vv 17-19 are causally linked by the conjunction **for** (*gar*). Paul is glad he baptized so few of them *for* Christ sent him to preach the message of the cross (v 17), "*for* the message of the cross . . . is the power of God" (v 18), *for* Scripture says God will destroy human wisdom. The wisdom of the cross (v 17) is thus a cord constituted of the triple strands of Paul's practice (v 17), the experience of those who are being saved by its power (v 18), and the word of God in Holy Scripture (v 19).

■ **20** This verse consists of four rhetorical questions, the fourth of which contains the reply to the first three. The three categories mentioned: the **wise man** (*sophos*), the **scholar** (*grammateus*), and the **philosopher** (*suzētētēs*) have been more concretely identified in various ways. Lightfoot takes the first to refer to the Greek sophist, the second to the Jewish scribe, and the third to both (Lightfoot 1895, 159). Hengel reads them as designations from the Pharisaic schools: the wise man, the scribe, the debater (1991, 42). However that may be, they are all bracketed together as representatives of the wisdom that God has made foolish.

Paul characterizes this wisdom in three different ways. First, he characterizes it as the wisdom that God **made foolish** (*emōranen*), using the aorist tense to indicate a specific event in which that folly was made clear. The context suggests that that event was the event of the cross. Second, Paul characterized the folly posing as wisdom as **the wisdom of the world**; that is, it is human wisdom. But Paul has already injected a third note into the description by characterizing the philosopher as the philosopher **of this age**. In Jewish thought, time was divided into two ages: this age and the age to come. If the event of the cross belongs to the age to come, the implication clearly is that in some measure the age to come has already arrived. An eschatological note is thus injected into Paul's thought, and it is the cross that marks the moment of transition.

■ **21** The truth underlying vv 18-20—that one must be saved in God's way or no way—now comes to its boldest expression. That the world did not come to know God through its own wisdom is, in fact, the outworking of God's wisdom. To know God, according to Paul, as indeed in Scripture as a whole, is not a matter of grasping intellectual information: a race that the best brains would win. Rather it is to perceive God at work in his revelation of himself and enter into the saving experience of him to which he invites us (*NIDNTT* 2:396, 398, 400). That revelation of himself reached its apex in the foolishness of the proclamation—namely, the message of the cross. We are not to choose between the proclamation as **what was preached** and proclamation or preaching as *an activity*. Paul proceeds immediately to use the term in an active sense in v 23: "we preach Christ crucified." A proclamation deserves the name only because it is proclaimed.

It was God's good pleasure to save humanity through the foolishness of the cross because in no other way could the folly of human wisdom be exposed. To have left humans to devise their own way to salvation would have been an atrocious self-contradiction in which humanity would have removed itself ever farther from God as it proudly worked out its own salvation. Only a way that overthrew human pride could be effective, and that is not the way of strenuous self-effort but the way of faith in the provision that God has made. Hence, God saves **those who believe**. Neither human wisdom, nor any other human activity, can effect salvation. Faith alone in what God has done can accomplish that.

■ **22** The aptness of God's demand for faith is shown in the fact that Jews and Greeks alike lay down the terms on which they will be convinced. Their terms do, indeed, differ. Jews demand mighty works, which their forefathers had seen, and nonetheless remained stubbornly unbelieving (e.g., Exod 17:1-7). Greeks demand wisdom: arguments to demonstrate the reality of the divine. To echo Conzelmann's words: both are requiring *proof* of the divine truth, thereby setting themselves up as authorities that can pass judgment on God. They expect God to submit to their measuring rods of truth (1975, 47).

■ **23** Against this Paul offers only **Christ crucified** (following Robertson and Plummer in giving force to the indefinite article [1914, 22]). This is what he *keeps on preaching* (present continuous). To Jews it is an *offense* (*skandalon*), a term that in the NT generally and in Paul particularly denotes that which constitutes an obstacle to faith (*TDNT* 7:352-55; *EDNT* 3:249-50). To Greeks it is simply nonsense.

■ **24** The old way of grouping humanity is now superseded. The key category is now **those whom God has called**. The language of *calling* has already been used in the chapter. The church is constituted of those "called to be . . . holy" (v 2), those whom God has "called . . . into fellowship with his Son" (v 9). This new way of categorizing is expanded into "those who are perishing" and those "who are being saved" (v 18), the latter being characterized still further as "those who believe" (v 21). So there must be a response of faith to the call of God. But the call of God is primary. The salvation of humanity was God's idea before ever it was ours. Those who respond in faith find that, contrary to all appearances, Christ is **the power of God and the wisdom of God**.

■ **25** The passage concludes with the rhetorical paradox that God's **foolishness** is **wiser than human wisdom**, and God's **weakness** is **stronger than human strength**.

FROM THE TEXT

Behind human juggling with words and ideas lies a far deeper issue: the desire to define salvation according to human tastes. This applies both to the way in which we need it and the way in which we think it should come. Jews and Greeks alike, for all their differences, see it as primarily an intellectual thing: the signs in the sky that will convince the mind; the scintillating arguments that will persuade the intellect. But this is altogether too superficial a plane on which to conceive the dilemma of the sinful situation and seek its solution.

Only a way that overthrows such shallow reasoning can meet the need, and this is what is presented in the foolishness of the message of the cross, and the summons to rest one's faith there.

At the same time it is to be noted that Paul is not commending no-power in place of human power, and no-wisdom in place of human wisdom. Paul's meaning is not that there is no sense in thinking as such: that we should put our brains in a box and leave them there. Rather he is directing the Corinthians to a power and wisdom that match their spiritual weakness and folly (vv 24, 30).

There is an emphasis throughout these verses (as in those that follow immediately) on God as the one who initiates and provides the salvation that humanity needs. It is of his good pleasure (v 21); the call comes from him (v 24). It is not said that some but not all are called, nor that all who are called believe. It is simply said that those who believe do so because they have been called. This constitutes the divine response to the human proclivity to dictate why we need to be saved and how.

2. The Composition of the Corinthian Church as Confirmation of the True Wisdom (1:26-31)

BEHIND THE TEXT

While these verses represent a new step in Paul's argument, illustrating his case regarding the true wisdom from the makeup of the Corinthian church, nevertheless they stand within the entire exposition of his argument from 1:18 to 2:5.

Several matters that lie on the surface of the text have deeper significance than might appear. First is the social background of Corinth, which rises to the surface most visibly thus far (for an overview of the social and cultural background of the epistle as a whole, → section A. of the Introduction). Whereas ethnicity is the stage on which the argument of 1:18-25 is played out, in vv 26-31 the setting is that of social distinctions. The Corinthian church was not composed by those who, by human standards, were clever (*sophoi*) or socially powerful (*dunatoi*) or of noble birth (*eugeneis*). On the contrary, it was the unlearned (*mōra*: "foolish"), the socially unimportant (*asthenē*: "weak"), the lowly (*agenē*), the nobodies whom God had chosen to put down those pretending to be and regarded as the movers and shakers. The implication of this is that, while there were some people of high social status in the Corinthian church, most were of no social consequence. The Corinthian church was not socially homogeneous. While this may well have given rise to some of the tensions among them, Paul does not make that point here.

Second, the highly contrived rhetoric noted in vv 18-25 continues here, if anything on a greater scale. Repetition (or parallelism, as it is technically called [BDF, 490]) is used to great effect: "not many" in v 26 (3x); "God chose" in vv 27 and 28 (3x); the verb "to shame" in v 27 (2x). Contrast is also present not only as between v 26 on the one hand and vv 27 and 28 on the other but as within the successive clauses of vv 27 and 28 ("the foolish things of the world to shame the wise," etc.). The whole unit is bound together by a glance at Jer 9:23 in 1 Cor 1:26 and a partial quotation from the same passage in v 31.

IN THE TEXT

■ **26** "Call" (*klēsis*) in the NT invariably denotes the call from God to salvation. Paul is therefore pointing to the basis on which God called them. It was not because they were clever **by human standards** or occupied positions of power or because they were of noble birth and therefore persons of wealth. Of some, these things might be true, but they were a minority (**not many**). Inevitably, such persons would stand out in a group consisting largely of less educated, less **influential**, and less-monied people, but that was not why God called them.

■ **27-28** These verses are bound together by language, grammar, and rhetorical form. Some terms are used three times over: **world, chose, God**; others twice: **shame**. Moreover, terms that denote qualities opposite to those favored in Corinth: **foolish, weak, lowly** stand first in the three clauses in these verses, as denoting God's chosen instruments for overthrowing the upstart wisdom, power, and pretension of Corinthian society. Further, *the three clauses of these verses are purpose clauses* (introduced by the Greek particle *hina*), with God as the subject. The rhetorical buildup reaches its height in v 28 where Paul departs from exact parallelism with the two preceding clauses to make his point even more forcefully: *the things lacking pedigree in the world, and the things that count for nothing—the things that are nothing—God has chosen to bring to nothing the things that are reckoned to be something.* What this amounts to is a huge reversal of human scales of valuation. In Corinth it was regarded as shameful for status boundaries to be breached. Yet Paul sees the overthrow of conventional measures of evaluation as the work of God himself.

■ **29** The demolition of this mindset had a specific aim in the purpose of God: **so that no one may boast before him**. In the NT, the word **boast** occurs chiefly in Paul's writings, and there mostly in 1 and 2 Corinthians. In this context it may well have been suggested by Jer 9:23-24, already drawn upon in 1 Cor 1:19 and again in v 31. God's use of precisely the reverse of all means held in human esteem is designed to kill any suggestion that humanity can effect its own salvation. The language is precise: it refers to everyone ("all flesh" [KJV]), whether Jew or Greek; and it defines its scope: **before** God. If humanity is to be saved at all, it can only be effected by God as a free gift.

■ **30** Paul now proceeds to define **wisdom from God** more exactly. Paul now proceeds to define wisdom from God more exactly. The three nouns used—"righteousness" (*dikaiosunē*), "holiness" (*hagiasmos*), and "redemption" (*apolutrōsis*)—do not appear again in the epistle. The changed order of the verb forms in 6:11 suggests that they are not arranged systematically (Conzelmann 1975, 52; Fee 2014, 90). "Righteousness" denotes both God's love for his covenant people in saving and delivering them (Ps 98:2-3; Isa 46:13; 2 Cor 5:21; Rom 1:16-17), but also in enabling them to fulfill their side of the covenant: living righteously (Isa 1:26; Amos 5:7, 24; Rom 6:13-14; Phil 2:12-13). Thus it has both a vertical and a horizontal dimension. "On the one hand God's *dikaiosunē* is pardoning action, and on the other a way of sharing God's character with believers, who then exhibit righteousness in the moral sense" (BDAG, 247b). "Holiness" gives explicit expression to the moral aspect. In 6:11 it is associated with washing or cleansing from the sins listed in vv 9-10. See also Rom 12:1-2; 1 Thess 3:13; 4:3-7. All of this is effected through Christ's work of redemption. The concept had a long history, denoting redemption from slavery (Deut 7:8; 9:26; Isa 41:14; 43:1, 14). It is used here to denote deliverance from the bondage of sin (Rom 3:22-23; Col 1:13-14). All of this is what is meant by being of God **in Christ Jesus, who has become for us wisdom.**

■ **31** If then there is to be any boasting, let it be in the things discussed by the worldly-wise as foolish, weak, and of no consequence (1 Cor 1:26-29). The words of Jer 9:23-24 form a perfect capstone to Paul's argument. Love, justice, and righteousness are the things in which the Lord delights, not wisdom, power, and wealth.

FROM THE TEXT

The Corinthian church was not a homogeneous congregation. It included a few who belonged to the intelligentsia, a few who were power brokers, a few of social distinction (1 Cor 1:26). By and large, however, they were run-of-the-mill types who would be reckoned as of little intellectual, social, or political consequence. Paul sees in this the hand of God reversing human canons of value. This has the effect of confounding human pretension and of removing any ground people may have for assuming that they have saved themselves by their own ingenuity and power. The purpose is not simply salvation, but the mental condition without which salvation is not possible—namely, **so that no one may boast before** [God] (v 29).

The meaning and nature of God's choice. There is no thought in these verses of eternal predestination or that God chooses to save some and damn others. The idea is rather that, in working out his saving purpose in history, God chooses the instruments best suited to fulfill his purpose. These are always those whose assumed self-importance does not obscure the solitary greatness of God as the sole source of salvation. Israel is the shining example of this in the OT (Deut 7:7-8). The principle is spelled out in Luke 1:51-53, and 1 Cor 1:27-28 is an application of it.

Justification by faith in Christ alone is presented in the Corinthian context. There is no mention here of "works" or "the works of the law." The challenge in Corinth was salvation by social pedigree or dependence on the miraculous (on the part of Jews) or wisdom (on the part of Greeks). To all alike Paul poses acceptance with God on one ground alone: faith in Christ crucified. "God was pleased through the foolishness of what was preached to save those who believe" (v 21). It is this Christ who has **become . . . our righteousness** (v 30). (The point is stated fully in Westerholm 2004, 364-66.)

3. Paul's Ministry in Corinth as an Example of the True Wisdom (2:1-5)

BEHIND THE TEXT

In 1:26-31 Paul appealed to the experience of the Corinthians themselves as validation of where true wisdom lies. Now in 2:1-5 he points to his own experience in Corinth for the same purpose. The Corinthians themselves could remember this since they witnessed his earliest preaching among them. In Roman Corinth, oratory was something of a popular form of entertainment. At local festivals, such as the Isthmian Games, not only the athletes would compete, but the sophists would also contend for applause at the multiplied feasts and banquets accompanying the games. Paul was inevitably measured against that competition, and clearly he was fully aware of it. Some of the terms he uses—such as "message" (*logos* [v 4]), "demonstration" (*apodeixis*), "persuasive" (*peithois*)—are borrowed from the enemy.

IN THE TEXT

■ 1 Paul now returns to the first-person singular, and in a most emphatic way. The Greek reads literally: "And I, brothers, coming to you, came." There is an undertone of urgency and mission in his words. This is confirmed by the concluding words of the verse, which describe *what* he came to do: **as I proclaimed to you the testimony about God**. Altogether the language has the ring of apostolic ministry. He came as one *sent*, and not to convey his own ideas, but to announce to them **the testimony about God**. (While a very strong group of manuscripts read "the mystery of God," and many commentaries and translations follow that reading, **testimony** fits the surrounding apostolic terms better than "mystery.") Paul's role was not to philosophize about what might or might not be, but to proclaim what God had done. This he did, however, not with imposing words or wisdom. He did not adopt "the grand style" (to borrow the expression from ancient rhetoric; see E. A. Judge [2008, 58-60]).

■ **2** Paul was a man of one theme. **I resolved to know nothing while I was with you except Jesus Christ and him crucified**. **Crucified** (*estaurōmenon*) is the perfect passive participle, expressing the permanent effect of the event. There is not, and never will be, any other Christ than the crucified Christ. Paul thus gathers up in this expression everything that he has said thus far about the cross. It was the crucified Christ (not Paul) who died for their salvation and into whose name they were baptized (1:13). It is the cross, the epitome of shame and defeat, in which the wisdom and power of God are seen most clearly (1:17-18, 23-24).

■ **3** Paul's presentation matched his message perfectly. **Weakness, great fear, and *much* trembling** characterized his ministry among them. These epithets stand in sharp contrast to the strength and self-assurance exhibited by the common run of orators. To try to pin them down to specific features of Paul's condition is probably misguided. **Weakness** need not refer to some physical malady from which Paul suffered (e.g., 2 Cor 10:10; 11:6; 12:5). The responsibility of proclaiming Christ crucified in a setting in which it could only be regarded as an absurdity explains sufficiently his fear and trembling.

■ **4** Paul continues the contrast between himself and the professional orators. His discourse (*logos*) and his preaching (*kerygma*)—denoting both *what* he proclaimed and *how* he proclaimed it—were not cast in persuasive words designed to impress. (The Greek manuscripts vary at this point as the translations, including the NIV, indicate. "Persuasive words of wisdom" renders the most likely reading, as followed by UBS[4]. For a full discussion of the options, see Thiselton 2000b, 215-16.) On the contrary, his proclamation was marked by **a demonstration of the Spirit's power**. The word **demonstration** occurs only here in the NT. As noted earlier, in Greek rhetoric it denoted a conclusive proof. Paul plucks it from its rhetorical surroundings to indicate the Spirit and power sufficient to transform lives. The convincing power of the Spirit at work in the conscience (rather than any miraculous demonstration) was what brought the Corinthians to faith.

■ **5** Paul's use of **faith** (*pistis*) may also (like "demonstration" in v 4) represent a play on meanings. In Greek rhetoric it was used to carry the sense of "logical proof" and so conviction. For Paul it carried the distinctive sense of the trust that led to salvation (1:21). Thus Paul is saying that his message was proclaimed in an unadorned way precisely in order that faith would not rest on rhetorical acrobatics, but on the moral power of the renewing Spirit.

FROM THE TEXT

The overall thrust of these verses is that the power of the gospel does not rest on the impressiveness of the preacher but on the simplicity and moral directness of the message. The conventional canons of acceptance—eloquence, magnetic personality, image (all occasions of boasting in Corinth)—are set aside as distractions when they compete with the message of Christ crucified. That message and proclamation (2:4a) were not decided by majority vote but by an act of God (v 5). The emphasis throughout the whole sequence from 1:18 to 2:5 is upon God as the actor and mover in the work of salvation (1:21, 25, 27-28; 2:1, 5). The cross is his doing.

The Spirit is mentioned—for the first time in the epistle (2:4)—as the agent of salvation. The task with which he is specifically associated is the confirmation of faith (v 5). This is the reverse of the emotional exhibitionism by which the Corinthians set such store.

It is possible to hold a correct theology, but neutralize it by presenting it in a frame that contradicts its essential meaning. It is possible that the Corinthians' soteriology stated in formal terms was sound enough (Litfin 1994, 171-80, 182-83, 187). However, their insistence that it must be presented according to the canons of rhetoric valued in Corinth had the effect of subordinating the message to its mode of presentation. This meant that something other than, or in addition to, the gospel was the power of God leading to salvation.

First Corinthians 1:18—2:5 has been regarded as the foundation of the whole epistle (Hays 1997, 36). It has also been seen as the central passage of chs 1—4 in which Paul sets forth his basic view of the wisdom debate that was convulsing the Corinthian church (Litfin 1994, 10, 188-92). There are good grounds for accepting this view. Throughout the epistle it will be well to keep this section in mind as the interpretative theological benchmark against which to measure Paul's treatment of the successive problems that he addresses. It is significant that it is this passage which Paul prefaces with the words: "Christ did not send me to baptize, but to preach the gospel" (1:17).

C. Worldly Wisdom versus the Wisdom Revealed by the Spirit (2:6—3:4)

BEHIND THE TEXT

The argument now undergoes a change of focus. So far Paul has assumed that the Corinthians accept his new definition of wisdom (1:30; 2:5). Now, however, he inserts a qualification. Paul will develop this progressively in the rest of this chapter and the next. Here he begins by simply introducing it: "wisdom," as he has just defined it, is perceived only by the perfect (NIV: "mature" [2:6]). Paul does not seem to regard many of the Corinthians as falling under that description (3:1).

Where does this language of perfection come from, and what does Paul mean by it? Apparently it was current among the Corinthian Christians—unsurprisingly since it seems to have been part of the stock of religious terminology in the religions of the Greco-Roman world. But Paul did not need to go there to learn it, for it is found in the OT. There it refers to God's way and those who walk in it (Heb. *tāmîm* in Gen 6:9; Deut 18:13) and to a heart that is wholly turned toward God and so is complete, whole, sound (2 Sam 22:26).

What Paul is doing here is something that, as a matter of strategy, he will do repeatedly throughout the epistle: correct the Corinthians' mistaken views by reinterpreting their language in fully Christian terms. At this point it is their (mis)understanding of perfection that he is reinterpreting. This explains the abruptness with which such language appears, the assumption being that the Corinthians will connect with what Paul is talking about.

IN THE TEXT

1. Wisdom: The False and the True (2:6-16)

■ **6** Paul speaks of a wisdom unlike that claimed by the pretenders to a superficial perfection. There is, indeed, an authentic perfection. But it is the reverse of what the powers that be regarded as perfection. To them wisdom was the power to make real differences in the real world. Ironically, this power is merely a facade: **The rulers of this age . . . are coming to nothing**.

Paul draws upon the idea rooted in the OT and developed in Judaism that saw time as divided between **this age** (when powers hostile to God were at work) and "the age to come" (when these powers would be overthrown) (Ladd 1993, 42-44, 66-67). Even now, these powers have been defeated and **are coming to nothing**. But it takes real wisdom—the wisdom of the truly perfect—to see this.

"The Rulers of This Age" in 1 Corinthians

The rulers of this age are evidently human, historical individuals. The same terms that describe them in ch 1 are used in ch 2. They are the wise, the powerful, the noble, who are being reduced to nothing (1:26-28). They "crucified the Lord of glory" (2:8). Paul speaks elsewhere of Satan as "the god of this age [*aiōn*]" (2 Cor 4:4). In 1 Cor 2:7 the "wisdom . . . decreed before the ages" (NRSV) seems to refer to knowledge on a supernatural plane possessed by supernatural beings. It appears, therefore, that behind the historical figures opposing Christ were ranged supernatural opponents, carrying out their evil designs in and through historical representatives (see Wink 1984, 40-45).

■ **7** The strong, adversative conjunction **But** (*alla*; NIV: No) introduces the emphatic contrast between pseudo-wisdom and true wisdom. Paul says it is "secret and hidden" (NRSV). Therefore, it is not accessible by human searching. God's eternal purpose, determined **before time began**, was to hide his wisdom from us **for our glory**. Glory (*dóxa*) is a term of wide meaning. Its sense here is evidently positive. Paul will argue later that the destiny of believers in Christ is sharing the glory of the resurrection (15:40-41, 43).

■ **8** The ignorance of **the rulers of this age** is stressed even more emphatically. If they had been as wise as they professed, **they would not have crucified the Lord of glory**. Paul thus returns implicitly to the conclusion he had reached already in 1:23-24: that "Christ crucified" is "the power of God and the wisdom of God." He thereby brings the understanding of wisdom from the level of ethereal speculation to the hard events of history. Paradoxically, the crucifixion is something that should never have happened. Yet it was always part of God's purpose. Only God's power of reversal makes the epitome of weakness the quintessence of power.

■ **9** Paul backs up his claims by quoting Scripture, as the introductory formula (**as it is written**) indicates. Precisely what scripture Paul had in mind is not completely clear. The citation comes closest to Isa 64:4 with allusions to other passages (e.g., Job 28:12-28; Isa 48:6) thrown in. The import of the passage is clear enough. God's saving work through the death of Christ surpasses all human imagination and expectation. Furthermore, its benefits are prepared not for those of superior intellectual powers but **for those who love him**. Once again, Paul grounds the knowledge of salvation in the moral, not the intellectual, realm.

■ **10a** If it be asked how we have come to know **these . . . things** that lie beyond human powers of perception, the answer is that **God has revealed** them **to us by his Spirit**. The pronoun **to us** (*hēmin*) stands in the emphatic position as first word in the sentence. It is intentionally nonspecific, referring to any open to the revelation of the Spirit. With the mention of the Spirit, Paul's argument acquires further definition. The key word used thus far has been "wisdom." Now Paul takes the further step of saying that the agent of revelation is the **Spirit**. Wisdom is thus directly linked with the Spirit, who becomes the controlling theme of the rest of the chapter.

■ **10b-11** It is sometimes suggested that these verses consist of a quotation of the ideas, if not the words, of the Corinthians (Thiselton 2000b, 252).

Certainly, the whole of 1 Cor 2:10-16 contains language that is not typical of Paul or else is used here in greater density. Terms such as "hidden" (*apokekramménēn* [v 7]), **know** (vv 8 [*egnōken* and *egnōsan*], 11 [*egnōken*], and 12 [*eidōmen*]), **searches** (*erauna* [v 10]), **judged** and **judgment** (vv 14 [*anakrínetai*: "discerned"] and 15 [*anakrínei*: "discern" and *anakrínetai*: "scrutiny"]), "human" (*anthrōpos* [v 11 (3x)]; *psychikòs . . . anthrōpos*: **those who are unspiritual** [v 14]), and "spiritual" (*pneumatikós* [vv 13, 14, 15]) are examples of these. It is probable that these verses are Paul's exposition of the Spirit of God as the source of wisdom. He uses terms and ideas favored by the Corinthians but recasts them in a way consistent with the gospel.

The conjunction **for** (*gar* [omitted in the NIV]) at the beginning of v 10*b* links vv 10*b*-13 with vv 8-10*a*. Paul explains the failure of the rulers of this age to understand the crucifixion of Christ as due to their lack of **the Spirit**. For **the Spirit** is the great explorer of everything, including the depths of God's own self. The personhood of the Spirit is strongly implied in these words.

Paul reinforces his point with a human analogy. A person's thoughts are fully known only by the person's inner **spirit** (v 11). In the same way God's thoughts are accessible only by the Spirit of God. The implications of this are twofold. First, if human beings are to know God, there must be a sphere of reality they share in common. Second, there is such a sphere—namely, spirit.

■ **12-13** These verses constitute a single sentence in Greek. They express a contrast between two spirits: **the spirit of the world** and **the Spirit who is from God** (v 12). The emphatic initial pronoun **we** means **we Christians**. As such, **we have received . . . not the spirit of the world**. **Rather** (*alla*: but) we have received **the Spirit who is from God**. Paul emphasizes that **the Spirit** is the gift of God, not simply some natural capacity. The gift of the Spirit is given **so that we may understand the gracious gifts** (*ta . . . charisthénta*) given to us by God. *Charisthénta* is broader than the term *charisma* used by Paul in 1:7. In particular, it includes the cross, which was perpetrated because of what "the rulers of this age" did not know or understand (2:8). Paul now (v 13) returns to the activity of speaking (vv 6, 7), which lay at the heart of the Corinthian problem: **We speak, not in words taught us by human wisdom but in words taught by the Spirit**. The use of the term **words** reinforces the reference to "speaking," while the forceful contrast between what is taught by human wisdom and what is taught by the Spirit maintains the antithesis between human wisdom and divine wisdom. The entire activity of Spirit-informed speaking is characterized as **explaining spiritual realities with Spirit-taught words**. While the Greek may be rendered as "interpreting spiritual truths to those who are spiritual" (as in the NIV mg.), it seems more likely that the force of the dative *lógois* in the first half of the verse carries forward into the second half. Commentators may be found on both sides. C. K. Barrett leaves the decision to the reader (1968, 76).

■ **14 The person without the Spirit** renders the Greek word *psychikòs*, which means the person controlled by their soul (Gk. *psyche*). The only other example of this word in Paul's writings is in 15:44-46 where he contrasts the "natural body" with the "spiritual body," basing the former on Gen 2:7 where the first Adam is said to have been created "a living *psyche*." The last Adam, on the other hand, has become a life-giving spirit (Gk. *pneuma*). *Psychikòs anthrōpos* is therefore correctly translated as **the person without the Spirit**. Such persons do **not accept the things that come from the Spirit of God** because they make no sense to them. The reason they make no sense to them is because "they are spiritually discerned" (NRSV). The Greek word rendered **discerned** (*anakrinetai*) is found sixteen times in the NT, ten of them in this epistle where it expresses the idea of evaluation of judging (1 Cor 4:3-5; 9:3; 10:25, 27). Spiritual discernment was not something for which the Corinthians were famous in Paul's eyes. He pointedly describes people like them as those who consider that the things that come from the Spirit as **foolishness** (*mōría*). This is the self-same word he has used to describe how the message of the cross is regarded by the worldly-wise, whereas in fact it is "the power . . . and the wisdom of God" (1:23-24).

■ **15** Verse 14 of ch 2 has given a definition of "the person without the Spirit." Verse 15 now gives a definition of the person **with the Spirit**: the *pneumatikos*. It is probable that the form of words used reflects the claims made by the "spiritual experts," as the Corinthians regarded themselves. On the contrary, says Paul, it is the truly spiritual person who is able to make judgments about everything (borrowing the Corinthians' favorite terminology). Moreover, an authentically spiritual person is not to be subject to merely human judgment: that is, the judgment of those who are unspiritual. It appears that the self-styled "spiritual" person in Corinth had been passing negative judgments on those they regarded as unspiritual, including Paul himself. Paul will say more of this later (4:3-5). For the moment he is saying that it is not for spiritual persons to be evaluated by those who do not know what "spiritual" means.

■ **16** Just as it is not for human beings to give instructions to the Almighty, so it is not for those without the Spirit or mind of Christ to give instruction to those who possess them. The bridge between "spirit" and "mind" is found in Isa 40:13 (LXX) where the Hebrew term for "spirit" (*ruah*) is rendered by the Greek term "mind" (*nous*). It follows that those possessed by the Spirit of the Lord are those who possess the mind of the Lord. Hence the conclusion: **But we have the mind of Christ**. That mind is the mind of the cross, as Paul has been arguing since 1:18—2:2. To have **the mind of Christ** is therefore to participate not only in Christ's thought but also in the attitude of spirit that animates that thought. Terms such as "mentality" or "mindset" bring out its meaning. On this understanding the mindset of Christ was exhibited in his whole life and ministry. To receive Christ is to receive the Spirit and vice versa. However, it is possible to have the Spirit and live at a subspiritual level: a form of spiritual infancy, as Paul will immediately go on to say (3:1-2). (For fuller treatment, see Sze-kar Wan, *NIDB* 4:90-91; Moisés Silva, ed., *NIDNTTE* 3:425-35; N. T. Wright 2013, 1120-25; Keener 2016.)

The Significance of the Plural in 1 Cor 2:6-16

The shift from the first-person singular in both pronouns and verbs in 2:1-5 to the first-person plural in 2:6-16 is striking. The singular is clearly appropriate in vv 1-5 since Paul is describing his preaching ministry among the Corinthians. It is probable that the plural is used with singular effect in vv 6-9, which seem best understood as expressing Paul's view of wisdom as the gift of the Spirit. Verse 10 ("things God has revealed to us") and v 12 ("what we have received") are generic references. Verse 13 would seem to refer primarily, if not wholly, to Paul. The shift to the third person in vv 14-15—which is taken in the commentary as Paul's reworking of Corinthian language and ideas—implies that the Corinthians may not be as spiritual as they think. The return to the first-person plural in the emphatic words of v 16 (**But we have the mind of Christ**) covers Paul and all those truly numbered among the perfect (*teleioi*). By this means Paul is able to make use of Corinthian terms and ideas while at the same time correcting misconceptions.

2. Perfection: The False and the True (3:1-4)

Paul now spells out in concrete terms the shortfall in Corinthian spirituality.

■ 1 These verses resume the autobiographical form of 2:1-5, beginning with the same emphatic phrase: **And I, brothers and sisters**. Paul is recalling his ministry in Corinth. His recollection was clear and—to the Corinthians—stunning: **I could not address you as spiritual**. He defines what he means by two further terms: "fleshly" (*sarkinos* [NASB]; NIV: **worldly**), meaning "belonging to the human order of things"; and *immature* (*nēpios*; NIV: **infants**), meaning "undeveloped" or "infantile"—the reverse of "perfect" or "not having reached completion." He does not say or mean that they are not Christians. He has already affirmed that they have received the Spirit (2:12) and are believers (3:5). Even if they are infantile, they are **infants in Christ**.

■ 2 Paul fed them the diet of infants, not that of adults—milk rather than meat, because they lacked the digestive power to assimilate meat. Not only were they **not yet ready for it** then, but they are **still not ready** for it now. But the phrase **not yet ready** shows that Paul has not given up hope.

■ **3** The evidence of their unreadiness is that **you are still worldly** (*sarkikoí*). The Greek term *sarkikoí* differs in only one letter from the Greek term *sarkinoi*, translated as "fleshly" in v 1 (NASB). Both are built on the Greek word *sarx*, meaning "flesh." But whereas *sarkinoi* in v 1 denotes "fleshly" in the sense of "belonging to the human and therefore weak," *sarkikoí* denotes "fleshly" in the sense of "belonging to the sphere of evil." (The NIV translates both as **worldly**, and indeed, both denote aspects of the same condition.) Paul now cites the evidence on which his accusation rests. This is the **jealousy** (*zēlos*) and "strife" (*éris* [KJV, NASB]) among them. This was typical of quarrels—often ferocious—between sophists and their respective groups of followers (Winter 2001, 38). Paul is thus deepening his implied definition of sin. It is sins of the spirit on which he now focuses. Hence he poses the question: Are you not fleshly and conduct yourselves like those who know nothing of the Spirit?

■ **4** The form of their strife is spelled out even more specifically. They are divided into contending factions: the Paul faction, the Apollos faction, the Cephas faction. To Paul this strife regarding leaders is conclusive evidence of their lack of the Spirit. They are "unspiritual, living on the purely human level" (v 3 REB).

Paul's argument has led him to the paradoxical conclusion that it is possible to have received the Spirit (2:12) and yet be unspiritual (3:1). He does not unchristianize the Corinthians; he implies rather that they are not Christian enough. There is a dimension of faith that they have not yet achieved: the dimension of spiritual maturity. Yet this is not because they have not been believers long enough. As Chrysostom put it: "The Corinthians' inability to receive solid food was not by nature but by choice, so they were without excuse" (ACCS VII, 28).

Pauline Perfection versus Corinthian Perfection

The idea and terminology of perfection were clearly familiar to the Corinthians. By perfection they evidently meant a stage of religious understanding and illumination beyond the level of the average. It apparently consisted more of imposing presentation—eloquence and sophisticated argument (2:1, 4)—than differences of substance. This mentality they brought with them into the church, and proceeded to apply it to the gospel message. Paul also had an understanding of perfection, derived from the OT, where the "way" of God was described as perfect (2 Sam 22:31), as were those who walked in it (Gen 6:9; 17:1). The sum of the matter was perfection of heart: a heart wholly aligned with God's will (1 Kgs 8:61; 11:4; 15:3, 14; 1 Chr 28:9). Jesus himself sounded the same note (Matt 5:43-48). In 1 Cor 2:6—3:4, Paul is building a bridge over the chasm between the Corinthian view and his own. Perfection thus changed its meaning from the Corinthian view, which was chiefly external and could readily tolerate wrong attitudes of heart (such as strife and jealousy), to his own view, where such attitudes bespoke the absence of the Spirit of God and a condition of spiritual immaturity. The shift in Paul's language from perfection (2:6) to the Spirit and spirituality in 2:10—3:1 shows that perfection and spirituality come with the inward presence of the Spirit of God. I have characterized this perfection elsewhere as "The Perfection of the Interim" (Deasley 2007, 218-20).

FROM THE TEXT

The overriding thrust of the passage is that there is a maturity or perfection of faith that not all Christians have attained. It is expressed in the passage in a variety of ways: in the contrast between "the wisdom of this age" (2:6) and "God's hidden wisdom" (1:7 REB); in the contrast between the spiritual (2:15) and the unspiritual or worldly (3:1-3); in the contrast between the adult (2:6) and the infantile (3:1-2). As Witherington says, "It does appear that Paul made it a practice to engage in wisdom teaching, at least *en tois teleois*, and this wisdom seems to have something to do with further explication of the initial preaching about God's salvation plan operating in and through the crucified Christ" (1994, 302). In Findlay's words, "The Corinthians are at fault in their Christian views, being as yet but half-spiritual men (3:1-3)" (1912, 740).

The heart of the wisdom Paul proclaims is not something in addition to the cross of Christ, but rather the apprehension of the full meaning of the cross. Were it an *addition* to the cross, Paul would contradict his earlier insistence that the crucified Christ alone is the means of salvation (1:30; 2:2). Paul is not proclaiming spiritual elitism but spiritual wholeness, and this consists not merely in accepting the death of Christ as a theorem but living the crucified life, which the Corinthians manifestly were not (3:1-3). To quote Findlay again, "Two things [Paul] strives to bring into full contact—Christ crucified and these half-Christianized Corinthian natures" (1912, 740).

The agent of this change is the Spirit of God. The reason Paul's argument moves from the language of wisdom in 2:6-10a to the language of the Spirit in 2:10b—3:4 is twofold. First, only the Spirit of God, who knows "the deep things of God" (2:10), can reveal these to the depths of the human spirit (2:13-14). Second, only the Spirit of God can bring the human spirit into alignment with the mind of Christ. The mind of Christ is the concrete definition and description of true spirituality (see Phil 2:5-11). Its opposite is the mind of the flesh, which judges by appearances and expresses itself in contentiousness, jealousy, and kindred unspiritual forms (1 Cor 3:1-4).

D. The Folly of the Corinthians' Wisdom (3:5-23)

BEHIND THE TEXT

The idea of wisdom is the cord that binds this section together, even though the term itself is rarely used. In vv 5-9 it comes to expression through the demonstration of the *unity* of the work of Paul and Apollos in the growth of the church in Corinth. Hence, to divide into factions on the basis of the work of two leaders who were working for the same end is folly. The word "wise" comes openly into view in v 10 where Paul describes himself as "a wise builder": "wise" because he builds in a way that ensures that his work will last. The interjection of vv 16-17 shows that nothing less than the temple of God is at stake. In vv 18-23 the idea of wisdom versus folly emerges explicitly as the controlling theme.

The issue of wisdom is thus worked out with specific reference to Paul and Apollos (Cephas seems to be mentioned as an afterthought in v 22). Behind all of this lies the Corinthian pattern of secular discipleship, characterized by intense competitiveness and the fierce loyalty of pupils to their teachers (Winter 2001, ch 2). The idea of teachers working together in unity for a common purpose that Paul expounds was utterly alien to the Corinthian mentality.

Equally noteworthy are the rhetorical devices Paul uses to express his argument. There are interjected questions, such as "What, after all . . . ?" (v 5) and "Don't you know . . . ?" (v 16). There are conditional clauses with the consequences flowing from them: *If this . . . then that* (vv 12, 14, 15, 17, 18). There is rhetorical listing (vv 22-23). The Corinthians would have recognized these as parts of the argumentative weaponry of the Stoic philosophers. Indeed, Paul will quote the Corinthians as saying, "His letters are weighty and forceful" (2 Cor 10:10). What Paul objected to was not the rhetoric as such. Things have to be said in some way, and they are better said clearly and pungently than obscurely and feebly. What Paul objected to was the valuation of rhetoric *for its own sake* as though *how* things were said was more important than *what* was said.

IN THE TEXT

1. The Folly of the Corinthians' "Wisdom" Demonstrated by the Subsidiary Role of Paul and Apollos as Servants of God (3:5-9)

Paul proceeds to demonstrate the folly of the Corinthians' "wisdom" in four ways. His tactic is not so much frontal attack as veiled reference (with which his readers will agree) followed by removal of the veil (which will open their eyes to the truth and so to the folly of their original view). This device, which is frequently referred to as "covert allusion" (Lampe 1990, 124-31; Witherington 1995, 130-31), enables Paul to secure the Corinthians' attention and approval and then close the trap by showing the inconsistency between their earlier ideas and what Paul has now shown to be their implications.

For all intents and purposes therefore, Paul goes back to 1:10 and draws out the implications of the Corinthians' divisions for the ministry, the church, and the gospel.

■ **5** The relative unimportance of Apollos and Paul, of whom their partisans had made so much, is "rubbed in" in successive ways. They are referred to by the impersonal pronoun "what?" rather than the personal pronoun "who?" (The textual evidence for the former is to be preferred, as by *TCGNT*.) They are further referred to by the socially demeaning term "servants." Finally, God is referred to as the source of their power to lead hearers to faith. Most significantly of all, they are placed on the same level: **to each** as the Lord gave.

■ **6** The last point is stressed yet again, with the important reversal of historical order (to which Paul will return): Paul did the planting, Apollos the watering, but throughout everything (the tense changes from aorist to imperfect) God caused the growth. In the Mediterranean world of the first century, in which the economy was predominantly agrarian, most of the population was employed on large plantations. Planting and watering was the work of the lower-ranking slaves. For Paul to apply these images to himself and Apollos is—in the expression of M. L. Soards—"far from flattering" (1999, 70).

■ **7** From the assertion in v 6 that God causes growth to take place, the irresistible conclusion is drawn that the planter and the waterer are ***nothing*** (→ v 5).

■ **8** It is now affirmed that the planter and the waterer are **one**. The NIV (**the one who plants and the one who waters have one purpose**) and NRSV ("have a common purpose") miss the point, which is rather to affirm the unity of the *action* of the two. To say that they are ***nothing*** is not to say that they are unnecessary, but that the effectiveness of their action depends upon God. This is confirmed by the second half of the verse, which states that each will be rewarded (at the last day, it is implied) according to his own work.

■ **9** Paul now summarizes the truth he has been expounding: **we are co-workers in God's service; you are God's field, God's building.** For all that "only God . . . makes things grow" (v 7) we are real sharers in his work. But the verb now changes from first-person plural to second-person plural, and the images are objective. If from one perspective they are fellow workers with God, from another they are his creation: **God's field, God's building.** The word **building** forms a bridge to the next section.

2. The Folly of the Corinthians' "Wisdom" Shown by the Security of the Foundation, Which Is Christ Alone (3:10-15)

The word "building" (*oikodomē*) and its compounds occur no fewer than four times in these verses, while "building" terminology occurs four more times. Whereas "growing" has been the controlling metaphor in vv 5-9, "building" is the controlling metaphor in vv 10-15. The vocabulary Paul uses: "work" (*ergon* [vv 13, 14, 15]), "wages" (*misthon*; NIV: "reward" [v 14]), "penalty" imposed for substandard work (*zemiothēsetai* [v 15]; NIV: "suffer loss") is the standard terminology for building (Collins 1999, 149).

■ **10** Paul describes himself as a **wise** [*sophos*] **builder**. The NRSV translates as "a skilled master builder." This is undoubtedly a correct rendering of the term as used in "building" contexts, but one may wonder if Paul did not find it a happy coincidence that he could apply the term *sophos* to himself, given his debate with the Corinthians. However, his skill/wisdom was not of his own making. It was the gift of God's grace. The founding of new churches was Paul's special gift (Rom 15:19-20). (The theme of gifts will occupy the letter increasingly.) While therefore he could say that he laid the foundation of the church in Corinth, it was really God's doing. Others are building on that foundation. While Paul uses the singular "another" (*allos* [KJV, NASB]; NIV: **someone else** [v 10]) he is not thinking of a single individual, such as Apollos or Peter. In effect, he means "others" as is shown by the widening of the pronouns into "each" and "anyone" (vv 10, 12-15). Hence the warning: **each one should build with care**.

■ **11** There is no need for another **foundation**, indeed, no possibility, for the one secure and lasting foundation has already been laid (the passive denotes that it has been laid by God)—namely, Jesus Christ. Paul has already made plain that the Christ he proclaimed in Corinth from the first was Christ crucified (1:23; 2:2).

■ **12-13** Materials varying from the most valuable (**gold, silver, costly stones** [v 12]) to the least (**wood, hay or straw**) may be used as the individual builder chooses, but none should deceive themselves that their worth—and durability—will not be found out. **The Day will bring it to light** (v 13). The Day of the Lord, understood as the day of judgment, goes back at least as far as Amos 5:18-20 and becomes a standard concept in the OT for the day when human accomplishments will be put to the final test. Paul's unqualified use of the expression shows that he assumes the Corinthians' familiarity with it, suggesting that it was part of his own teaching. The testing will be by fire.

■ **14-15** Two outcomes are possible. If the building **survives**, the **builder** will be rewarded (v 14). If the building goes up in smoke, the builders will pay the penalty for inferior work (v 15). However, they will not be destroyed along with their substandard work but will be saved though only as those **escaping through the flames**. Paul gives no reason as to why they will be spared, unless it is to be found in v 16. F. F. Bruce takes it to mean that "(their) salvation depends on God's grace, not on (their) own works; but (they) would have nothing to show for all (their) labour" (1976, 44). This fits nicely with Paul's earlier comment that God saves those who believe (→ 1:21 with the note) as well as with his characterization of the frenzied efforts of Jews and Greeks to find salvation through signs or syllogisms (1:22-25).

The emphasis on individual responsibility is very forceful in 3:12-15. The double use of the pronoun "each" (*hekastou*) in v 13, and the triple use of the singular generic pronoun "anyone" (*tis*) in vv 12, 14, and 15 is striking. Collins states that nowhere else in Paul or the NT is individual eschatological scrutiny stressed so strongly (1999, 159).

3. The Folly of the Corinthians' "Wisdom" Shown by the Danger It Poses to the Temple of God (3:16-17)

Paul now moves from the horticultural metaphor of vv 5-9 and the building metaphor of vv 10-15 to a religious metaphor: that of the temple of God.

■ **16** The Greek word translated **temple** (*naos*) is the term used regularly in the NT to denote the shrine or holy of holies as distinct from the entire temple complex. It was the unique locus of the presence of God. The Corinthian believers are the temple of God, hence it follows that God dwells in them. Paul's question **Don't you know . . . ?** implies that they do know. Paul uses this formula at least nine times in the epistle (5:6; 6:2, 3, 9, 15, 16, 19; 9:13, 24) to refer either to matters in which he had given them instruction (as here) or matters of common knowledge. In either case they ought to have known.

■ **17** Paul now draws a solemn inference from this. It is possible for an individual (*tis*, **anyone**) to destroy the **temple** of God. But if anyone does, they will suffer the same fate. The verb translated "destroy" (*phtheirei*) has a wide field of meaning, including "defile" or "damage." The language is clearly metaphorical. What is in mind is not destruction in the sense of annihilation but loss of effective operation. The offense in question appears to be creative fissures in the church, destroying its unity. This violates the holiness of the church as well as of the transgressor. There is a continuation of the interplay between the corporate and individual dimensions begun earlier with the reference to the church as God's building (3:9), but built by the labors of individual believers (vv 10-15). Similarly, believers collectively are God's temple (v 16) but the individual believer is capable of damaging it. (Paul will apply this again in 6:18-20.)

4. The Folly of the Corinthians' "Wisdom" Shown by the Deceitfulness of Worldly Wisdom (3:18-23)

These verses are a recapitulation of the whole argument thus far (Horsley 1998, 66). The idea of the contradictory views of wisdom is picked up from 1:18-25; and the idea of boasting in general, and in leaders in particular, from 1:31 and 3:4-5. Paul rounds off his argument by an appeal to Scripture (vv 19-20), and by drawing the logical conclusion that, since there is only one wisdom, they need not pick and choose among their leaders: all belong to them; and leaders and Corinthians alike belong to Christ and to God.

■ 18 Paul now takes a further step in clearing the air. What the Corinthians face is not simply an alternative though equally acceptable option. Rather they confront a choice between two mutually exclusive value systems, representing two mutually exclusive "ages." Judaism distinguished sharply between the "present age" in which the rule of God was resisted by the forces of evil and the "age to come" in which God's will and rule would triumph. The "present age" had its own values and standards of success and Paul placed squarely among them the superficial wisdom and display of eloquence cherished by the Corinthians. It must have been a riveting shock to them to discover that Paul placed them among those whom he had branded as foolish at the beginning of his discourse (1:20-21). His argument has thus come full circle. Those who regard themselves as wise by the standards of this age **should become "fools" so that [they] may become wise**. What he had said covertly in the first chapter, he now says openly and explicitly.

■ 19-20 The paradoxical injunction of v 18 is now expressed plainly (note the connective **for** [Gk. *gar*]): **For the wisdom of this world is foolishness in God's sight** (v 19). There is no way in which the world's wisdom can be upgraded so as to become God's wisdom. Paul now calls in Scripture to support him: significantly two passages from the Wisdom books of the OT. First is Job 5:13, which (in the LXX, which Paul was apparently using) stands in a context that denounces the scheming of the wicked. Paul therefore links **the wise in their craftiness** with Ps 94:11 [93:11 LXX]: "The LORD knows all human plans; he knows that they are futile."

■ 21-23 With the verdict of Scripture clear, the argument is now closed, as the NIV aptly indicates with the rendering **So then** (*hōste* [v 21]). The Greek text reads: "Let no one boast *in* men" rather than "*about* [men]" (as NIV): the former denoting if anything a deeper dimension than the latter (compare 1:31). The reason Paul gives for banning boasting in specific human persons is that **all things are yours**. To be a camp follower of Paul or Apollos or Cephas is to confine oneself within a very small sphere indeed. The whole world is theirs for the taking—life and death, the present and the future. The reason the world is theirs is because they are Christ's who, through his sacrificial death, is Lord of this age and the age to come (2:8-9). The point is clinched by the concluding phrase: "Christ is God's" (KJV). Everything falls within the divine lordship, including Christ himself (compare 8:6; 15:27-28).

Paul's Rhetorical Strategy in 1:18—3:23

First Corinthians 1:18—3:23 constitutes a unity, bound together from a literary perspective by the use of the verb "to boast" (*kauchasthai*) in 1:29, 31 and 3:21. Paul begins by drawing a sharp distinction between folly and wisdom, and he includes the Corinthians among the wise (1:18, 26-31). However, as his argument develops, it becomes clear that the Corinthians' definition of wisdom differs considerably from Paul's (2:12-16), to the extent that they could only be regarded as in their spiritual infancy (3:1-2). The evidence of this is their quarreling over rival leaders on the basis of their powers of argumentation (3:3-4). It transpires, therefore, that the Corinthians themselves are among those whom Paul has branded from the start as mistaking foolishness for wisdom. The trap that he has loaded in 1:18-25 he now closes with the Corinthians well and truly in it. This form of disguised speech or covert allusion was popular among orators in the middle of the first Christian century (Lampe 1990, 128-31).

FROM THE TEXT

Among the ways in which this ancient text speaks to today's church are these:

The growing of the church is God's business (3:6-7). There is, indeed, a role for us to play, but it is as God's agents and instruments (note the threefold use of "God" in v 9). The foundation of the church has already been laid: Jesus Christ (v 11). Our task is to ensure that the materials we use are durable (vv 12-15). The history of the church is littered with the wreckage of schemes, programs, and fads that were asserted at the time to be "the only way" to ensure the church's growth. Now they are forgotten, buried beneath the latest schemes that are likewise touted as "the only way." The test is: Is there concinnity between the foundation—the crucified Christ—and what is being built on it? And is it recognized that only Christ can build the church (Matt 16:18)?

There is a strong emphasis on the holiness of the church. This is implicit in identification of the church as the temple of God. The Greek word *naos* denotes not the complex of buildings including courts and colonnades that constituted the Jerusalem temple, but rather the inner shrine, the holy of holies, where God was uniquely present. Stunningly, Paul identifies the Corinthians as the temple, because God's Spirit dwells in them. It follows that as the dwelling place of the Spirit they are holy, and to defile the temple of God with the jealousy and quarreling present among them is to destroy it (1 Cor 3:3). This exposes them to divine judgment (v 17).

There is a striking interplay between the corporate and the individual in Paul's understanding of the church. When he writes in v 16 that **you are the temple of God and God's Spirit dwells in you** he uses the plural (which the NIV brings out by rendering "you yourselves are God's temple"). In v 17 he immediately moves into the singular: "If anyone destroys God's temple" and then returns to the plural at the end of the verse: "you together are that temple." (Collins notes that all the references to judgment in 1:10—4:21 are individualized. See 3:8, 12-15, 17; 4:4-5 [1999, 146].) Witherington's comment is apt:

> One of the great challenges to understanding Paul's thought is the relationship between the one and the many. Paul affirms both, holding them in tension. To be a Christian is to be a member of the body of Christ, not an isolated saved individual. At the same time, Paul holds individuals responsible for their behavior, expecting the community to discipline them. (1995, 133)

The underlying problem in the Corinthian church was the tension between the fashionable and the enduring, the transient and the eternal. What passed for wisdom in current fashion (3:18) was folly from the eternal perspective (vv 19-20). For the Corinthians this meant boasting about their favorite preachers (v 21) and quarreling with those who favored others. That is the path to an impoverished and, indeed, sub-Christian mode of life. In truth, everything is theirs, because they and their leaders and the Christ they proclaim are all gifts of God (vv 21-23).

E. Paul's Apostleship as Exemplifying True Wisdom (4:1-21)

BEHIND THE TEXT

The argument about factiousness might seem to have come to an end at the close of ch 3. However, this is not the case. Not only does it continue in ch 4, but it continues with even greater intensity. It appears that Paul himself has suffered a put-down, to which he responds in vv 1-5 by saying that he does not much care about their opinion: God's opinion is what counts. Evidently their attachment to a given leader led them to conclude that this showed their superiority in choosing the best. Paul replies with an ironical outburst in which he contrasts their alleged superiority with the inferior status of the apostles (vv 8-13). The mood changes in vv 14-17 where he reminds them that he (not Apollos or anyone else) was their father in the faith. The mood swings yet again to sternness when he tells them that he will be visiting them soon. The language shows how far things had regressed in Corinth when he describes his opponents as "these arrogant people" (v 19). What is implied in all of this is that the focus (if not the substance) of the matter is their attitude to Paul. They are not only pro-Apollos but anti-Paul, rejecting both his teaching *and* his authority (Fee 2014, 169). Paul therefore had to find a way of asserting his authority as an apostle in order to secure his teaching, but in such a way as not to undermine the central truth of the message of the cross—namely, that the power of God is revealed in weakness.

A notable feature of ch 4 is the series of ironical references by Paul to the claims apparently made by his critics. **Already you have all you want! Already you have become rich! You have begun to reign—and that without us! . . . We are fools for Christ, but you are so wise in Christ! We are weak, but you are strong! You are honored, we are dishonored!** (vv 8, 10). Such claims were not unknown among philosophers in the Greco-Roman world. In the words of Horace: "The sage is second only to Jupiter, rich, free, noble, handsome, finally a king of kings" (translation of Fitzmyer 2008, 217ff. [see 218 for further quotations]; also Hays 1997, 70-71). Paul also proclaimed the presence of the kingdom but as having come in power but not in fullness (2:4; 4:20). It is possible that some of the Corinthians may have baptized their Stoic understanding into Paul's message, and concluded that the kingdom had come "already." Those who did not share their view (which included Paul and others) simply showed by this that they were not fully "spiritual." Chapter 4 is devoted to correcting such misapprehensions.

IN THE TEXT

1. God's Verdict as the Verdict That Counts (4:1-5)

The idea of judgment has been in the wings since the reference to "the Day" (of judgment) in 3:13. It now assumes more prominence in 4:1-5 where the issue is the judgment that the Corinthians have been passing on Paul.

■ **1 This, then** captures the sense of the Greek adverb *houtōs* by resuming the discussion of the status of Paul and Apollos in 3:5-9. But the purpose is somewhat different. There the intent was to stress the subordinate role of the apostles as servants (*diákonoi*) who planted and watered, and therefore were not to be lionized as leaders (3:21-23). Here the accent falls on their authority as God's appointees. Two different Greek words are used to express this, better rendered as **assistants** [*hypērétas*] **of Christ and stewards** [*oikonómous*] **of the mysteries of God**. It is not that they are less servants, but rather that they are answerable to God, because appointed by him. The "assistant" was not a slave (like the *doulos*), but he worked under orders, while the "steward" had to give account of his performance to his master (Rengstorf in *TDNT* 8:532-33, 542). In a word, they were responsible but to God, not to their Corinthian critics. This is underlined by their job description as being **stewards of the mysteries of God**: clearly a reference to the gospel (2:1, 7). Thus the apostles were not to be viewed as social superiors. On the other hand, neither were they to be disparaged, for they had been commissioned by God. Paul is treading a fine line, leading to what he will say in 4:2-5.

■ **2** The supreme quality required in a steward is fidelity. Stewards are nobodies in themselves. Their worth derives entirely from their divine commission and their **faithful** fulfilling of it. For Paul that means faithfulness to the message of the cross.

■ **3-4** Consequently, it means nothing to him that the Corinthians, or indeed any other human body, pass judgment on him. This shows clearly—for the first time—that the Corinthians had been sitting in judgment on Paul. Paul dismisses their judgment—or that **by any human court** (v 3). The Greek literally reads **by any human day**, evidently meaning "day appointed for a court hearing." (→ 1:8.) Paul presses his point further. His own judgment of himself is of no consequence. Even though he is conscious of nothing against himself, he is not thereby placed in the clear (NIV: **innocent** [4:4]; NRSV: "acquitted"). The Greek verb is *dikaioun*, meaning to "justify" or "make right with God." Human conscience cannot make such a pronouncement, for while it can adjudicate between right and wrong (Rom 2:14-15), it can also be bludgeoned into silence (Rom 1:21-25) (Thiselton 2000b, 340). The only trustworthy judge is the Lord, and it is to his judgment that Paul submits.

■ **5** Hence, no one should judge anything **before the appointed time**—that is, **until the Lord comes**. With these words the futurist eschatology hovering over these verses comes into plain view. At the Lord's coming the things hidden in the dark will be brought into the light and the deepest wishes (NIV: **motives**; NRSV: "purposes") **of the heart** will be exposed. Paul thus injects a profound moral dimension into the issue. The differences between the Corinthians and himself are not mere matters of style and mode of presentation; they involve assertions of position and pride, whether or not the Corinthians acknowledge it. By placing ministry in the present under the judgment of the last day, Paul brought together two nostrums that ranked high among the Corinthians: first, that as already belonging to the age to come, they had attained superior spirituality; and second, in consequence they did not need advice about the practice of ministry from subspiritual guides such as Paul. Paul uses future eschatology to correct both errors at the same time. It is on the last day that the accomplishments of ministry will become known, which means in turn that not everything has been revealed even to the spiritual. Paul is using futurist eschatology to correct an exaggerated present eschatology. The ultimate and only worthwhile reward is praise from God, and this will be forthcoming **at that time** (*tóte*, "then"), when it will be measured out to **each**. The ultimate unit is the individual (see 3:13) (Collins 1999, 181).

2. The Folly of Judging by Appearances (4:6-13)

The general drift of these verses is clear; some of the details less so.

■ **6 These things** (*tauta*) clearly refer to matters pertaining to Apollos and himself, as, indeed, Paul goes on to say. This has in mind at least everything from 3:5 onward. However, those verses themselves look back to 1:10-12 and the whole matter of disputes among the Corinthians, as well as Paul's sustained reply in 1:18—4:5. Verses 6-21 of ch 4 seem to be Paul's summing up and application of that reply both to himself and Apollos and also to the Corinthians. When he writes that he has **applied these things to myself and Apollos for your benefit**, he appears to mean that he has been citing the harmonious way in which he and Apollos have worked together (→ 3:6-9) as an example for the Corinthians to follow (→ 4:16 and *TDNT* 7:958; for a review of other possible interpretations—of which there are many—see Garland 2003, 131-33). Expounding the problem by "transforming" (the literal meaning of the Greek word *metaschēmatizo*) or "transferring" it to himself and Apollos has had the added advantage for Paul of avoiding naming the name-callers, and so of avoiding increasing antagonism. His method has been: "if there are those whom the cap fits, let them wear it."

The remainder of the verse elaborates Paul's meaning via two purpose clauses. The first reads: **so that you may learn from us . . . not to go beyond what is written**. The NIV's **from us** and the NRSV's "through us" both reflect the meaning, though the original Greek is *in* (*en*), which seems to have a distinct depth in this context. The NIV translates the entire clause: **so that you may learn from us the meaning of the saying, "Do not go beyond what is written."** This assumes that **what is written** was, if not a proverb, at least a saying well-known in the Corinthian church, meaning "Keep to the book!" (Bruce 1976, 48). If one asks what lies behind it, the clue is almost certainly to be found in the words **what is written** (*gégraptai*), which Paul uses thirty times (apart from 4:6) to introduce quotations from Scripture and never anything else. Eight of these examples occur in 1 Corinthians, five of them in chs 1—3 (1:19, 31; 2:9; 3:19, 20). All share the theme of the superiority of divine wisdom over human, and implicit in all, and explicit in 1:31, is the folly of human boasting. The thought then is that the Corinthians are not to rate Apollos over Paul or vice versa, since either involves boasting in someone other than the Lord. This thought is expressed even more pungently in the second clause, which elaborates in pointed language the thrust of the first clause: **Then you will not be puffed up** [*phusiousthe*] **in being a follower of one of us over against the other**. Paul will use this term again in the epistle five times (4:18, 19; 5:2; 8:1; 13:4) to expose the Corinthians' self-inflation for what it is.

■ **7** Paul proceeds to puncture Corinthian pride by a series of three direct questions that essentially amount to one: "Who do you think you are?" They are no **different from anyone else**—the primary reference presumably being to Paul and Apollos. What they are they have become by what they have received—namely, the grace of God in Christ crucified. That being so, what have they to **boast** about?—"boast" having already established itself as a key word in the epistle, denoting the antithesis of the humility of the message of the cross (1:29, 31; 3:21). Since it is unlikely that the superior attitudes referred to would have been adopted by the poorer members of the church, it seems probable that social distinctions played a significant part in the problems of the Corinthian church.

■ **8** Paul now launches into deep irony in his description of Corinthian pretensions. Two words especially bear the burden of his attack. First, the word *basileuō* (meaning "reign as kings"), which occurs (including a compound form) three times; and second, the word *ēdē* (**already**), which occurs twice. The Corinthians were claiming that they were already full (**you have all you want**); already rich; already reigning as kings: things that Paul and Apollos had not attained. With biting sarcasm Paul says that he wishes their claims were true, for it would then mean that he and Apollos would share this regal status with them. Clearly, the Corinthians were marching to a different drummer than Paul, or living on a different planet.

■ **9** Paul develops the contrast by reference to the rough treatment received by the apostles. He clearly regards them as a defined group, as well as a unified group (Soards 1999, 94), thereby scouting any Corinthian preference for one above another (his own apostleship had evidently been questioned by some [9:1]). On the basis of his knowledge and experience Paul has concluded that **God has put us apostles on display at the end of the procession, like those condemned to die in the arena**. There is a degree of interpretation in this translation, but it is probably justified. The picture in mind is either of a gladiatorial contest or a general's victory parade in which the bedraggled remnants of a defeated foe were dragged through the streets of Rome on their way to execution. As such the apostles have become a spectacle to three audiences: the world, angels, and humankind. No wider audience is possible. The apostle of the suffering Christ becomes a sufferer himself.

■ **10** The contrast between the Corinthians on the one hand, who preened themselves on their superiority, and the bedraggled apostles on the other hand is elaborated in a list of twelve specific items. Such lists were common in the rhetoric of the day. This list is constructed in a chiastic pattern (A-B-A¹) in which the first and third units (A [v 10]; A¹ [vv 12b-13]) consist respectively of three contrasting members; and the central unit (B [vv 11-12a]) consists of six descriptive statements.

The language echoes that of 1:26-30, even though the Greek terms are different. The supposed wisdom, strength, and glory of the Corinthians stand in contrast to the foolishness, weakness, and shame of the apostles. It is significant, however, that for all their misguidedness, Paul does not disfellowship them, and he allows their claim to be "in Christ," even though their understanding of being "wise in Christ" falls well short of the truth.

■ **11-12a** This central part of Paul's description of the adversity faced by the apostles lists six items, which are largely self-explanatory. The language is striking to the point of being stunning: **To this very hour we go hungry and thirsty, we are in rags, we are brutally treated, we are homeless. We work hard with our own hands** (4:11-12a). All of them can be readily documented from other accounts of Paul's ministry (see 2 Cor 11:23-27). But two matters are of particular note. One is the reference to manual labor (1 Cor 4:12a). This was evidently Paul's standard practice as a means of supporting himself (9:6, 12, 15, 18; 1 Thess 2:9; Acts 18:1-4). It was not unknown among pagan philosophers (Hock 1978, 562-64), especially the Stoics and Cynics. Among the rabbis, supporting oneself by learning a trade was not unknown. However, throughout the Greek world manual labor was regarded as degrading and contemptible. Against this Paul regarded earning his living as "a studied expression of his mission" (Fee 2014, 195). This involved being treated (and therefore regarded) as little better than a slave. The language of 1 Cor 4:11-12a is to be taken at face value (Hock 1980, chs 3, 4; Hengel 1991, 15-17). Paul preferred to earn his living, and this gave offense to some of the Corinthians, who apparently saw it as demeaning. (Paul will elaborate his case in ch 9.) The second matter of note is the emphatic phrase with which 4:11 begins: **to this very hour**. This stands in ironic contrast with the twice-repeated "already" in v 8, creating a stark contrast between the lofty position claimed by the Corinthians and the current humiliation of the apostles.

■ **12b-13** The list concludes with three contrasting statements. The apostles answer cursing with blessing, face persecution with endurance, and meet slander with conciliation. The thought, including some of the words, echoes the teaching of Jesus (Luke 6:27-29). Paul crowns this catalog of apostolic humiliation by saying that the apostles have become the **scum** (*perikathármata* [1 Cor 4:13]) and "refuse" (*peripsēma* [RSV]) of the world. The former Greek term is used of the impurities thrown away when a vessel is cleaned, but in a derivative sense of the scapegoat on whom the guilt of a community was unloaded. (See Prov 21:18 LXX; NIV renders it **ransom**.) The latter Greek term carries much the same meaning. Undoubtedly, it carries its primary sense here. Lightfoot thinks it also bears its secondary sense of those sacrificed as expiatory offerings to atone for the guilt of the nation: a custom preserved in Athens (Lightfoot 1895, 201). The idea is found elsewhere in Paul's work (see Col 1:24). Verse 13 of 1 Cor 4 ends with the note with which v 11 begins: **right up to this moment**. This has the effect of intensifying the contrast with the Corinthians' claims to have wealth and honor "already" (v 8).

Eschatology and the Corinthians

Eschatology comes into view most clearly in 4:8ff. (→ Behind the Text for 4:1-21, above.) It is probably present earlier under a different disguise. The language of "wisdom" and "spiritual" is found in Stoic and other sources from that time. It is not impossible that the Corinthians simply reinterpreted the views they had derived from pagan philosophy in terms of Paul's proclamation that the kingdom had come (4:20). This could have been misunderstood to mean that the kingdom had come in its fullness so that its members were already possessed of ultimate wisdom and occupied an exalted spiritual state. They therefore needed no instruction from anyone, and certainly not Paul. This exaggerated (or as it is commonly called "overrealized") eschatology spilled over into multiple areas of Corinthian life, including most of the problem areas dealt with in the epistle. In chs 1—4 it covers both the heart of the gospel message and those who proclaimed it, leading to the conclusion that the last days had arrived, so one "spiritual man" was as good as another (Thiselton 1978, 513). It could lead to the disparagement of the material, leading to sexual immorality (ch 5) and the denial of bodily resurrection (ch 15). It could lead to an exaggerated emphasis on the ecstatic or charismatic (chs 12—14). Paul's eschatology, by contrast, was both present *and* futurist, combining both realization and expectation. It has been questioned by some scholars whether eschatology (particularly in an exaggerated form) was present in the Corinthian situation at all (Hays 1997, 70; Horsley 1998, 69). David Kuck's observation that in vv 9-13 "Paul answers their view with ethics, not with eschatology" (1992, 217) is sometimes taken as fatal to an eschatological interpretation (Garland 2003, 138; Ciampa and Rosner 2010, 179). But this overlooks the fact that Paul regularly places ethics in an eschatological setting (see 1 Cor 1:7-8; Rom 6:8-14; Col 3:1-14; Thiselton 1978, 510-26; 2000, 357-59; Fee 2014, 187-89). The emergence of eschatology at various points throughout the epistle suggests that it played a significant role in the Corinthian troubles.

3. Paul's Fatherly Affection for the Corinthians (4:14-17)

Paul's tone now changes from irony to paternal concern. In Paul's world, both Jewish and Greek, fatherhood was a hierarchical relation, the father being clearly the head. He was expected to rule, educate, and be imitated. However, affection was also understood as part of the paternal role. This emerges clearly in these verses.

■ **14-16** Paul's intent was not to shame them (as vv 6-13 might well have done) but to admonish (NIV: **warn**) them (v 14). The word translated **warn** (*nouthetein*) is unique to Paul in the NT and denotes trying to correct without arousing hostility (J. Behm in *TDNT* 4:1021). Addressing them as his **dear children** explains his tone. Paul preferred the language of family over the language of friendship, which he never used. So he draws a contrast between **guardians** (*paidagōgoi* [v 15]), of whom they might have had many, and their **father**, of whom, by definition, they could have only one. The guardian was responsible for ensuring that a child attended school and kept out of trouble until he or she reached maturity. Guardians varied greatly in their ability (Young 1987, 157-68) as well as in their attitude toward their charges, but even at their best they could not come close to the place of fathers. For the Corinthian believers Paul held that solitary role, encompassing their conception (lit. "I have begotten you" [KJV]) and his authority and love. The fatherhood in mind was spiritual fatherhood **through the gospel**. For this reason Paul urges them to **imitate** him (v 16), an exhortation he will repeat (7:8, 9; 11:1).

■ **17** In case they had forgotten Paul's manner of life in Christ, he is sending someone who can remind them. Timothy is not only a beloved child of Paul's (as are the Corinthians [4:14]) but also **faithful in the Lord** (something Paul pointedly does not say of the Corinthians). He can therefore serve as an example of what Paul wants the Corinthians to be. An apostolic agent could serve with the power second only to that of the sender (compare 2 Cor 8:22-24; Phil 2:19-23). Paul directs the Corinthians to note two things: first, **my way of life in Christ Jesus**. The accent appears to fall on the ways in which he conducted himself as a preacher of Christ—yet another indication that the cause of dissension lay in mode of presentation. Second, he affirms that his conduct in Corinth did not differ from his conduct everywhere else: a claim that affirms not only Paul's consistency but also the unity of the church (compare 1:2).

4. Paul's Forthcoming Visit to Corinth (4:18-21)

■ **18** Paul had evidently indicated that he would pay a return visit to Corinth. Some had dismissed the possibility that he would do so—an implicit rejection of his authority—and had **become arrogant**. The word translated **arrogant** means literally "have become puffed up," the same word used in 4:6. Clearly, vanity was a large element in the problem in Corinth.

■ **19** Paul rebuts the implied charge that he has cold feet about the idea of a return visit. When he comes he will find out not the bluster of his critics but their power. The contrast between word and power, already made in 2:1-5, is an important clue to the nature of the problem in Corinth. For Paul's critics the important thing was high-sounding talk; for Paul it was transformed lives (as the rest of the epistle will show).

■ 20 This verse sums up Paul's point succinctly. Paul does not speak often of the **kingdom of God** (but see Rom 14:17; 1 Cor 6:9; 15:50; Gal 5:21); but when he does, he means by it the domain in which God's sovereign authority is acknowledged—that is, in which his will is done. What counts is not windy rhetoric but spiritual power. The contrast has already been expressed in 2:4-5.

■ 21 The Corinthians can choose the spirit in which Paul will come: to remonstrate and discipline, or to show gentleness and love.

FROM THE TEXT

Behind what may look like a local church squabble lie some large-scale practical theological principles.

The danger of premature judgment (vv 1-5). The point Paul is discussing is not whether the truth of his message (which the Corinthians had grasped very imperfectly) is something that should await God's verdict on judgment day. Nor is it that believers should suspend judgment when confronted by what are plainly matters of right and wrong. Rather it is whether Paul's powers as a preacher are as effective as those of Apollos or Cephas. His reply is: "I am not aware of anything against myself" (v 4a NRSV; a vastly better translation than "my conscience is clear" [NIV]). This is further elaborated in v 5, where it is said that judgment day "will bring to light what is hidden in darkness and will expose the motives of the heart." This may imply that Paul had been accused of harboring self-serving designs. There are areas where we lack the calculus to pass judgment. In these, it is best to leave them to the judgment of the Lord in his good time (v 5a).

The danger of either underrated or exaggerated eschatology (vv 8-13). The Christian message is built squarely on the belief that in and with the coming of Christ, the kingdom of God was inaugurated. We have the authority of Jesus for believing that this was so (Luke 11:20; 7:18-23). Hence, the power of the kingdom is presently available. To deny this is to destroy the foundation on which the message of salvation in Christ rests. Paul declared this in his own preaching in Corinth (1 Cor 2:1-5; 4:20). At the same time, the kingdom has not yet come in its fullness, though the Corinthians were parading themselves as though it had (v 8). But trusting in Christ does not put an automatic end to poverty and ill-health any more than it confers upon the believer the wisdom to understand all mysteries, past, present, and future. These gifts await the day of the Lord.

Right thinking is not enough; there must also be right behavior (vv 14-21). As we have seen, Paul did not accept that the thinking of the Corinthians was right. Not the least of his reasons was that it did not lead to right behavior. Hence, his urging of the Corinthians to imitate him (v 16) and his sending of Timothy to remind them of his "way of life in Christ Jesus" (v 17). He does not describe the precise shape of his ethical instruction. Some interpreters see echoes of the Sermon on the Mount in vv 12-13 (Barrett 1968, 112; Bruce 1976, 50). We may infer from the context that for Paul the way of the cross was the criterion for Christian living. The power Paul embodied and taught was not the power to move the crowds with the finely tuned rhetoric and sharply honed arguments cherished by the Corinthians. It was the power to transform people to embrace acceptance of rejection, humiliation, and suffering for the sake of the Christ who did the same (v 20).

Paul as a Servant-Leader

Throughout 3:5—4:21 (to look no earlier) Paul has repeatedly described his role in unprepossessing, not to say demeaning, terms. He is a servant (lit. "slave" [3:5; 4:1]); a mere planter of the seed (3:6); a spectacle to the whole universe (4:9); a fool for Christ (v 10); decked out "in rags" (v 11); "the scum of the earth" (v 13), and so on. But he has embraced this because the Corinthians are his "brothers and sisters" (v 6), indeed, his "dear children" (v 14), for he is their father "in Christ Jesus" (v 15).

At the same time Paul does not hesitate to put the Corinthians in their place. He cares very little if he is judged by them (v 3). He addresses them sarcastically as being "wise" and "strong" and "honored" (v 10). He brands some of them as "arrogant" (vv 18-19) and asks if they prefer the whip over the embrace (v 21).

This has been branded—in no measured terms—as an illustration of how a leader, anxious about his own authority, can become authoritarian (Horsley 1998, 77). This overlooks the unique character of Paul's role. He was not merely a servant *leader*; he was a servant *apostle* (v 9). As such he bore a special role as a witness to the risen Christ (9:1-2; 15:8; Acts 1:21-22) and the gospel with which he had been entrusted (1 Cor 4:1; see also Rom 1:1; Gal 1:1, 11-12; 1 Thess 2:4). Still more, his call was to preach the gospel *to the Gentiles* (Rom 1:5; Gal 1:15-16; 2:7-8), thereby bringing to fulfillment the Abrahamic covenant that through Abraham all the nations of the earth would be blessed (Gen 12:3; Rom 4:16-18; Gal 3:6-9). It is more than personal pique that evokes Paul's strong response. It is his awareness of having been commissioned uniquely by Christ to bear witness to Christ as raised from the dead and therefore as the Conqueror of death and Savior from sin for all humanity (Barnett 1993, 45-51).

III. THE GOSPEL AND MORAL FAILURE IN THE CHURCH: THE SUMMONS TO HOLINESS OF LIFE: I CORINTHIANS 5:1—6:20

BEHIND THE TEXT

There is widespread agreement that 4:21 marks the end of the first section of the epistle. F. F. Bruce goes further and sees it as the conclusion of the epistle as Paul first intended to write it. He points out that the announcement of Timothy's forthcoming visit and his own intended visit (4:17, 18-19) are items normally found in the concluding elements of Paul's letters (e.g., 1 Cor 16:10-11; Titus 3:12-14; Philemon 22). He suggests that before Paul could dispatch it fresh news arrived from Corinth (16:17) requiring a much longer letter (Bruce 1976, 52ff.).

There are marked indications that 5:1—6:20 are to be regarded as a unity. This follows not only from the features suggesting that 4:21 marks the end of a section, but also from the opening words of ch 7: "Now for the matters you wrote about." In addition, there are internal features that appear to bind chs 5 and 6 together. They begin and end with the topic of sexual immorality (5:1; 6:18), which thereby serves as an inclusion or literary bracket. There is a common concern with the adverse impression that the antics of the Corinthians will have on unbelievers (5:1; 6:6). Or to put the same point from the inside: there is doubt as to how far the Corinthians can continue in these ways and remain a Christian church (5:2, 4, 7; 6:5, 15-16, 19-20).

If the foregoing has any validity, it goes a fair way to answering the question as to why Paul treats these matters first, before taking up "the matters you wrote about" (7:1). Assuming that Stephanas, Fortunatus, and Achaicus delivered the Corinthians' letter to Paul (16:17), they were probably also the bearers of the news of the goings-on in Corinth that Paul found so disturbing. What that news demonstrated was that the state of affairs which Paul had addressed in chs 1—4 (not to mention his letter to them referred to in 5:9) was continuing—if anything, on a more outrageous scale than before. There was toleration of immoral behavior (5:2). The boasting that characterized their earlier behavior (1:31; 3:21) was present still (5:6), as were the divisions (6:1, 4). Such conduct threatened the very survival of the church (6:15-17). It is a fair conclusion that the holiness of the community is the central theme of these chapters (Collins 1999, 203; Sampley 2002, 844). Indeed, it has been plausibly suggested that Paul not only picks up the theme of the danger of destroying the temple from 3:16-17, but that behind it lie the OT laws of excluding from the temple anything that would defile its holiness (Deut 23:1-8; Pss 15; 24:3-5; Ezek 44:6-9) (Rosner 1991). It is hardly surprising, therefore, that these issues are the first to receive Paul's attention.

Underlying Paul's argument in both chapters are features that seem best understood against the social-legal background of Roman Corinth. The idea of "equality before the law" was foreign to the Roman Empire. The guiding principle was rather respect for status. This gave an immediate advantage to persons of wealth and position. Moreover, the laws of evidence took a distinctly second place to bribery and unrestrained verbal attack. Court proceedings became a theater for rhetorical gladiatorial combat in which the most eloquent (and unscrupulous) party won. It is possible that the "boasting" over the immoral man in 5:1, 6 originated in this way. The lawsuits in 6:1-6 may well reflect this same background, initiated in order to give visibility to, and enhance the reputations of, those who brought them.

IN THE TEXT

A. The Problem of Fornication (5:1-13)

The problem Paul confronts is narrower than "sexual immorality" (v 1). The Greek word used here (*porneia*) can, indeed, be used "of various kinds of 'unsanctioned sexual intercourse'" (BDAG, 854), but it can, and in the NT frequently does, have a narrower connotation, as is the case here. In the decree of the Jerusalem Council (Acts 15:20, 29; 21:25) it most probably denotes marriage within the prohibited degrees of relationship: a sense that it may also have in the so-called exceptive clauses of Matt 5:32; 19:9 (Deasley 2000a, 110-21). By the time the argument of 1 Cor 5:1—6:20 is reaching its conclusion, the word *porneia* has acquired the wider sense of any kind of illicit sexual relationship (6:13, 18). Paul's argument develops in three main steps: a statement of the problem and how it should have been dealt with (5:1-5); a description of the danger to the church (vv 6-8); and a clarification of Paul's meaning with a repetition of his earlier directive (vv 9-13).

1. Corinthian Toleration of Fornication Denounced (5:1-5)

■ 1 The particular problem Paul addresses is one he has learned of by report: probably from the bearers of the Corinthians' letter to him (7:1). The report was of an illicit sexual relationship that would scandalize even pagans: **a man is sleeping with this father's wife**. The woman in question was presumably the man's stepmother. This practice is forbidden in Lev 18:8; 20:11 under penalty of death. In Roman law whether the father was still living (in which case the offense would be both adultery and incest) or if he had divorced his wife or was dead (in which case the offense would be incest) the action constituted a punishable crime (Winter 2001, 45-47). Perhaps as important as the legalities, such relationships were regarded as repugnant to decency, as is well indicated by Cicero's comment on a case known to him, that they were "incredible and, apart from this one instance, unheard of" (*Pro Cluentio*, 14).

■ 2 Paul's incredulity expressed in v 1 comes to even more intense expression in v 2: **And you are proud!** (or as the verb would be more literally rendered, "puffed up"). Why might the Corinthians have been proud of something so egregiously offensive? It is possible that the reference is perfectly general: "You are full of yourselves, yet this kind of thing is going on among you." It is also possible that it may have been a by-product of their claim to super-spirituality, implying that what was sin for others was not sin for them (Barrett 1968, 122). It is significant that this section concludes with a stern warning against immorality and lending the body for immoral uses (6:12-20). At the same time it seems unlikely that the Corinthians would applaud an action that was against the law. Another possibility is that the Corinthians were boasting about the social (and financial) status of the son while ignoring his immoral behavior. Such an individual would be likely to have belonged to the "not many . . . influential" (1:26) minority in the church whose ranks would be likely to have supplied those vocal in their opposition to and criticism of Paul (Chow 1992, 139-41; Clarke 1993, ch 6; Winter 2001, 53-57). These factors need not have been mutually exclusive.

The response that should have been forthcoming from the Corinthians was twofold: (1) grief that such an act of moral turpitude was found within their fellowship and (2) expulsion of the offender. The fact that the woman is not mentioned may indicate that she was not a believer.

■ **3** Paul now spells out his own response: **For my part**. Though not present in body, he is present in spirit and has already passed judgment on the offender. The language is judicial in tone.

■ **4-5** What Paul has already done he now calls upon the Corinthians to do. The series of clauses in these verses may be read as an addition to v 3 or an expansion of it. (The options are set out in Conzelmann 1975, 97.) The NIV is probably correct in adopting the former view (i.e., Paul has already passed judgment though absent in body from the Corinthians); he now calls the Corinthians to repeat his action though absent from him. What he has in mind is an act of spiritual debarment or expulsion. The operative elements are: (1) the assembling of the Corinthians in the name of the Lord Jesus; (2) the presence of Paul in spirit; (3) the presence of the power of the Lord Jesus; (4) the handing over of the offender to Satan. Several points are noteworthy.

First, the act of expulsion is not Paul's alone nor the Corinthians', but both "in the name of our Lord Jesus" (v 3); that is, it is the act of the whole church. Second, the action takes place when **the power of our Lord Jesus is present** (v 4). This does not simply repeat the phrase "in the name of our Lord Jesus" (v 3). The theme of power has already surfaced in the epistle in a way that shows that Paul's understanding of it differed radically from that of the Corinthians (1:17, 18; 2:5; 4:20). The present context shows that the power of Christ operates not only on a moral plane but also through an obedient church. Third, the expelling of the offender is not retributive in its ultimate purpose but redemptive. This is not to say there is no retributive element, as 5:11 shows; sin must be labeled for what it is and treated accordingly. The means by which this retributive-redemptive act will be accomplished is to **hand this man over to Satan for the destruction of the flesh, so that his spirit may be saved on the day of the Lord** (v 5). To be handed **over to Satan** seems to be akin to being given up by God (Rom 1:24, 26, 28) and thereby discover the havoc that sin can wreak and so turn back to him again (2 Cor 12:7-9; 1 Tim 1:20). The concrete form by which this takes place is exclusion from the church (1 Cor 5:2, 13). In line with this **the destruction of the flesh** denotes the reorientation of the actions and inclinations away from sin and self and turning toward God. The purpose and end of this is the saving of the individual **on the day of the Lord**. In the thinking of Paul—as in the teaching of the NT as a whole—salvation is a gift received in measure here and now and in full measure on the day of the Lord (Rom 5:9-10; 8:24-25).

2. The Danger to the Church (5:6-8)

Paul's words thus far have not been directed to the offender but to the Corinthian church. He has not minced his words in describing "the man who has been doing this" (v 2) and the atrociousness of his conduct, but his primary target has been and remains the church that has accepted such behavior not merely without protest but with approval. Paul now turns from the danger to the offender to the consequences for the church.

■ **6** Such conduct was not anything to boast about, as the Corinthians ought to know. It is noteworthy that of the twelve occurrences of the question: "Do you not know?" in Paul's letters, seven appear in this section (5:6; 6:2, 3, 9, 15, 16, 19). Ignorance was the last excuse the Corinthians could use. This is particularly the case here, since the phrase "a little leaven leavens the lump" (NASB, RSV) appears to have been a popular proverb (see Gal 5:9). While it could be used as a metaphor for good (as in Matt 13:33), it was more commonly used as a metaphor for evil, as is the case here.

■ **7** The quotation of the proverb apparently reminded Paul of Jewish Passover practice, though it is entirely possible that his thought was influenced by OT accounts where the cleansing or restoring of the temple was consummated by the observance of the Passover (see 2 Chr 29:5, 35; 30:1-4; 35:1-19; Ezra 6:13-15, 19-22). It was possible for a new batch of dough to be leavened by kneading in a small amount of the previous batch, guaranteeing that the bread was leavened continuously throughout the year. But the Jewish Passover Festival was also the Feast of Unleavened Bread, hence the custom of clearing out the old leaven before the Passover so that a completely fresh start could be made (Exod 12:15; 13:6-7). Paul applies this to the Corinthians, calling them to cleanse out the old leaven so that they might be a completely new batch. Astonishingly, Paul then adds: "as you really are unleavened" (1 Cor 5:7 NRSV).

There are two aspects to the life of Christian believers. On the one hand they are "sanctified in Christ Jesus" (1:2), and thereby *a new creation; the old has passed away, behold, the new has come* (2 Cor 5:17 RSV). At the same time they are also "called to be . . . holy" (1 Cor 1:2 NRSV; i.e., to live out the life of those who belong to God). The command to be holy (the imperative) is based on the fact that they are already set apart in Christ Jesus (the indicative). In C. K. Barrett's words, "The people of God have in fact been freed from sin; because this is so, they must now avoid sin and live in obedience to God's command" (1968, 128). Christians, by their profession of faith, are Passover people. Henceforth, they are to live as such. It is on this basis that Paul exhorts the Corinthians to clean out the old leaven. There is a power available that expels the old, making the new possible. This is the dominant note in Paul's thinking.

There is a particular urgency about this. Our Passover Lamb—Christ—has already been sacrificed. In the Greek text the word "Christ" is stressed by being placed at the end: **our Passover . . . has been sacrificed—Christ**: but there is still leaven in the house! But the law required that the leaven be removed before the Passover lamb was slaughtered! It is remarkable that Paul could assume that the Corinthians would be familiar with the details of Jewish Passover observance. Evidently the Exodus story was used as a scriptural analogy for the story of Christian salvation.

Equally notable is the explicit understanding of Christ's death as sacrificial. The multiple references thus far to Christ's crucifixion as the means of salvation have given no explanation of *how* his death was saving. This was part (not to say the heart) of Paul's gospel, and Paul could take it for granted that the Corinthians already knew (15:1-4). The equation of the Passover lamb with Christ implies that his blood offered in willing sacrifice (unlike that of the Passover lamb) saves believers from destruction. Once again Paul brings the problems of the church in Corinth to the touchstone of the gospel. The way of the cross is the way of holiness.

The *old leaven* to be removed is, therefore, in its primary application, the guilty offender. This is made clear in v 13*b*, although it is already implied in v 5.

■ **8** However, the Corinthians themselves by no means have clean hands. It is they who are called upon to **keep the Festival, not with the old bread leavened with malice and wickedness**. "Malice" (*kakía*) and "wickedness" (*ponēría*) tend to occur in the NT in lists of evils (see Rom 1:29; Col 3:8; Titus 3:3), the former denoting the disposition to evil, the latter the practice of it (Lightfoot 1892, 212). They are rather to keep the festival **with the unleavened bread of sincerity and truth**: **sincerity** (*eilikríneia*) denoting a right disposition and **truth** (*alētheia*) denoting an attitude in accord with moral reality. "Both terms indicate an authentic transparency, a perfect correspondence between their profession of faith and their new life" (Ciampa and Rosner 2010, 215). Neither the behavior of the Corinthians in general nor their response to the particular situation of the incestuous man has been distinguished by either of these. In 2 Cor 1:12 Paul declares that, in contrast, "we have behaved in the world, and still more toward you, with holiness and godly sincerity, not by earthly wisdom but by the grace of God" (RSV).

The Significance of the Indicative and the Imperative

It is impossible to miss the paradoxical element in v 7: **Get rid of the old yeast, so that you may be a new unleavened batch—as you really are**. The sentence consists of two elements: a command, expressed in the imperative: **Get rid of the old yeast**; and a statement, expressed in the indicative mood: **as you really are**. While in this case (as in a few others) the imperative comes first, followed by the indicative (Phil 2:12-13), more commonly the order is reversed (Rom 6:2, 11-12).

On the surface this might be taken to mean that the redemptive work in our salvation is God's, while the life of obedience is something done in our own strength. But this is certainly not Paul's meaning. "Work out your salvation with fear and trembling" is immediately followed by the explanation "for it is God who works in you to will and to act in order to fulfill his good purpose" (Phil 2:12-13). The grace of God that provides salvation also includes the power to obey him.

Schreiner observes that "all attempts to formulate the relationship between the indicative and the imperative seem to reflect partial truths" (2001, 254-55). More forcefully, N. T. Wright sees it as an oversimplification that fails to do justice to Paul's inaugurated eschatology, particularly that Christ's resurrection and the gift of the Spirit have created a new world. With these a new power has become available for transformed living (2013, 1097-1101). Udo Schnelle offers a stringent critique, concluding that the basic paradigm in Paul's thought is "transformation and participation" (2005, 546-51). Stanley E. Porter finds indicative-imperative language misleading, as failing to do justice to the believer's condition in Christ (1993, 401). A broad generalization might be that the indicative affirms the priority of grace, the imperative the indispensability of faith. The two are distinguishable but inseparable.

3. A Clarification and a Command (5:9-13)

Paul has discussed earlier the issue of associating with those of questionable character. It appears that his teaching was misunderstood. He now attempts to correct this.

■ **9** The first clause is best translated **I wrote to you in my letter**, taking the Greek verb (*égrapsa*) as a genuine past tense rendered by the simple past tense in English. Apparently the letter we call First Corinthians was not, in fact, his first letter to them. In his earlier letter (frequently called "the previous letter") he had warned them **not to associate with sexually immoral people**.

■ **10** This directive had been misunderstood. If Paul's counsel was expressed in the simple form given in v 9, it is not impossible that he was responsible for the misunderstanding, because of the unqualified character of his statement. It is, however, more probable that, in their arrogance, the Corinthians swept aside his teaching as nonsensical. Therefore, he now clarifies his original words, saying that he did not mean they were to have no contact whatever with the degenerate people **of this world**. The latter expression is the key to the distinction Paul is making. To avoid all association with the **immoral, or the greedy and swindlers, or idolaters** would seriously reduce their conversation partners.

■ **11** He is now **writing** (*égrapsa* as in v 9, but now functioning as an epistolary aorist, in which the action of writing is present to Paul but will be past by the time the Corinthians read it) that they are to avoid any who bear the name of brother or sister but still live in the style of the old life. That style he now describes by listing a series of specific vices: sexual immorality, greed, idolatry, slander, drunkenness, and swindling (a partial list of four of these has already been given in v 10).

It has often been argued that such vice lists were common in the ancient world and Paul simply pulled items at random from such traditional sources. They tell us nothing specific about the situation in Corinth. However, it is significant that the lists in vv 10 and 11 begin with the term **sexually immoral** (*pórnos*), which Paul says he wrote about in his previous letter (v 9). This in turn establishes a link with the case of sexual immorality (*porneía*) in v 1, which is the theme of the whole section.

Further, v 11 begins with the prepositional phrase **but now**, indicating that he is amplifying the instruction given in his previous letter (v 9). The items that he includes (in addition to **sexual immorality**) are greed and idolatry, for both of which Corinth was notorious in Paul's day; and slander, drunkenness, and swindling, to which he will return in the fullest vice list of all (6:9-10). Indeed, every one of these vices will reappear in major sections of the letter.

The ban on associating with any so-called brother or sister who practices such things now receives sharper focus: **Do not even eat with such people**. The scope of this prohibition is uncertain. Certainly it would include the Lord's Supper. It could also include any kind of meal since dining was regarded not merely as a sign of friendship but also as a sign of approval (Winter 2001, 56ff.).

■ **12-13** The note of judgment is picked up from 5:3, where Paul declares he has already "passed judgment . . . on the one who has been doing this." He also assumes the distinction he has made in v 10 between "the people of this world" and Christian believers, a distinction that he expresses as between **those inside** and **those outside** (v 12). It is not Paul's business to judge those outside. But he poses the other side to the Corinthians in the form of an emphatic question: ***Is it not your business to judge those inside?*** Outsiders can be left to the judgment of God. It is a solemn consideration that God has entrusted the judgment of the church (which means the purity of the church) to the hands of its members. What that involves in this case Paul makes perfectly clear. **Expel the wicked person from among you** (v 13). This is a Pauline adaptation of a phrase that is virtually a standing formula in Deuteronomy for the removal of an evil that, if not acted upon, will bring destruction upon the whole community (Deut 17:7; 19:19; 21:21; 24:7). There may be a wordplay here between the word ***evil*** (*ponerón*) and ***sexual immorality*** (*porneía*) to emphasize Paul's point still more (Zaas 1984, 260).

Holiness as Corporate and Individual

Paul has already written of the power of individual sin to compromise the holiness of the church (3:16-17). The immoral man of 5:1-5 is now taken to be a concrete example of that fact, expressed in terms of the lump of leaven and the batch of dough (5:6-8). The old leaven is to be got rid of (5:7, 13). The underlying theme is the indwelling of God in and among his people, which is "fundamental to the biblical tradition" (McKelvey 2000, 806). The vehicle through which this was realized in the OT was the temple in its successive forms. The tabernacle in the wilderness was "a sanctuary for me, and I will dwell among them" (Exod 25:8). God's promise regarding Solomon's temple was that, if the people obeyed his commands, "I will live among the Israelites" (1 Kgs 6:13). The destruction of that temple in 587 BC meant the loss of God's presence (Ezek 10:18—11:25). The building of the new temple would be marked by the ingathering of all the peoples of the earth, making offerings to the Lord in holiness (Isa 66:18-21). As E. P. Sanders has put it: "The temple was holy not only because the holy God was worshipped there, but because he *was* there ... Jews did not think God was there and nowhere else ... Nevertheless, he was in some special sense present in the temple" (1992, 70-71).

It is clear from the foregoing that the temple had never been regarded as consisting exclusively of timber and stone. The indwelling of God was linked inseparably with the holy character of God's people. This prepared the way for the spiritualization of the temple. If a temple building did not necessarily create a holy people, was it not possible for people to be holy without a temple building? The Qumran sect apparently believed that it was, and regarded themselves as such (1QS VIII, 1-16a; Deasley 2000b, 83-87).

That same step was taken by Paul—if anything a stage further than by the Qumran sectarians. Paul may well have been drawing out the implications of the teaching of Jesus (McKelvey 2000, 808; Peter Marshall 1987, 207-12). He states flatly that "you [plural] are God's temple and that God's Spirit dwells in you" (3:16 NRSV). He goes on to say that "if anyone destroys God's temple, God will destroy that person. For God's temple is holy, and you [plural] are that temple" (v 17 NRSV). But Paul presses his point to the last degree when he writes: "Do you not know that your body is a temple of the Spirit within you, which you have from God, and that you are not your own?" (6:19 NRSV). The context is singular (6:17-18), having the act of fornication in mind (6:17). Paul thus sees the church and the individual believer alike as temples of the Lord, just as in 3:16-17 he has seen the unholiness of the individual as a threat to the holiness of the church.

B. The Problem of Lawsuits (6:1-11)

The sudden change of topic from incest to lawsuits prompts questions as to the connection of thought. There are certainly some links of language with ch 5, notably that of judging (5:3, 12-13; 6:2, 3, 4). There are also links of theme, particularly that of the purity of the community (5:6-8, 11-13; 6:9-11). If the occasions of the lawsuits were "trivial cases" (6:2) or "the things of this life" (6:3), they might well have shared the same surface character as the bickerings Paul rebukes in chs 1—4 (though both had deeper implications). Perhaps the most immediate link is the mention of the obligation of judging those inside the church while leaving the judging of outsiders to God (5:12-13). The Corinthians are now confounding confusion by allowing outsiders to judge the insiders.

Attempts to show that the lawsuits were brought by a party or parties aggrieved by the case of incest (Richardson 1983) are hardly convincing. It appears rather that the Corinthians' failure to take any action in that matter contrasted so sharply with their taking of each other to court on much lesser issues that Paul uses the latter to rub in their failure in the former. He almost certainly had a further concern. The law in Roman Corinth was not the even-handed, equal-justice-for-all instrument that it is (at least in principle) in developed societies today. It was rooted in a society in which wealth, social position, and clout had as much to do with determining a verdict as abstract principles of justice. The oft-quoted words of Seneca, in which a rich and powerful man dares a poor man to take him to court, illustrate the situation perfectly. The poor man replies, "Am I, a poor man, to accuse a rich man?" (quoted in Winter 2001, 62-64). Name-calling and character-assassination in court were not only expected but also permitted. Clearly, encouragement in such legal proceedings could only exacerbate the divisions in the Corinthian church and apparently had already done so. It is against this background that these verses are to be read.

Paul's argument in this section consists basically of a series of rhetorical questions. He is merely reminding the Corinthians of what he has already taught them and therefore they should already know. Note the recurring formula: "Do you not know?" (vv 2, 3, 9).

■ 1 Paul's sense of outrage is perhaps best brought out by translating: **How dare any of you having a dispute with a brother go to law before the ungodly** *and not before the saints?* What is envisaged is not a lawsuit against anyone (as the NIV's **another** might suggest) but a lawsuit against a fellow believer. Such cases are not to be brought **before the ungodly** (*adikoi*). The term probably has a double flavor. On the one hand it denotes the unrighteous (see v 9), but it may also reflect the crookedness of the judicial system of Corinth, which was typical of courts in the eastern part of the Roman Empire at that time (Winter 2001, 58-64).

■ 2 The mention of seeking judgment before **the Lord's people** triggers a series of rhetorical questions interspersed with exclamations: all directed now not to the litigating individual of v 1, but to the church as a whole. The idea that **the Lord's people will judge the world** is present in the teaching of Jesus (Matt 19:28), which in turn echoes Dan 7:13 where the figure "like a son of man" receives universal dominion himself (v 14), which he shares with "the holy people of the Most High" (v 18). With this there is introduced an eschatological note into Paul's teaching. The church is the judgment court of the age to come and exercises part of that role here and now. Hence Paul's second question: **if you are to judge the world, are you not competent to judge trivial cases?** Those who are competent to do the greater are, by that argument, competent to do the lesser. It is most improbable that by **trivial cases** Paul is referring to the case of incest in 1 Cor 5:1. The inference then is that what is in mind in 6:1 is a pettifogging lawsuit: an argument for the sake of an argument, which was all too typical of Corinthian society.

■ 3 Paul moves on to a third question to which the Corinthian Christians knew the answer. Since they are to **judge angels**, how much more should they be able to judge the ordinary matters of this life. The idea that Christian believers would judge angels seems to have been an inference from Dan 7:13-14, 18; 10:4-20 where the angel-princes over the nations are in mind. See also Heb 2:5-9 and Jude 6, where the angels who rebelled against God are spoken of. In either case, evil angels are in mind.

■ 4 Paul presses his point still further, with yet another question. If they persist in having squabbles about trivial matters, why do they take them for judgment to **those whose way of life is scorned in the church** (i.e., pagan judges; lit. *those regarded as nobodies* [*tous exouthenēmenous*])? If they are to have disputes among themselves, they should settle them among themselves, not have them settled by unbelievers.

■ 5-6 In a shame and honor culture like that of Corinth where the sense of belonging was everything, Paul is saying that resorting to pagan courts amounts to disowning their Christian identity. He drives the dagger in still further by asking if there is not one among them **wise enough to judge a dispute between believers** (1 Cor 6:5)—a deadly thrust to those who claimed to be wise (*sophos*: see 1:18-25). The question continues in 6:6 (though the NIV reads it as an exclamation) where the term "believers" is replaced by the mere intimate term "brothers": **one brother takes another to court—and this in front of unbelievers!** Following in the steps of Jesus, Paul interprets the Christian community in family terms (Matt 23:8-9).

■ **7-8** Paul now turns to a still deeper consideration. It is better to suffer wrong and be cheated than to engage in any kind of litigation at all. While this echoes the teaching of Jesus (Matt 5:40-41), it is by no means without parallel in contemporary pagan moralists. The Stoics held that the truly wise person would rather be wronged than do wrong. The difference between Paul and the Stoics lay in the Christian view of the community as a family, rather than simply in the moral principle. That the lawsuits in question involved suing for monetary damages seems to be implied by the term **cheated** (1 Cor 6:7; NRSV: "defrauded"). The charge Paul levels against the Corinthians is that they would rather do the cheating—and that against fellow members of the Christian family.

■ **9-11** Paul resumes not only the rhetorical question mode but the specific form that he has used earlier in vv 2 and 3: **or do you not know?** (v 9). The reappearance of the term **wrongdoers** (*adikoi*) provides a link with the verbal form "be wronged" and "do wrong" in vv 7 and 8. The trap is now about to close upon the Corinthians, who are the wrongdoers in v 8: **wrongdoers will not inherit the kingdom of God** (v 9). The expression **the kingdom of God** is more common in the teaching of Jesus than in the teaching of Paul, presumably because it carried more meaning to Jews than it did to Gentiles. However, Paul uses it thirteen times in all the letters that bear his name (it has already occurred in 4:20), chiefly in the eschatological sense of the kingdom that will come in the future (e.g., 15:24, 50; Gal 5:21; Eph 5:5; 1 Thess 2:12; 2 Thess 1:5). Equally significant is the fact that in many of these examples it has ethical overtones: it is those who live lives of purity who will inherit the kingdom. In Collins' words: "The coming of the kingdom required a change in one's life, a radical conversion" (1999, 235).

Paul warns the Corinthians to be under no illusions on this score. Now follows another vice list (see 5:10-11), naming those sins that exclude one from the kingdom. Significantly, the sins are not named in abstract form but in personal form: **the sexually immoral, idolaters, adulterers**, and so forth. Equally significantly for his Corinthian audience, the emphasis falls upon sexual sins. Sexual immorality (*pornoi*, already mentioned in 5:11 and a verbal relative of *porneia* in 5:1) is named first, followed by idolatry and adultery. Idolatry often led to, where it did not directly involve, immorality. The next two terms are rare (*malakoi* and *arsenokoitai*) and are translated in the NIV by the phrase

men who have sex with men. (See footnote to 6:9 in the NIV.) Their meaning is more precise. Greek *malakos* means "soft" and came to denote the passive role in male homosexual activity. Greek *arsenokoitai* is apparently a Pauline coinage (possibly based on the LXX of Lev 18:22; 20:13) and denotes the active role in male homosexual activity. Taken together they are perhaps best translated as **homosexuals, both passive and active partners.**

The list of five sexual sins (1 Cor 6:9) is followed by a list of five nonsexual sins (v 10). At first sight these appear to be run-of-the-mill sins that could be found anywhere in the Greco-Roman world. However, it is interesting that four of the five (the **greedy**, the **drunkards**, the **slanderers**, and the **swindlers**) have appeared already in 5:11; while defrauding or cheating, which is a form of theft, is mentioned in 6:7-8. Moreover, with the exception of **drunkards**, all appear to have figured in the unprincipled practice of litigation in Corinth. Paul's list seems, therefore, to be on target. Such persons are not strong candidates for the kingdom of God.

Paul continues with the stunning declaration: **And that is what some of you were** (v 11). Some at least of the Corinthians would recognize themselves as the list was read. But the incriminating charge was removed before the sentence was completed. The verb is in the past tense: that is what they were. The nature of the change and the means of its accomplishment are now spelled out. Three verbs describe it, each introduced by the emphatic conjunction **but** (*alla*; the NIV weakens the force by omitting the second and third occurrences). The first verb (**you were washed**) taken in conjunction with the phrase **in the name of the Lord Jesus Christ** suggests that baptism is in mind. However, the standard verb for baptism (*baptizō*) is not used, suggesting that the inner meaning, "cleansing," is in Paul's mind. The second verb (**you were sanctified**) recalls the expression "sanctified in Christ Jesus and called to be . . . holy" in 1:1 where the idea of being set apart for holy and godly living is in mind. The third verb (**you were justified** [*edikaiōthēte*]) presents a striking contrast to earlier uses of the negative form of the same root (*adik*) in 6:1, 7, and 8 where it denotes "being in the wrong." The meaning here will then be, "You have been made right." The three terms therefore denote not three separate realities but three aspects of a single reality—namely, the spiritual, moral, and ethical changes that come through belonging to Christ and through the work of the Spirit of God. This meaning fits perfectly with the subject matter of the whole section—namely, immoral conduct that scandalized the pagans, and behavior that was not fit for the kingdom of God. Significantly, this three-sided saving work is said to involve the three persons of the Trinity.

Paul, the Corinthians, and Homosexuality

Paul's references to homosexuality in v 9 (using uncommon terms) must be read against several backgrounds. First, Roman law penalized homosexual acts in which the passive partner was a Roman citizen, apparently in the belief that this undermined the masculinity of Roman manhood. It did not ban citizens from the active role. This meant that slaves were prime targets for active homosexuals. This view appears to have carried over into Roman Corinth, although in pre-Roman times slaves had been banned from engagement in homosexual activity in Greece (Raditsa 1980).

In Judaism homosexual practice was absolutely forbidden by the law (Lev 18:22; 20:13). As noted, the unusual term Paul uses in 1 Cor 6:9 to denote the role of the active partner appears to be derived from the Greek version of the OT passages just referred to. Hence, Paul is taking over the OT law banning all forms of homosexual activity, and applying it to his Corinthian readers in terms that would be meaningful in their cultural setting.

That Paul grounded his view on more than simply the quotation of a piece of legislation is clear from his fuller treatment of the subject in Rom 1:24-28, where he sees same-sex relations as a violation of God's order of creation (Rom 1:20; compare Gen 1:27; 2:24). Paul does not quote the Genesis passages in the vice list here (the literary form does not allow for it), but he applies the principle to female prostitution in 1 Cor 6:15-16, where he quotes from Gen 2:24.

It is inadmissible to narrow the scope of Paul's teaching by restricting its reference to pederasty, or by drawing inferences from its silence regarding lesbianism. The prominence Paul gives to sexual sin here (in addition to its presence in the Corinthian setting) is that it constitutes rejection of God's order and design in the creation of persons. That design finds its expression in the differences, physical and emotional, between the sexes, and consequently in their complementarity.

Two further points may be made. First, while Paul would not have been familiar with the idea of "orientation" as it is used today, he knew something akin to it. The idea of "effeminacy," used to characterize passive homosexuals, was well recognized in the world of his day (Winter 2001, 116-18). Paul knew only too well that sin is more than a matter of choice. It has an inward dimension (Rom 7:14-20). But it does not become acceptable merely because, in whatever form (pederasty, promiscuity), it is desired. It is therefore the more striking—and this is the second point—that the overriding tone of 1 Cor 6:9-11 is that of optimism. Paul's emphasis rests not on the inward power of sin, but on the power of God in Christ to bring deliverance. Clearly, Paul preached the gospel to homosexuals, and he expected a change in the lives of those who responded to it.

(For fuller discussion, see Schmidt 1996b, Grenz 1998, Thiselton 2000b, 440-53; Gagnon 2001, 303-39; 2005, 745-47; Winter 2001, 110-20; Fitzmyer 2008, 254-58.)

Thus Paul's argument in 6:1-11 drives progressively more deeply. First, Paul reproaches the Corinthians for calling in judges who are both unbelieving and corrupt to adjudicate matters of dispute between believers (vv 2-6).

Second, he reproves them for having lawsuits at all—even where there has been injury—since this is contrary to the spirit of the gospel, let alone the good name of Christ (vv 7-8). Paul is not saying that they should wash their dirty linen in private, since doing so publicly was damaging the good name of the gospel. Presumably he believed that to be true, but his point was deeper. He was saying that it was better to accept being wronged rather than have the church rent by disputes at all. In accepting undeserved suffering they would be following in Paul's own footsteps (4:11-13), as well as those of Jesus (2 Cor 4:10). First Corinthians 6:9-11 takes the argument deeper still. Wrongdoers will have no place in the kingdom of God. In these verses the accent rests on sexual sins and the sin of greed. The latter appears to have been at the bottom of many of the lawsuits (vv 7-8). As believers they have been cleansed (v 11). They should not pollute themselves all over again.

C. The Problem of Sexual Immorality (6:12-20)

Overview

This passage has been regarded as one of the most intractable, if not the most intractable, in all of Paul's writings (Ciampa and Rosner 2010, 245). The problems arise on at least two counts.

(1) There is no doubt that some aspect of sexual immorality is in mind. The frequency of the term *porneia* and its cognates makes that clear (vv 13, 15, 16, 18), not to mention complete statements, such as vv 16a and 17. The question is whether this picks up the earlier treatment of *porneia* in the sense of incest (5:1); or the more general sense of sexual immorality (5:9-10); or any (or all) of the specific forms of immorality referred to in 6:9-10. In different terms, the question here is the developing form of the argument of the letter.

(2) A second problematic issue in this section is the precise meaning of frequently recurring terms. Most notable in this section is the term "body," which appears eight times in as many verses. Particularly challenging are statements such as **the Lord [is meant] for the body** (v 13) or **all other sins a person commits are outside the body, but whoever sins sexually, sins against their own body** (v 18b). Again, the term seems to carry more than one meaning. In the context of sexual immorality the reference is clearly to the physical body (vv 13b, 16), but a metaphorical sense emerges where the body is spoken of as a member of Christ (vv 15-17).

Several things seem clear and may be taken as guidelines in the interpretation of the passage.

(a) The specific form of sexual immorality addressed is prostitution. While the term *porneià* can be used "of various kinds of 'unsanctioned sexual intercourse'" (BDAG 854) and is used in that sense in v 13, it clearly assumes the narrower sense of "prostitute" in vv 15 and 16. Whether a particular kind of prostitution is in mind—"temple prostitution" as at cultic festivals and pagan feasts (Rosner 1998, 350-51) or secular prostitution—it is impossible to know for certain. The language of the text is not specific (Ciampa and Rosner 2010, 246-49). In the end it makes little difference to Paul's argument.

(*b*) The background of the problem in the Corinthian church appears to have been the nature of Christian freedom. The repeated statement in v 12 ("I have the right to do anything") together with v 13 ("Food for the stomach and the stomach for food, and God will destroy them both") are best understood as Corinthian slogans affirming their freedom to do with their bodies as they pleased. (Paul essentially repeats v 12 in 10:23.) Such views were not uncommon in Stoic-Cynic thought, giving rise to the conclusion that the enlightened wise man was free to do anything he chose. This mentality was present among the Corinthians (4:8), possibly encouraged by (a misunderstanding of) Paul's insistence upon his own freedom (9:1, 19; 10:23). (For this reason, some scholars argue strenuously that 6:12 and 13 are Paul's words in their entirety. See B. J. Dodd 1995, 39-58, Garland 2003, 219-29 and the commentary below.)

(*c*) There is also a possibility that a Corinthian misunderstanding of the timing and nature of the age to come may have been at work. The reference to the resurrection of the body as something yet to happen (v 14) may be an indication (and correction) of a Corinthian view that it had happened already. Paul will take this up at length in ch 15, where he affirms the permanence of the body as well as its changed nature. In many respects 6:12-20 is an applied example in miniature of the problems and principles enunciated in ch 15 at greater length.

(*d*) Paul emphasizes that he is not telling them anything new. Three times he poses the question: "Do you not know?" (vv 15, 16, 19). The three items Paul expects them to know are that faith in Christ involves union with Christ (v 15), that union with Christ involves sharing his Spirit (v 17), and that consequently their bodies are temples of the indwelling Holy Spirit, and they are not their own (v 19). This demonstrates that the distinction between *kerygma* (the gospel proclamation) and *didache* (ethical instruction) cannot be pressed absolutely. Clearly it was not pressed in Paul's ministry in Corinth since he *reminds* them of matters he had every reason to expect them to know.

Most of these ideas (sexual immorality, the nature of Christian freedom, and the nature of the age to come) will emerge again—some of them more than once—later in the letter. Lightfoot's comment that these verses contain "the germ of very much which follows in the Epistle" (1895, 215) is very apt.

■ **12** It seems clear that this verse is constructed around a slogan popular among many of the Corinthians, which Paul quotes twice, and then inserts a qualifier of his own each time. The Corinthians' slogan was "All things are lawful for me" (NRSV), which the NIV renders as **I have the right to do anything**. The claim probably reflects Stoic influence, as indicated in the saying of the Stoic philosopher Epictetus (late first century AD to mid-second century): "That man is free, who lives as he wishes, who is proof against compulsion and hindrance and violence, whose impulses are untrammelled, who gets what he wills to get and avoids what he wills to avoid" (*Discourses IV* i.1-4, as in Barrett 1961, 68). The title of the work by the first-century Jewish philosopher Philo of Alexandria, *Every Good Man Is Free*, echoes the same influence. Paul also believed in freedom (9:1), but for him it was defined by moral principle: in particular, by the principle of self-surrender, embodied in the cross. Hence he replies by saying that **not everything is beneficial** (*sympherei*): "beneficial" being itself a common philosophical term denoting what is helpful. Paul's second rejoinder strikes deeper still: **I will not be mastered by anything**. The ongoing argument indicates that sex indulgence is at issue. Paul replies that free indulgence in sex can very quickly result in bondage to sexual activity and therefore the very reverse of freedom. We have here yet another example of Paul's argumentative strategy. He does not respond by squashing the Corinthians, telling them (for example) to stop talking nonsense. Rather, he goes as far as he can in accepting the principle they are asserting, but corrects their misuse of it.

■ **13-14** Paul now quotes another Corinthian slogan. The NIV is correct in taking this to include **and God will destroy them both** (v 13; the NRSV punctuates the words quoted as Paul's, but this would imply that Paul regarded the body as destined for destruction, which is the reverse of what he says in 15:35-49). The Corinthian claim was that the bodily organs were merely functional: food is made for stomachs, stomachs for food and—it is implied—sexual organs for sex. All are headed for decay and have no higher value. Accordingly, we may use them as we please. Significantly, Paul's reply is expressed not in the physiological terms used by the Corinthians but in terms of **the body**, which, for Paul, has a far deeper meaning.

His reply is in two steps. First, he asserts that the body falls under the lordship of Christ. His statement that it is **not meant for sexual immorality** shows that this has been his primary target from the beginning. But this is merely an application of the overarching principle that **the body . . . is . . . for the Lord, and the Lord for the body**. The way in which the body is **for the Lord** he will develop in 6:15. The assertion that **the Lord is for the body** appeals to the fundamental principle that both in creation and redemption the Lord is the life-giving power (Gen 2:7; 1 Cor 2:12). Accordingly, the body is not to be used for purposes that defy the will of the life-giver.

Second, he affirms that, rather than being destined for destruction, the body has a future. The same God who raised Christ will resurrect us also **by his power** (v 14). The verb translated "will resurrect" (*exegerei*) is an intensive form of the verb "raise" (*egeirō*). Despite the varied tenses in the manuscripts, the future tense of **will destroy** (v 13) requires the future here (see *TCGNT*, 486-87). Significantly the word **body** in v 13 is replaced by the pronoun **us** here, indicating that the body, while physical, is more than a thing. It is the habitation of a *person* and its actions are the actions of a person. In overlooking the *future* eschatological dimension, the Corinthians lost sight of the ethical dimension. As elsewhere in his writings, Paul sees the resurrection as the supreme demonstration of the power of God (Rom 6:4; 8:11; Eph 1:19-21; Phil 3:10-11).

■ **15** Paul now begins to take the Corinthians to task for their ignorance of what he had taught them and had every right to expect them to know. In this first question, introduced by the formula **Do you not know?** he returns to the opening topic of v 13*b* that "the body . . . is not meant for sexual immorality but for the Lord." The reality underlying this is that the bodies of believers are **members of Christ himself**. The term **members** (*melē*) is used in a much more sharply defined sense here than in 12:12, 27. The sense here is that the bodily members of the individual believer are Christ's instruments carrying out his actions. In an important measure the "not yet" has become the "already." It is therefore unthinkable that the bodily members of a believer should be given over to a harlot. "God forbid!"—as the Greek expression "may it not be so!" is vividly (if freely) rendered by the KJV (see Rom 6:2).

■ **16-17** A second question follows. **Do you not know that he who unites himself with a prostitute is one with her in body?** (v 16). Something more takes place in sexual intercourse than the conjoining of two physical entities. A union of persons is involved in which *one body* is created. This truth rests on the scriptural declaration of Gen 2:24*b*: **The two will become one flesh**. That "flesh" has a more than simply physical sense is shown by Gen 2:24*a*, in which the creation of "one flesh" is said to take place by the departure of a man from his parents and being united with his wife. This being so, Paul is able to state the obverse of being united with a prostitute—namely, being united with the Lord, which means being **one with him in spirit** (1 Cor 6:17). This paves the way for him to pick up the idea of the believer as one indwelt by the Spirit (v 19).

■ **18** Paul now resumes the note of command with which he concluded his reprimand regarding the treatment of the immoral man in 5:1-13. There he gave the peremptory order: "Expel the wicked person from among you" (5:13*b*). Here he writes: **Flee from sexual immorality**. The next sentence is difficult. What does Paul mean by the words: "Every sin that a person commits is outside the body" (as the Greek text reads)? The NIV translates: **All other sins** a person commits are outside the body, but whoever sins sexually, sins against their own body. The meaning in this case would be that sexual sins are damaging to the individual in a way that other sins are not. There are several difficulties with this interpretation. First, the word **other** is not in the Greek text. Second, how can sins including sexual immorality and drunkenness, which Paul has declared will bring exclusion from the kingdom of God (vv 9-10), be regarded as **outside the body**? It is probable, therefore, that v 18*b* should be regarded as yet another notion embraced by some of the Corinthians. Their view then was that sexual sin was a misnomer because the body is material whereas sin is a matter of the spirit. Paul's reply is that, on the contrary, the body is not to be regarded as a material (and therefore submoral) entity. It can be both the instrument and the locus of sin. Thus sexual immorality is also a sin against the sinner in that he defiles himself by his illicit action. Differing understandings of **the body** thus lie behind Paul's disagreement with the Corinthians.

■ **19-20** Paul presses his point by reminding the Corinthians of yet another truth that they ought to know—the third example in this context of the question: **Do you not know?** In 3:16 (which is introduced by the same formulaic question) he has reminded them that collectively they are the temple of God, indwelt by his Spirit. Now he gives that truth individual application. Each of them (lit. "your body") is a temple of the Holy Spirit. The point is emphatic. Rendered literally the text reads: "your body is a temple of the within you Holy Spirit whom you have from God." Three points are stressed. First, the Holy Spirit dwells within them as believers. Second, whereas Paul normally in Greek places the adjective "holy" after the noun "spirit," here he reverses the order, so as to accent the word "holy." Third, he affirms that the Holy Spirit is given by God himself.

Holiness of life is not an optional extra. It is part of the plain logic of God's saving work in us. Accordingly, they are not free to live as they please. The ground of this claim is that they have been **bought at a price** (6:20*a*). The force of the image here—which would have been clear at once to the Corinthians in a slave-owning society—is that they have been purchased from slavery to sin, and the cost was not small. Elsewhere Paul identifies the price as the blood of Christ (see also 7:23, and Rom 3:24-25; Eph 1:7). Their obligation therefore is to **honor God with your bodies** (1 Cor 6:20*b*). (Some manuscripts contain the additional words: "and with your spirit which is God's." This represents a true understanding of the word "body," though the aspect of the body in mind here is the physical. In any case, the addition is not present in the earliest and best manuscripts. See *TCGNT*, 487-88.) Once again Paul has brought his readers back to the truth of the gospel as the touchstone of their lives. Just as the message of the cross ruled out the divisions among them, so—as they should already have known—the message of the cross, the resurrection, and the gift of the Holy Spirit rule out sexual immorality.

FROM THE TEXT

The overriding message of chs 5—6 is that *there is a sharp distinction between the church and the world inasmuch as the church is characterized by purity of heart and life*. The illustrations—taken from the Corinthian church—are those of illicit sexual relations (5:1-13; 6:12-20) and church quarrels (6:1-11). Both are condemned as inconsistent with the purity of Christ (5:6-8) and the indwelling Holy Spirit (6:11, 19-20). This message, which unifies these chapters, is worked out in detail in terms of these topics.

1. 1 Cor 5:1-13 has a triple focus and application:
   (a) *The toleration of sexual sin has a destructive effect on the offending individual*. This is the primary or initial focus. The motivation of the church's discipline is the salvation of the sinner (v 5).
   (b) *The failure of the church to act has a destructive effect on the church*. The toleration of flagrant sin places the whole body at risk (vv 6-8), just as leaven permeates the whole lump. Sexual immorality among its members is something the church cannot condone and from which it must dissociate itself. The precise form of dissociation may vary from one setting to another. In Corinth, where the offending individual remained publicly identified with the church and the church expressed not merely approval of him but pride in him (v 2), strong measures were needed.

   The action called for was therefore positive in intent: saving the offender and saving the church. Holding the two principles together is not always easy, but it is a responsibility the church cannot shirk: not least in times like the present when sexual immorality is as much a byword as it was in Paul's Corinth.
   (c) *The church's attitude to the world must be one of tempered realism*. An exaggerated separation is not only illogical but impossible (v 10). The judging of the world in the last analysis is the work of God (vv 12-13*a*). Nevertheless, just as the toleration of sin within the church is the judgment of the church, so also the purity of the church is the judgment of the world.

2. *The unity of the church is more important than the personal gain or loss of the individual member* (6:1-11). The differences between the legal situation in Corinth and in developed countries today rule out any parallel between believers battling out differences in the lawcourts, though in less developed countries it could be otherwise. But the principle that Paul expounds for the

settling of grievances still applies very much, even if it does not involve lawsuits. Is it not better to be wronged rather than collapse the church into a welter of backbiting and strife (vv 7-8)? Here Paul is appealing to the crucified Christ who, when maltreated, did not return injury in word or deed (1 Pet 2:21-23). This is the wisdom of the cross (1 Cor 1:23-25).

3. *The holiness of the body is to be prized and preserved as the gift of the indwelling Holy Spirit* (6:19). The aspect of the body primarily in mind is the physical, as the application to prostitution shows (vv 15-16), though throughout the passage the word "body" and the personal pronoun are used interchangeably (vv 14, 19-20). Commenting on v 13*b*: "The body is meant not for *porneià* but for the Lord, and the Lord for the body," J. Paul Sampley writes: "Without using the term, this is holiness talk" (2002, 866). William Barclay strikes the same note when he writes: "The great fact of the Christian faith is not that it makes us free to sin, but that it makes us free *not* to sin. . . . When we really experience the Christian power, we are no longer slaves of our bodies but take full charge of them" (2002, 67). The incarnation is the ultimate declaration of the sanctification of the body. For believers that sanctification takes place by the indwelling Holy Spirit (v 19). Consequently, they are not their own to use their bodies as they please. As purchased and possessed by God and destined for resurrection, their obligation is to live in accordance with God's will and design.

4. One of the challenges the church faces today is how to proclaim the gospel to homosexuals. On the one hand the church cannot betray the gospel by declaring as acceptable a practice that biblical teaching declares to be sinful. But neither can it betray the gospel by placing beyond its reach any particular group of sinners. It was precisely the refusal to do this that distinguished the ministry of Jesus and caused him to be branded by the religious establishment as "a glutton and a drunkard, a friend of tax collectors and sinners" (Matt 11:19; Luke 7:34). To condemn sin while loving the sinner is what the gospel is all about. Paul's preaching on the subject had been forthright. He had also seen some of his hearers "washed . . . sanctified . . . justified" (1 Cor 6:11). Such a combination of the realism of truth and the optimism of grace should inform the church's proclamation still. For how this may work out in practice, see Hays 1996, 400-3; Gardner 2018, 264-69, 287-92; McGowan 2017, 188.

IV. THE GOSPEL AND HOLY LIVING IN A PAGAN SOCIETY: I CORINTHIANS 7:1—11:1

Overview

Now for the matters you wrote about (7:1*a*) clearly marks off ch 7 from what precedes, at least in the sense that Paul now turns to questions raised by the Corinthians rather than questions of his own choosing. Two issues immediately present themselves. First, how much of the rest of the letter consists of responses to the Corinthians' questions? It has been argued on the basis of the introductory phrase "now about" (*peri de*) that the rest of the letter falls under this description (see 7:25; 8:1; 12:1; 16:1, 12). But while this expression clearly indicates a change of topic, it cannot by itself indicate that the new topic was raised by the Corinthians. Moreover, there are clear indications in later parts of the letter that Paul chose some of the topics he addresses (see 11:2-3, 17-18). Indeed, this very feature at 11:2-3 marks the conclusion of this section and the beginning of the next.

Second, 7:1—11:1 seems to find coherence around the theme of the avoidance of immorality. In that sense ch 7 follows naturally from chs 5—6. However, the perspective is different. Whereas chs 5—6 are directed to a mindset that did not particularly object to sexual immorality, ch 7 reflects a mentality that, though anxious to avoid it, in Paul's opinion was following a course likely to promote it. This mood continues in ch 8, which deals with eating food offered in idol temples and the dangers involved for immature Christians. Paul makes his point in a long discourse (ch 9) on his own circumscribing of his apostolic freedom, concluding with warnings against idolatry and the immorality to which it invariably led (10:6-10, 18-22). He urges the Corinthians to follow his example in the exercise of their freedom (10:23—11:1). Thus the overriding theme of 7:1—11:1 is how to live holy lives in a pagan society. Unlike chs 5—6, whose mood is predominantly mandatory, the mood of 7:1—11:1 is predominantly advisory. Further, while chs 5—6 are concerned directly with the effect of sin on the church, ch 7 is concerned with the life of the individual believer. In many respects ch 7 functions as a bridge between chs 5 and 6 (which deal with immoral conduct) and chs 8—11, whose concern is the danger from involvement in morally ambiguous practices.

It is significant that once more Paul brings everything he teaches to the touchstone of the gospel (7:17; 9:12, 23; 11:1-2). There is not one gospel for the Corinthians and another for everyone else. It appears that the Corinthians regarded themselves as a special case, with a gospel tailored to their dimensions and tastes. Paul will have none of it. As he has insisted from the start, there is but one gospel (1:17; 2:1-2), and it is the same for all.

A. Christian Married Life in a Non-Christian Culture (7:1-40)

BEHIND THE TEXT

Not the least of our problems in interpreting this chapter is that, while we have Paul's answers to the questions asked by the Corinthians, we have no clear record of the questions themselves. It would have helped greatly if their inquiries, which were either written or transmitted by messengers, had survived so that we could know for sure when Paul is quoting them (as in 7:1) or the exact point he is addressing (as in vv 25-35). As it is, we are left to infer these, which it is not always easy to do with precision. This makes exact interpretation difficult and casts a degree of tentativeness over the entire enterprise.

It is of the utmost importance to read ch 7 in its own context and in terms of its own purpose. The questions the Corinthians were asking about

Christian marriage (as far as we can ascertain them) were not necessarily the questions that we would ask. Several factors apparently at work in the Corinthian setting are of crucial importance for the understanding of the chapter. (On the whole question, see Deasley 2000a, 122-25.)

Sexual morality in Corinth. The Corinth of Paul's day was the Roman city refounded by Julius Caesar in 44 BC. As such it differed from its Greek predecessor of which the Greek playwright Aristophanes (450-385 BC) had coined the term "to live like a Corinthian" (*korinthiazesthai*) as a synonym for committing fornication. This is not to say that Roman Corinth was a temple of moral purity. However, the marriage laws of Augustus (dating from 18 BC onward), which laid down legal procedures for marriage and divorce, had imposed a measure of order and even stability in marriage. In the earlier Greek city, as throughout Greece, marriage meant little more than living together, and divorce no more than leaving. However, the legalization of marriage was no guarantee of fidelity. The multiplied temples and feasts provided ample opportunity for sexual license. First Corinthians 5—6 shows how this mentality had survived in the Corinthian church.

The social make-up of the Corinthian church. The Corinthian church was composed of converts from Judaism (see 7:18 and Acts 18:1-8) as well as from paganism. Within Judaism views of divorce varied from those who held that it was permissible only on the grounds of the wife's immorality (the school of Shammai) to those who regarded it as permissible for any reason (the school of Hillel). In either case remarriage was permitted. From the side of paganism marriage breakup was perfectly possible (1 Cor 7:15), as was remarriage following divorce. Hence, divorce with the possibility of remarriage was part of the mentality with which all Corinthian Christians would have been familiar.

Tendency toward sexual abstinence. A tendency toward sexual abstinence seems to have been a factor in those seeking Paul's counsel. Most obviously it was present in some sense in Paul himself. He wishes that the Corinthians were as he was: unmarried (vv 7, 8, 38, 40). Some of the Christians in Corinth believed that withholding sexual relations with their married partner was "good" (v 1). This may have been prompted by Paul's example. More probably, other influences were at work. Greek philosophy from the time of Plato onward had harbored a deep divide between matter (as being evil) and spirit (as being good). Moreover, there was an ongoing debate between Stoic and Cynic philosophers closer to Paul's time about the desirability of marriage. The Stoics viewed it as beneficial to the city-state, while the Cynics downgraded it as a distraction from the pursuit of philosophy. In addition Egyptian cults known to have been present in Corinth in Paul's day (such as the cult of the goddess Isis) required sexual abstinence.

With so many influences in the direction of abstinence and even of asceticism, it is not surprising that it should have infiltrated the Corinthian church. This means that Paul's entire treatment has a particular slant to it that arises not from his view of marriage as such but from Corinthian attitudes to it. Will Deming observes aptly that Paul writes of "*being* married versus *becoming* celibate, *being* married to a non-Christian versus obtaining a divorce, *remaining* celibate versus *marrying* a Christian, and *marrying* a Christian versus *marrying* a non-Christian" (2004, 211).

Eschatology. A further complicating factor in the Corinthian situation was eschatology. This seems to have been present in two forms. First, there was the Corinthian misunderstanding that, in belonging to the kingdom of God, they must divest themselves of things belonging to the present age. Marriage was a prime example, especially if the words of Jesus that marriage had no place in the age to come (Mark 12:25; Luke 20:35-36) were known to them. This would chime in easily with their preoccupation with being "spiritual" as well as with the pervasive influence of Platonic dualism. Second, there was Paul's warning about "the present crisis" (1 Cor 7:26), by which he meant the shortening of "the time" (v 29) and the "passing away" of the "present form" of the world (v 31). These demanded single-minded concentration on "the Lord's affairs" (v 32), which marriage rendered difficult (v 33).

Variation in tone. Throughout ch 7 there is a notable variation in the tone in which Paul responds to the Corinthians' questions. Whereas in chs 5 and 6 his tone is peremptory throughout, in ch 7 there are differences of tone in his treatment of different issues. First, where Jesus has pronounced on a matter, his pronouncement is taken as conclusive and final (7:10-11). Second, where no specific teaching of Jesus exists, Paul gives his own ruling as an apostle (v 12), which is to be regarded as authoritative (v 17). Third, in some matters Paul speaks by way of concession (v 6); while, fourth, in other matters he leaves the decision to the choice of those involved. Allied with this is Paul's argumentative strategy. This was to go as far as he could in accepting the Corinthians' view, but then to point out practical consequences of it that could be disastrous if it were accepted in an unqualified way.

Henry Chadwick points out that there is no mention in the chapter of the doctrine of creation according to which marriage is a divine institution. This would have placed a decisive gulf between Paul and the Corinthians (Chadwick 1955, 268). Paul preferred to pick out the acceptable elements in their view and reshape it in the light of Christian principles. Sexual abstinence was acceptable, but not if it led to fornication. We shall attempt to trace this out in detail in the commentary.

Putting all of this together, we may say that Paul has two overriding but related concerns in ch 7. The first is ridding the Corinthian church of sexual immorality. The starting point of his case is that sexual immorality was occurring (v 2). His fear is their lack of self-control (vv 5, 9, 36-38). Accordingly, he sees Christian marriage, in which sexual relations find legitimate and appropriate expression, as the right framework for the avoidance of immorality. But second, he is concerned about the stress of the times in which he and the Corinthians live. In such times marriage and the responsibilities it brings militate against serving the Lord with unrestricted freedom. To reconcile these contending claims is something that cannot be done by everyone in the same way. Paul himself has done it by ruling out the responsibilities of marriage and family, and he would prefer to see the Corinthians do the same (vv 7, 8, 26-27, 29-35, 38). But he recognizes that all are not made like him, nor have they received the same gifts and calling (vv 7, 9, 17, 20, 24), hence the right thing for these is to marry, accepting its privileges and responsibilities (vv 2-7, 9, 27-28, 36-38). Chapter 7 is an exercise in holding together views that stand in a degree of tension, yet both have undeniable validity.

IN THE TEXT

There are distinct marks of structure in the text indicating the steps or stages in the argument. The expression "Now for" (*peri de*) indicates a change of topic at v 1, introducing a number of questions raised by the Corinthians. Verses 1-16 seem to fall into four subsections. Verses 1-7 address the question of the place of sexual relations within marriage. Verses 8-9 are addressed to "the unmarried and the widows." Verses 10-12 are directed to "the married"; and vv 12-16 to "the rest" who are evidently believers married to unbelievers. The occurrence of the expression "Now about" at v 25 suggests that a new topic is picked up there. This is confirmed by a marked change in vocabulary. The word "virgins" occurs six times in vv 25-40, and nowhere else in the chapter, while the verbs for "getting married" (*gameō, gamizō*) occur eight times in these verses and only twice earlier (in v 9). Verses 17-24 constitute a bridge between the two main sections in which Paul expounds the guiding principle he commends to all the groups addressed.

The guiding principle that Paul recommends to the various categories of people indicated by the structure may be summed up as: "Remain as you are—unless." Undoubtedly, the accent falls on the first part: "Remain as you are" (vv 8, 17, 20, 24, 26). In some cases indeed, he leaves elbow room for individual situations (vv 6, 9, 15, 28, 35, 38), but his preferred principle is clear. This principle is based on the twin factors of "gift" and "calling." Indulgence in, or abstinence from, sexual relations are gifts from God, and the presence of either gift should be the determining factor in conduct, not a one-size-fits-all approach (vv 7, 36-37).

Closely related to the idea of "gift" is that of "calling." This appears to refer to believers married to unbelievers. Paul's rule is that such marriages are not to be either terminated or held together by force, since **God has called us to live in peace** (v 15). He applies the same principle to slavery and circumcision (vv 17-24), under the overriding rubric that **keeping God's commands is what counts** (v 19b). (For further discussion, see Deasley 2000a, 28-34, 122-25.)

From all of this it seems clear that the Corinthians' questions ranged all the way from whether sex within marriage was Christian to whether it was Christian to get married at all. The strangeness of these questions arose partly from the mindset of first-century Corinth and partly from their (mis)understanding of Paul's teaching. These factors must be kept in mind in seeking the message of the chapter for today.

1. Christian Married Relationships (7:1-16)

BEHIND THE TEXT

As noted above, these verses are bound together structurally. But is there a bond that ties them together in thought? The answer appears to be that there is—namely, whether continuance in the married state is fully Christian. This question (which seems bizarre to us) was apparently prompted by the contemporary currents in Hellenistic thought noted above. It was accentuated by the exaggerated understanding of spirituality that many Corinthian believers had derived, partly from Paul's teaching, that they had already entered the kingdom of God; partly from his teaching that in the current crisis one could serve God more effectively if one were free from the obligations of marriage (vv 29-35); and partly from his own example as unmarried (vv 7-8).

It has sometimes been suggested that the problem originated among women believers in Corinth, often referred to as "eschatological women" (Fee 2014, 299). However, it is remarkable that Paul is careful to address both parties in each case, and that in three of the four cases (vv 2, 8, 12) men are addressed first. Only in the area of divorce are women addressed first (v 10).

Paul's reply that they should all remain in their present marital state is qualified by the observation that it would be better if they were all unmarried like himself (vv 7-8). But he holds this view for very different reasons from those seeking to minimize involvement in marriage (sometimes to the extent of avoiding it), as will become clear (vv 29-35).

IN THE TEXT

a. The Place of Sex within Christian Marriage (7:1-7)

■ **1** The matters Paul now turns to are those raised by the Corinthians in their letter to him. Hence the NIV places v 1b in quotation marks: **It is good for a man not to have sexual relations with a woman**. These words have been understood in several ways. They have been taken to indicate that celibacy was preferable to marriage. Hence, the 1984 edition of the NIV translates: "It is a good thing for a man not to marry." This was Calvin's understanding (even though he hedged it to avoid the conclusion that marriage was good only for those who could not control their sexual appetites [1960, 134-36]). But the Greek verb translated "marry" (*haptesthai*) means literally "to touch" and was widely used in Greek literature to denote physical intercourse. (The suggestion has been made that it denoted extramarital dalliances on the part of married men, their wives being kept only for the procreation of family [Ciampa and Rosner 2010, 268-69, 272-75].) This hardly explains why Paul proceeds to treat celibacy within marriage as a mutual problem (v 5). Minds that were capable of contemplating permanent engagement (vv 36-38), or viewing marriage as a sin (vv 28, 36), were presumably perfectly capable of seeing celibacy within marriage as a spiritually desirable state of existence. Hence, the words are to be taken at their face value—namely, that abstinence from sexual relations within marriage is **good**. However, since Paul proceeds to qualify this statement (see vv 2-5), it is possible that—as on other occasions—Paul is using the Corinthians' words, but with his own meaning. While they used the phrase **it is good** to mean "it is best," Paul used it to mean "it is not necessarily bad or evil." These verses are addressed to the married, not the unmarried. It is also significant that the statement is framed from the male perspective alone. This contrasts sharply with Paul's statements in vv 2-4, which include both female and male. This is further confirmation that the statement in v 1 is Corinthian in origin.

■ **2** Paul now proceeds to qualify the statement that avoiding sexual relations is "not bad." The reason he gives is (to translate the Greek literally) "but on account of the acts of fornication" (*dia de tas porneias*). The term translated "fornication" (KJV) is the same term used in 5:1, 10, 11; 6:13, 18. The use of the definite article suggests that it is the acts of fornication that have taken place in the Corinthian church which Paul has in mind. The NIV is therefore correct in translating: **But since sexual immorality is occurring** (compare NRSV: "But because of cases of sexual immorality").

In these circumstances, what is called for is not abstinence from sexual relations, but rather normal sexual relations between husbands and wives. **Each man should have sexual relations with his own wife, and each woman with her own husband**. The verb **have** (*echetō*) is a standard term for "have sexual relations with" (see Matt 14:4; John 4:18). The use of the reflexive personal pronouns **his own** (*heautou*) and **her own** (*idiou*) reinforces the conclusion that what Paul has in mind are recent instances of fornication in the Corinthian church. This makes clear that the question Paul is addressing is not whether sexual relations should be avoided by all, but whether they should be avoided by those who are married.

■ **3** Paul now proceeds to set forth his view of a normal marriage. This is that each partner owes the other the physical intimacy of intercourse. It is a matter of obligation (*tēn opheilēn*); that is, it is part of what marriage is about. Significantly, Paul says nothing about procreation, though some of his Jewish contemporaries maintained that procreation alone justified conjugal relations (e.g., Josephus: "The Law recognizes no sexual connexions, except the natural union of man and wife, and that only for the procreation of children" [*Ag. Ap.* 199, ET 24, Loeb edition 373]; similar views were held among Stoic philosophers, of whom Musonius is a good example; see Ward 1990, 281-89). Equally significantly, Paul specifies that this obligation rests upon each partner for the sake of the other. The husband's obligation to his wife is stated first, reinforcing the point that the purpose of sexual union is not to gratify the husband's sexual desires but those of his wife. The same obligation rests upon the wife. This is a frank recognition of both the reality and propriety of the sexual urge in male and female. But it is expressed not in terms of a right to be claimed but an obligation to be freely honored. It is possible that the refusal of sexual relations for "spiritual" reasons lay behind the immorality Paul denounces in chs 5 and 6.

■ **4** The mutual obligation expressed in active terms in v 3 is now expressed in passive terms. Both partners are again mentioned, but this time the wife first and the husband second. Neither has authority over their **own body but yields it to** the other. The NIV paraphrase brings out well the intended meaning that the literal meaning "has authority over" (*exousiazei*) overstates. This carries two important implications. First, the obligation rests on both partners. This completes the stress on mutuality that runs throughout vv 2-4. It is underlined by the alternation of first female then male in v 2, followed by male then female in v 3, and female then male in v 4. This recognition of a wife's claims in this regard was nothing short of revolutionary in a world in which women were regarded as beings of the second order. Second, the import of this mutuality is the expression of the intimacy of love in and through sexual relations. This was distinctively Pauline in the world of his day (Ward 1990, 286-87).

■ **5** Paul's directive not to **deprive each other** confirms both the aspect of mutuality as well as that of love. To have said merely that "each belongs to the other" would have reduced marriage to a matter of possession. To describe it as an expression of mutual care points to the deepest dimension of love. Against this background Paul now takes up the question of abstinence, which has been agitating the Corinthians. He is prepared to countenance it but only under certain conditions. First, that it is **by mutual consent**. Second, that it is for a short period of time. Third, that it is motivated by the desire to make time for prayer.

But perhaps most significant are the expressions with which his statement begins and ends. It is prefaced by the conditional phrase **except perhaps** (*ei mēti an*). Abstinence is permitted; it is not enjoined. The verse concludes with what is enjoined: **Then come together again so that Satan will not tempt you because of your lack of self-control.** Paul recognized the reality and the validity of the sexual urge.

■ **6** Despite vigorous arguments that the **concession** Paul speaks of refers to v 7 (Winter 2001, 233-38; Garland 2003, 268-71), it more probably refers to vv 5-7 where he permits abstinence within marriage, but within prescribed limits.

■ **7** Paul's personal preference is that they would all be as he was: unmarried. Exactly what form of "un-marriage" Paul occupied is unclear. It is improbable that he had never married since marriage was viewed in Judaism as the norm, even if there were exceptions. He could have been a widower. It is also possible that his wife may have left him on account of his conversion to Christianity. Whatever the explanation, it certainly was not that he regarded marriage as subspiritual or evil.

In 9:5 Paul will go on to argue that, like the other apostles and Cephas, he had the right to be accompanied by his wife (if he had one) on his missionary travels. The determining factor was the gift (*charisma*) received by the individual. Strikingly, Paul regards both marriage and the single life as gifts from God: a telling thrust at the gift-minded Corinthians. Accordingly, Paul is not expressing the wish that marriage should be abolished, which would be absurd. Rather, he is saying that those who have received the charisma of marriage should live in keeping with that charisma, and not inject the charisma of abstinence where it does not belong. Why Paul would prefer the Corinthians to be unmarried like himself he will explain more fully later (vv 17-35).

b. Advice to Widowers and Widows (7:8-9)

■ **8** It is probable that the term **unmarried** (*agamois*) refers to widowers (see NIV mg.), given that Paul has just addressed the married in vv 1-7 and that he links it to the term **widows** (*chērais*) in this verse. His counsel to both repeats his generalized advice in v 7. What is expressed there as his "wish" is expressed here as what is **good** (*kalon*). Paul thus picks up the term **good**, which the Corinthians used (v 1) regarding abstinence from sex within marriage to describe the single life that he himself followed. He will use it again to describe other options (vv 26, 38). It is difficult to avoid the conclusion that Paul is thereby indicating that the Corinthians' definition of **good** is not the only one available. The **good** that Paul recommends to the widowers and widows is that they remain single like himself. Presumably he recommends this for the same reason as in v 7.

■ **9** Nevertheless, there is another side to the matter. Where widowers and widows are engaging in sexual immorality, it is better for them to marry. The Greek text does not read **if they cannot control themselves** but "if they are not controlling themselves." It is not a generalization about Paul's view of marriage, but a specific application to the Corinthian situation. It is far better (*kreitton*, the comparative form of *kalos*)—that is, a far greater good to marry than to avoid marriage and be ensnared by immorality. In keeping with this, **to burn** means to allow sexual passion to have its way.

c. Directions Regarding Divorce (7:10-11)

Paul now addresses a third category of celibates: those who become such by divorce. Since the one remaining group—"the rest" (v 12)—are those caught up in mixed marriages, it is probable that the divorced referred to in these verses are believing Christians. If this is correct, then it is likewise probable that the motive behind the divorce was the same as that behind the quoted statement in v 1—namely, the desire to be truly spiritual. It would seem that the logic of spirituality was thus being pushed to its final limit: if sex was the cause of immorality, then the Christian answer was no sex at all. This was how you became the best type of Christian: separated from the flesh and wholly spiritual.

■ **10** There is a marked change of tone from what Paul wishes or advises in vv 7-8. Now he speaks in tones of **command** (*parangellō*). The reason is that the Lord has pronounced on this subject. Taken with the disclaimers in vv 12 ("I, not the Lord") and 25 ("I have no command from the Lord"), this seems clearly to mean that regarding divorces between Christians, Paul had knowledge of an actual pronouncement of Jesus. The content of this command was: **A wife must not separate from her husband** (v 10*b*) and "a husband must not divorce his wife" (v 11*b*). This is essentially the same as the saying of Jesus in Mark 10:11-12: "Anyone who divorces his wife and marries another woman commits adultery against her. And if she divorces her husband and marries another man, she commits adultery."

Several points should be noted. First, the use of the term **separate** in 1 Cor 7:10 is not a reference to "legal separation" as this is understood today—that is, as referring to something less than divorce. The Greek term rendered **separate** (*chōristhēnai*) is best taken reflexively: "separate herself." In Greco-Roman society to leave a partner was a standard form of divorce: the terms were interchangeable (see Deasley 2000a, 127 n. 117; Instone-Brewer 2002, 198-201). Second, it is interesting that Paul directs the command to the woman first, the reverse of the order in Mark 10:11-12. We have noted that Paul addresses male and female alternately in an intentional way in 1 Cor 7:2-5. It is possible that the command against divorce in vv 10-11 is addressed to a wife first because women were pressing for divorce—or had already effected it—in Corinth and were doing so for spiritual reasons. (In this context it may be possible to speak of "eschatological women.")

■ 11 A third point of note is that, no sooner has Paul quoted the command of Jesus against divorce than he immediately takes account of the fact that it will be—or perhaps already has been—broken. **If she does, two courses are open to her—she must remain unmarried or else be reconciled to her husband.** It is significant that she is not *commanded* to reverse the divorce. Allowance is made for the fact that reconciliation might not be possible either because the divorced husband refused to resume the marriage or because the divorcing wife did the same on the grounds of her call to a celibate life. What Paul is intent on ensuring is that the call to a celibate life does not become a smokescreen for acquiring a change of husband for less than spiritual reasons. Paul is thus seen to be affirming the Lord's command against divorce, but doing so in a pastoral rather than a literalistic or legalistic way. The divorced were not outlawed or unchurched. The law was honored even where it could not be completely fulfilled (Deasley 2000a, 128-29).

A fourth point is that the command against divorce is also directed to husbands (v 11*b*). The question arises as to whether a husband who found himself divorced by a wife who refused to reverse a divorce and be reconciled was bound by the order to remain unmarried. On the basis of the teaching in vv 2-6, 8-9, and 15 (see below) the answer would appear to be no. Paul thus appears to be recognizing the validity of the law as well as the fact that there were cases in which it could not be fully implemented without subverting its own intent—namely, to protect and safeguard meaningful marriage. It is—to borrow Dunn's phrase—an example of "living between two worlds" (Dunn 1998, 692).

d. Instruction to Those Married to Non-Christians (7:12-16)

The question of true spirituality surfaced most acutely here. If sex within Christian marriage was being questioned, what was to be said of sex where one partner was an unbeliever? This is an important clue to the mindset of the Corinthians. It suggests that their basic concern was the extent to which contact with the world could compromise their spirituality (→ 5:9-10). This reached its apex in mixed marriages. We cannot know, though we can guess, the pressures of living with an unbelieving spouse in Corinth. If believers could be endangered by eating food offered to idols (8:7-8), then what of a pagan marriage partner to whom idols were part of his or her mental furniture and daily practice?

■ 12-13 Paul now turns his attention **to the rest**. Since he has thus far been addressing those who either were or had been married, presumably he now turns to another group within that category. In contrast with his statement in v 10, he indicates that the teaching he is about to give is his own (**I, not the Lord**) and does not rest on any word of Jesus. This does not mean it lacks authority: Paul writes as an apostle (→ 7:40; 14:37; 15:50, 51; 2 Cor 13:10). This is to be distinguished from contexts where he is explicitly expressing his personal wish or preference (→ 1 Cor 7:7). Paul deals respectively with a believing husband with an unbelieving wife, and a believing wife with an unbelieving husband. Since he taught that believers must marry only believers (→ 7:39), the mixed situation must have arisen through the conversion of one of the partners after they married. Paul's language in addressing both believing spouses is identical and his directive is the same: if the unbelieving spouse is willing to continue the marriage (lit. *is well pleased to make home with him or her*), the believing partner must not resort to divorce. The initiative in either continuing or terminating the marriage thus rests with the unbelieving spouse.

■ 14 Paul now addresses the Corinthians' underlying fear of being married to an unbeliever: that it would pollute their spiritual purity. Since his argument concludes with a reference to the holiness of the children of such marriages, it appears that the focus of the Corinthians' concern lay in the realm of sexual relations. Paul's reply is that, far from the unbelieving partner polluting the believer the "infection" works the other way round. The unbelieving partner is **sanctified through** the believing partner. In what sense is the unbelieving partner sanctified? Clearly not in the sense of being saved (→ v 16). Evidently, in the same sense as the children of such marriages who are said to be **now holy**. Whereas if the Corinthians' argument were sound, they would be **unclean**.

Paul has written earlier of the believers as God's holy temple both collectively (3:16-17) and individually (6:19). He now draws upon another aspect of that image. Everything used in the temple became holy by virtue of its association with the temple (Exod 29:37; Lev 6:18). Paul transfers this idea to the unbeliever married to a believer as well as to their children. These now stand within the sphere of holy influence by virtue of relationship to the believer. (The Greek preposition *en* may denote both sphere and agency, hence the NIV's **through**.) There were therefore no grounds for the believing partner to dissolve such a marriage for fear that it would defile the temple of God. The truth was rather the reverse. The power of the gospel was such that it could neutralize the power of the pagan influences on the lives of unbelieving partners and children. That this, and no more than this and no less, is Paul's meaning is shown by his statement in 1 Cor 7:16 that such relationships might well lead to the salvation of the unbelieving spouse.

The Holiness of Unbelievers and Children

It is stated that the unbelieving partner is sanctified through the believing partner, and the children of such marriages are holy. Paul is evidently drawing on OT temple ideology. Their persons became "holy" by virtue of contact with the temple (Exod 29:37; 30:27; Lev 6:18, 27; see Hartley 1992, lvii-lxiii; Wenham 1979, 18-25). The holiness in mind in 1 Cor 7:14 denotes living in a sphere where holy influence is at work. (For an extended treatment see Ciampa and Rosner 2010, 296-302.)

■ **15** This resumes the main issue of vv 12-13—namely, divorce. While divorce is not an option for the believing partner, the unbelieving partner may choose it and leave. The use of the term **leaves** in parallel with **divorce** in vv 12-13 shows clearly that divorce is what is meant. The believer's response to such a divorce must be to accept it. **Let it be so.** What is meant by this is further explained by the statement that **the brother or the sister is not bound in such circumstances.** This has been understood in several ways. At the very least it means that the believer is not bound to try to hold together a marriage that the unbelieving partner wishes to dissolve (Barrett 1968, 166). This would be confirmed by the following statement that **God has called us to live in peace.** (In the Greek text **in peace** stands in the emphatic position as first word in the clause.) There is no sense in making futile exertions to maintain a marriage that one party has ended.

However, it is possible that "not being bound" means much more than this: specifically, the freedom to remarry. Several considerations favor this interpretation. First, in the earlier context where divorce is contemplated and permitted between Christians (vv 10-11), specific limits are placed on the options of the divorcing wife: celibacy or reconciliation. It would be odd if nothing were said about remarriage in case of divorce by a pagan partner. Second, the term **bound** (*douloō*) is a much stronger term, denoting enslavement, than that normally used by Paul (*deō*, "bind" as in 7:39) to denote the marriage bond. This suggests that Paul is stating emphatically that the believer is wholly freed from the previous relationship. It is possible that Paul is drawing upon his Jewish heritage where the language of bondage and freedom was used to denote divorce. The Mishnah reads:

> The essential formula in the bill of divorce is: "Lo, thou art free to marry any man." R. Judah says, "Let this be from me thy writ of divorce and letter of dismissal and deed of liberation, that thou mayest marry whatsoever man thou wilt." The essential formula in a writ of emancipation is, "Lo, thou art a freed woman: lo, thou belongest to thyself." (Danby 1933, 319)

(For fuller discussion and documentation, see Deasley 2000a, 133-34.) On this view being **called . . . to live in peace** means accepting the decision of the unbeliever to depart. **Let it be so.**

■ **16** At the same time the possibility that the unbeliever may be saved is not to be discounted. While v 16 is sometimes taken pessimistically in view of v 15*b*, it is possible that it may be picking up the thought of v 14. The use of the conjunction "for" (*gar* [omitted in the NIV]) implies a link with something earlier. The most probable antecedent is v 15*c*, which in turn refers to both the continuance of marriages with unbelievers (vv 12-14) as well as the breaking of them (vv 15*ab*). In that case the emphasis in v 16 will fall upon the former. That is, it is perfectly possible that marriage to a pagan may lead to his or her salvation. This possibility is not to be dismissed unless the unbelieving partner brings the marriage to an end (v 15*a*).

Paul's Teaching on Marriage and Divorce

The baseline of Paul's view of marriage and divorce is stated clearly in vv 10 and 11*b*—namely, that marriage is permanent and lifelong. He held this view because it was the view taught by Jesus (v 10*a*). In substance it reproduces the content of Mark 10:11-12. The Marcan context shows that Jesus went behind the Mosaic permission of divorce (Mark 10:2-4; Deut 24:1-4) to the divine design for marriage at creation (Mark 10:5-9). At the same time Matthew's account of Jesus' teaching injects exceptions to this absolute position (Matt 5:32; 19:9). These seem to be directed to Jewish converts to Christianity who had been divorced and remarried before their conversion. (See Deasley 2000a, 116-21.)

Paul follows this same principle in applying Jesus' teaching in a pagan setting where it could not be enforced or applied in a literal or legalistic way. In a case where an unbeliever ended a marriage to a believer, the believer was left "in a state of what amounted to widowhood" (Bruce 1976, 70). In such cases there was no alternative but to accept divorce, and remarriage was an acceptable option. In Thiselton's words: "We see Paul the pastor setting forth a dialectic between principles and circumstances" (2000b, 537).

FROM THE TEXT

This passage is directed to a situation and mindset in some ways dissimilar from, and in others similar to, those of today.

1. A high and deep view of marriage is presupposed everywhere. Marriage is a gift (*charisma*) from God (1 Cor 7:7b) and is to be regarded as permanent and lifelong on the authority of Christ (vv 10-11).

2. A central element in marriage is the mutual enjoyment of the sexual relationship, in which each partner accepts the claims of the other to sexual intercourse (vv 3-4). This was revolutionary in Paul's world. Sex is not surrendering to a lower aspect of human nature (vv 1b-3). There is no approval of asceticism for its own sake (v 5).

3. While Paul's preference was for the single life (v 7a), he recognized that it was not for everyone. For those who had not received the gift of self-control (vv 7-8), marriage was the course to be followed (v 8b). To live against the grain of one's gifts was simply to invite disaster (v 9).

4. Marriages between believers and unbelievers are not to be dissolved on grounds of spiritual incompatibility. On the contrary, such is the power of the holy influence of the believer, that both the children and the unbelieving partner fall within the sphere of its sanctifying power and may well be brought by it to salvation (vv 13-14, 16).

5. While Paul clearly affirms the permanence of marriage as God's intent, he does not apply the law rigidly. So if believers find themselves divorced by a pagan spouse, they can only accept the divorce and are free to remarry.

2. The Underlying Principle: Remain as You Are (7:17-24)

BEHIND THE TEXT

First Corinthians 7:1-16 is held together by a principle that, though never stated in so many words, is the core of the whole argument. This principle is that they remain in the marital state that they occupied when they were called by Christ (vv 12, 13). In vv 1-16 Paul applies this principle to the specific cases that had arisen in Corinth, in some instances making allowance for exceptions (vv 5, 9, 11, 15). Now, however, he turns from the specific cases to the principle underlying them, which is his main concern. This he expresses three times (vv 17, 20, 24), in the latter two using the key word "remain" (*menetō*). He illustrates the principle by two analogies: circumcision and slavery. Circumcision was well known throughout the Greco-Roman world as the distinguishing mark of the Jew. Slavery was the social status of 50 million of the 250 million populating the Roman Empire.

The import of Paul's argument is that social status has no relevance to one's relationship with God. This, indeed, was the heart of his gospel (Gal 3:26-29; 1 Cor 7:17b). This shows that Paul's concern in 7:1-16 has been largely (though not entirely) with sexual status as a means of commending oneself to God. His argument in vv 17-24 now makes clear that this is not so. The Jew was neither helped nor hindered by his circumcision in becoming a Christian. The slave was neither aided nor obstructed by his slave status in becoming a believer. In terms of salvation, these states were irrelevant. They might remain facts of life, but spiritually they were powerless. They were no longer the controlling factors of their existence.

This comes to particular expression in the idea of "calling," which occurs in various forms in these verses no fewer than eight times. The term, in itself, in its various forms, denotes both the call to salvation as well as the situation (or calling) in which the call came (see Fee 2014, 339-42). Paul's repeated point is that the call to Christ makes irrelevant the situation in which the call was received (vv 18, 20). But equally, if the situation is changed, the call to Christ remains unaffected (v 21b). *The important point is that a change of situation (or calling) is not to be sought as if it were religiously significant.*

In many respects, these verses throw light on the angle from which the Corinthians were raising questions about the place of marriage in the spiritual life, as well as the angle of Paul's response. This is not, however, to overlook the moral implications of the Corinthians' behavior and questions or of Paul's reply.

IN THE TEXT

■ **17** Paul now proceeds to elaborate the principle underlying vv 1-16; namely, remain as you are. **Nevertheless** is misleading as suggesting that he is about to develop a contrasting view. Paul is rather simplifying by gathering together the various cases in vv 1-16 under the unifying principle that they embody. Verse 17a might be translated: **Only as the Lord has assigned to each, (and) each as the Lord has called, so let them walk**. Two aspects are distinguished. The first is the **situation the Lord has assigned to them**. The reference here is to their social status. The second is to their calling to faith in Christ. Both together are part of the Lord's calling, and they are not to seek a change in social status in the belief that this would bring spiritual bonuses. Paul concludes by stating, **This is the rule I lay down in all the churches**. Once more he brings everything to the touchstone of his proclamation.

■ **18** Circumcision was a social marker in the Greco-Roman world. The evidence suggests that it was not only the occasion of ridicule but also a barrier to promotion in the professions (Winter 1994, 147-52). It was possible to have it surgically reversed (epispasm). Paul rules against this. Still more piquant is his ruling that those uncircumcised at the time of their calling should not be circumcised. This had been the occasion of the Jerusalem Council (Acts 15:1-35) and an early source of conflict in the church (Gal 2:6-10; 6:12-15).

■ **19-20** Quite stunning is his flat statement of the reason for his rejection of circumcision and epispasm: that circumcision and uncircumcision are **nothing** (v 19). Even more startling is the positive claim that **keeping God's commands is what counts**, with its implication that circumcision is not a divine command. This stands in flat opposition to Gen 17:10-14 where circumcision is given to Abraham as the sign of God's covenant with him and his descendants for all time, on pain of death. It was on this basis that some Jewish Christian leaders affirmed that without circumcision salvation was impossible (Acts 15:1). The same view had found its way into the churches of Galatia. Paul responds in essentially the same terms (Gal 5:2a, 6).

Interestingly, Paul draws a sharp contrast between circumcision and the cross (Gal 6:12, 14): the controlling theme of 1 Cor 1:18—4:21 and, in many respects, of the entire letter. However, he goes further. In 1 Cor 7:19b he places in opposition to circumcision **keeping God's commands**. In Gal 5:6b he does the same: "The only thing that counts is faith expressing itself through love." In Gal 6:15b he repeats the thought in different, highly significant terms: "what counts is the new creation." The implication of all of this is that a new era has dawned in the history of salvation. This does not mean (as some Corinthians apparently thought) that they were to live the life of angels, treating sex as nonexistent. That road would lead only to immorality. But it did mean that the life of a new era had dawned, marked by the power to live a life pleasing to God, which is what **keeping God's commands** appears to mean (this is the only example of the phrase in Paul's writings). Being circumcised or uncircumcised would do nothing to improve this.

■ **21** Paul turns now to his second illustration of his guiding principle—namely, slavery. Again, his principle leads him to exhort the slave to be untroubled by his situation. But immediately he inserts a qualification. This has been understood in opposite ways, largely because of the absence of an object of the verb in the original. The Greek text may be rendered literally: "but if indeed you are able to become free, rather make use of ____." The NRSV translates: "Even if you can gain your freedom, make use of your present condition." That is, remain as you are—namely, a slave—and use that condition as your appointed place to serve the Lord. "For" (*gar* [v 22]) is taken to reinforce that line of argument. It is much more probable, however, that Paul's meaning is the opposite of this. First, the natural object of the phrase "rather make use of" is the subject referred to in the first part of the sentence—namely, becoming free. Again, the emphatic conjunction **but** (*alla*; NIV: **although**) leads one to expect a marked contrast with what has just been said. Once more, the use of the aorist tense "make use of" (*chrēsai*) suggests a single action. For an ongoing condition, the continuous present would be more appropriate. (For a clear and comprehensive treatment of this difficult phrase, see Garland 2003, 308-14.)

■ **22** Following the interjection Paul returns to the main point he is making: that slavery and freedom as social conditions make no difference to the believer's relationship to Christ. There is a remarkable double application both to those called to faith when slaves and those called when free. The slave becomes **the Lord's freed person**. This translation is an attempt to avoid gender prejudice by referring to the Roman slave category of freedman (*apeleutheros*), which denoted a slave emancipated ("manumitted" is the technical term) by his master. While socially and politically free, he could and usually did owe certain obligations to his erstwhile master, who now became his patron. On the other side the person called while free (*apeleutheros*) becomes Christ's slave (*doulos*). Paul thus leads his readers to the paradoxical conclusion that the slavery and freedom in which slaves and free lived when called to faith in Christ are exchanged for a bond to a new master "whose service is perfect freedom."

The divide between the socially enslaved and the socially free is thus transmitted into a service of a new order where both stand on level ground, owning allegiance to the same Lord. In this way Paul accomplishes three things. First, he baptizes into Christ the demeaning category of slavery in much the same way that he has earlier done with the category of crucifixion. He will use it regularly to describe himself (Rom 1:1; Gal 1:10; Eph 6:6; Phil 1:1) and his fellow workers (Col 4:12). In particular it denotes the redemptive salvation brought by Christ to those whom he has rescued. Just as the slave-born is redeemed from slavery by the freedom given by his or her master, so all who own Christ as master—whether born slaves or free—are emancipated by him into a new relationship with him as Lord. (It is misguided to see the reversals of status in the verses as the establishment of a new hierarchy of Christian slavery. Paul's point is the straightforward one that those hitherto separated by social status are now united in common service to the Lord Christ.)

Second, following from this there is an analogy between slavery and salvation in that both come to fulfillment in an emancipation that paradoxically culminates in service. There is no liberty that does not involve acceptance of lordship. This was true of emancipated slaves who, notwithstanding, still owed obligations to their erstwhile masters. And it is true of Christian believers who, liberated from the power of sin, are now bondslaves of Christ (Rom 6:17-18). The meaning of slavery is thus changed from subjugation to willing submission. (In this sense D. B. Martin is correct in affirming that "Slavery is Salvation" [1990, ch 1].)

Third, the example of slavery enables Paul to reinforce the point he has been making throughout the chapter: "Remain as you are—unless"; unless, that is, there are circumstances in which change is possible and consistent with Christian teaching. Paul clearly regards emancipation from slavery as falling within that description.

■ **23** Since both categories addressed in v 22 now share the status of servants of Christ liberated by him from bondage to sin, Paul is able to address both in the same terms: **you were bought at a price.** He has already used this expression in reference to believers being possessed by the Holy Spirit (6:19-20). He uses it now in regard to their ownership by God. The purchase of slaves in the market could be a costly business. That was so with them. Redemption may be free, but it is not cheap. God paid top price to purchase them from their previous owner. Hence, they are not to become **slaves of human beings.** While this paragraph begins by referring to literal slavery, it broadens as it progresses. The meaning here probably covers the entire sweep of the term from literal slavery to becoming a slave to popular opinions and habits (5:6-8; 6:9-11, 18-20; 2 Cor 11:20; Gal 5:1).

■ **24** Paul repeats the substance of 1 Cor 7:17, with which this verse constitutes an inclusion. This serves to remind us that Paul's primary concern is with marriage. Verses 17-24 reflect primarily on vv 1-16 and are an illustration and reinforcement of what he says there. Verse 24 restates the principle laid down in v 17, that each person should remain in the situation they were in when God called them.

Slavery in the Roman World and Paul's Attitude to It

Slavery had a long history before NT times. Race and inferiority were no part of it. People became slaves as prisoners of war, both male and female. By the first century AD, the children of women in slavery were the prime source of slaves. An important factor in the creation of a slave system in the Greco-Roman world was the absence of a work ethic in which each man earned his own living. One took orders only from military or state figures. Households survived through the labor of slaves. Slavery was thus a crucial mechanism in the structure of society. Its removal would have required a complete recasting of the shape of society.

In the Greco-Roman world, slavery was both simple and complex. It was simple in that slaves had no legal rights and existed simply as tools for their master's use. It was complex in that slaves could own property (including slaves) and save money, enabling them to buy their freedom. Some were better educated than their owners, who depended on them to manage the business of the household. This meant they could be treated well: so much so that some people sold themselves into slavery to provide themselves with money to pay their debts, and also to guarantee for themselves a secure living. Manumission (emancipation) within ten or twenty years was common. Slavery could thus be a means of upward mobility.

At the same time slavery had its dark side. Flogging was perfectly admissible, and sexual availability was assumed. The treatment of a slave depended largely on the character of the master. The fundamental offensiveness of slavery was its denial of human dignity. Slaves were not free to make their own choices and decisions.

This was evidently the view underlying Paul's advice in 1 Cor 7:21—that if slaves could gain their freedom, they should not miss the opportunity. He affirms this even while going on to use slavery metaphorically of the believer's service of Christ (vv 22-23). The Epistle to Philemon presses this point to the last degree. How is it possible for a Christian slave-owner to treat his slave who is a Christian brother in a way that denies his personhood? (See I. Howard Marshall 1993, 185-91. For overviews of the historical and biblical material on slavery, see Bartchy in *ABD* 6:65-73; and Webb in *DThIB*, 751-53.)

FROM THE TEXT

1. Social status is ultimately of no consequence before God. Because our lives are determined by God's call, not by our situation, we are to live as before God (v 24). The concepts of "call" and "service" differ radically from secular notions of self-direction or self-fulfillment.

2. This does not preclude the possibility or desirability of changing one's social situation for the better if the opportunity presents itself (v 21*b*). But this leaves our relationship with Christ unaffected: we are still "bought at a price" and are not to become slaves to any notions of hierarchical superiority (v 23*b*).

3. Slavery is baptized into Christ, becoming an image of salvation (v 22). (See D. B. Martin 1990, 64-65.) This was, and is, as countercultural a move as the use of crucifixion as a figure of the life of salvation (1 Cor 1:22-24; Gal 2:20). It is—in the words of the Book of Common Prayer—"when we are His willing bondsmen, then only are we truly free."

3. The Question of Those Engaged but Not Yet Married (7:25-38)

BEHIND THE TEXT

Commentators are agreed that this is one of the most complex passages to interpret in Paul's writings. This is indicated by the number of varying interpretations that have been put forward (Fee lists three: 2014, 359-62; Thiselton lists six: 2000b, 569-71). At least three have attracted a significant measure of support in the history of interpretation. (1) What may be regarded as the standard view until recent times sees the reference as being to fathers responsible for giving their daughters in marriage. However, 7:25-35 refers to those who *marry* rather than *give in marriage*, and there is no mention of fathers or daughters anywhere. (2) Some have taken the passage to speak of "spiritual marriages"—that is, marriages that intentionally foreswore sexual intercourse. But Paul has already ruled against such a practice in vv 1-5. (3) Most scholars at present adhere to some form of the view that what is in mind are engaged couples who, under pressure from those of an ascetic bent in the Corinthian church, are wondering whether they should renounce marriage but live in a state of permanent engagement. (For a full exposition and critique of these three views, see Garland 2003, 336-41.)

At the risk of oversimplification, one may say that the difficulty resides in two problems. First, what is meant by the term "virgins" (*parthenoi*), which is used six times in these verses (vv 25, 28, 34, 36, 37, 38 [2x]) and nowhere else in the chapter? The answer has been said to be self-evident (Conzelmann 1975, 131). However, in vv 27-29 the common Greek word for "woman" (*gunē*) appears to be used in the sense of "woman" and "wife" (vv 27, 29), while "virgin" (*parthenos*) is used also in reference to a "woman" (v 28). In v 34 a virgin is distinguished from "an unmarried woman" (*hē gunē hē agamos*). Further, vv 36-38 are concerned with the right conduct of a man toward "his virgin" (*tēn parthenon autou*), implying some recognizable relationship to her. The alternatives open to men in such relationships are marriage or non-marriage. Indeed, the term "getting married" (*gameō*) occurs in various forms eight times in these verses (vv 28 twice—the third instance in the NIV is used for smooth translation; vv 32, 33, 34, 36, 38 [2x]) as against twice in the rest of the chapter (v 9).

These data suggest that Paul's argument has moved on to yet another category of persons beyond those addressed in vv 1-16—namely, betrothed couples not yet married. However, the underlying mindset addressed appears to be the same as in the earlier verses, if anything, in a more extreme form. There the mentality addressed was proscribing sexual relations within the marriage. Here it is recommending avoidance of marriage altogether: even among those already engaged (v 28). As before Paul goes as far as he can to meet their mindset, to the point of agreeing with their position. Yet he differs from them in two significant respects: (1) he affirms that exceptions are to be admitted; (2) the reasons for which he agrees with them differ greatly from theirs. He argues not that sex is unspiritual, but that the current situation makes marriage and family life a heavy burden; and moreover, that it constitutes an impediment in the service of the Lord.

Second, why does Paul deal with the problem of those not yet married at this point? It is unlikely that news of it had only just reached him. It is an entirely natural growth from the issues addressed earlier, particularly in vv 1-5. The undertone of his counsel earlier—"Remain as you are unless"—is present here also (vv 26, 29-31). What is present in these verses in greater measure is a positive exposition of the reasoning behind his advice: the present crisis and the shortening of time. His earlier concern was the avoidance of immorality among the Corinthians. But while not overlooking that (vv 36-37), he also has positive grounds for urging them not to marry—their greater freedom to engage in the service of the Lord (v 35).

IN THE TEXT

a. The Options Open to Betrothed Persons and Paul's Recommendation (7:25-28)

■ **25** The phrase **Now about** (*peri de*) indicates, as elsewhere, a change in topic. It does not necessarily indicate a new topic raised by the Corinthians (as in 7:1; but → v 26), but it is evidently one stirring agitation among them. Paul clearly considered that it called for intervention by him. Against suggestions that "virgins" could refer to males as well as females, or that the problem addressed was that of "spiritual marriages" in which sex was avoided, it does most justice to the language of the section as a whole to see the problem as involving those betrothed but not yet married (→ Behind the Text). Five of the six examples of the word "virgin" in vv 25-38 are explicitly feminine.

Paul prefaces his statement with the acknowledgment that he had no command of Jesus on this subject (contrary to his statement in v 10 regarding divorce). However, he was giving his **judgment as one who by the Lord's mercy is trustworthy** (v 25). Paul uses similar (if not identical) language to describe his calling in general (1 Tim 1:13-14) and his apostolic vocation in particular (Gal 1:15-16; 1 Cor 15:9-10). Hence, while he does not assert his apostolic authority in this passage, neither does he expect his view to be treated as one among others. The stupendous measure of the grace shown to one with a record like his marks him out as one to be listened to.

■ **26** Paul's advice is addressed first to engaged men. It is the advice given throughout the chapter regarding other marital states. They should remain as they are. He describes this action as **good** (*kalon*). The NIV smooths the original, which in fact repeats itself: *I think this to be good because of the present distress, that it is good for a man to remain as he is*. The expression "it is good" has already appeared in 1 Cor 7:1, where it is a quotation from the Corinthians' letter to Paul. It is possible that they went on to apply it to betrothed persons.

Paul now quotes it back to them with the addition of what he regards as a sound reason: **Because of the present crisis**. Clearly, the Corinthians knew the nature of this crisis. The word *anangkē* commonly denotes "necessity" in the sense of "stringency" (as in v 37) but can also convey the sense of "distress" or "tribulation" (2 Cor 12:10). Sometimes it is used in harness with the word "trouble" (*thlipsis* [1 Thess 3:7; 2 Cor 6:4]) to denote Paul's afflictions as an apostle and preacher. Paul will develop (and clarify) his meaning in 1 Cor 7:28-31.

■ **27** The verse should be interpreted within the framework of Paul's developing argument. This means that it is addressed to betrothed couples. Hence "bound to a woman" means **pledged** by troth. Release from this commitment is not to be sought. Conversely, those who have made no such commitment should not enter into one—that is, **look for a wife**. The language of binding and loosing is unusual and may reflect the seriousness with which betrothal was then regarded.

■ **28** Verse 27 expresses the "remain as you are" principle. However, Paul proceeds to allow an exception. Applied literally to betrothed couples, remaining as they were would mean living in a state of permanent betrothal. This would be tantamount to sexless marriage, while not seeking a wife would amount to a sentence of celibacy. Paul has already made clear his recognition of the realities of human sexuality, and does so again here. The form in which he expresses it may well be dictated by the language and ideology of some of the Corinthians that sex was sinful. Paul rebuts that specifically in regard to both male and female. However, he adds the rider that those who marry will endure trouble (*thlipsin*) in this life, which he would rather see them spared.

A new term is thus added to "crisis" or "distress" (*anangkē*) as Paul builds up his picture of the hardships facing the Corinthians. What these were he does not spell out. They appear to involve the responsibilities incumbent on caring and providing for a family—that is, obligations belonging to the married state. There is evidence that Corinth was affected by acute famine several times in the early 50s (Winter 1989, 86-106). However, more than simply material want appears to be in Paul's mind. Famine was a stock feature in predictions of the end-times (Matt 24:7-8; Luke 21:11). The fact that Paul goes on to speak in explicitly eschatological terms suggests that he had a larger problem in mind.

b. The Pressures of the Present Eschatological Situation (7:29-31)

The argument makes a distinct advance at this point. The references to "the present crisis" (v 26) and the **many troubles in this life** (v 28) are placed against a broader eschatological backdrop. This explains why he has given the advice he has in vv 25-28.

■ **29a** The beginning words are emphatic, as indicated by the demonstrative *this* (rendered **What** in the NIV) placed as the first word, and the direct form of address: **What I mean, brothers and sisters**. The thrust of what Paul means is indicated by the momentous expressions with which this stage of his argument begins and ends: **the time is short**; and "this world in its present form is passing away" (v 31). The former is better rendered in some such way as "the time of opportunity has been shortened," the reference being to the era of salvation introduced by the death and resurrection of Christ. Time is therefore no longer simply clock time, but salvation time for the fulfilling of the redemptive purposes of God. The implication of this for the present order of things is not merely that it *will* pass away but that it *is* passing away. Christian life is therefore not to be lived simply for an eschatological future, but in an eschatological present.

■ **29b-31a** Paul now proceeds to apply this to the Corinthians in a series of five illustrations constructed around the pivotal phrase "as not" (*hōs mē*).
1. **Those who have wives should live as if they do not** (v 29b).
2. **Those who** weep and **mourn** (should live) **as if they** do **not** (v 30a).
3. **Those who are happy** (should live) **as if they** are **not** (v 30b).
4. **Those who buy** (should live) as if they owned nothing (v 30c).
5. **Those who use** worldly possessions (should live) as those who have no use for them (v 31a).

The sayings are clearly paradoxical, affirming a dimension of reality, while denying that it constitutes the whole of reality. The Christian therefore lives at a point of tension between two eras, both of which are real, but only one of which will last. To take his first illustration: the last thing Paul is saying is that marriage is unreal and that husbands should treat their wives as though they did not exist. This is precisely what he has argued against in vv 1-5. What he is saying is that marriage, and the other items he has listed, stand within the temporal sphere, which will one day be superseded.

■ **31b** The basis on which he rests his case is that **this world in its present form is passing away**. With the coming of Christ and his death and resurrection not only has a decisive judgment been passed upon the present world order, but a decisive terminus has been set for it. That terminus is the second coming of Christ. It is in this sense that the time has been shortened. The temporal world order will not go on forever. Life will be played out on another stage where eternal values prevail. The Corinthians should not live as though the temporal, transient order is the only one that counts. In Calvin's words: "we ought to be living as if we might have to leave this world at any moment" (1960, 160). Paul thus broadens his focus—and that of the Corinthians—in these verses beyond their preoccupation with the rights and wrongs of living married life or even of being married at all. There is a larger frame of reference within which not merely marriage but the whole of life is to be viewed. This must not be lost sight of.

c. The Claims of the Service of the Lord (7:32-35)

Paul now broadens the frame of reference still further by invoking another matter affected by marriage—the claims of the service of the Lord. At the same time it is important not to sunder this matter from vv 29-31 with its eschatological setting, and read vv 32-35 as though they represented Paul's comprehensive view of marriage. There appears to be a reference back to "the present crisis" (v 26) and the troubles it entails for the married. There is also a link with the idea of his concern to see them spared trouble (vv 28, 32), though the vocabulary is different. The verb stem translated "concern" (*merimna*) occurs six times. Paul uses it in a variety of senses. He addresses the effects of marriage on the Christian service of men first (vv 32*b*-34*a*), then on women (vv 34*b*-35).

■ **32-34a** Following on his five paradoxical illustrations in vv 29*b*-31*a* in which he has expressed the tensions of living with a foot in two different eras—living "as if not" as he calls it—he now states his overriding desire for them that they **be free from concern** (v 32*a*). Remarkably, he then proceeds to present them with two options, both of which he describes as forms of concern! In v 32*a* **concern** clearly denotes anxiety. But he changes immediately to a positive meaning: concern for the things of the Lord. If there is a kind of concern which is destructive, there is also a kind of concern which is productive. In this context it is described as how one can **please the Lord** (v 32*b*). Paul uses this expression elsewhere as a summary of what the aim and object of the Christian life is (1 Thess 4:1; Rom 8:8), including his own (2 Cor 5:9; 1 Thess 2:4). In this context he speaks of it as being the particular faculty of the **unmarried man**. In contrast, the man who has married (*ho de gamēsas*) **is concerned about the affairs of this world** (1 Cor 7:33)—a world that Paul has just described as "passing away" (v 31)—at least in its present form. The thrust of the contrast is expressed even more sharply in the phrase **how he can please his wife** (v 33). Consequently, his focus and **interests are divided** (v 34*a*).

The language and the contrast expressed between pleasing the Lord and pleasing one's wife, resulting in a division of energies and loyalties, is very strong. This would be consistent with the intensity of "the present crisis." It has been argued that Paul is reflecting Stoic language and teaching in his references to **concern** (Balch 1983, 429-36). It is true that there are some striking similarities (e.g., Epictetus, the late first-century Cynic, saying CXVI in Crossley 1968, 159-60). At the same time, the language of anxiety and concern (using the same root *merimna*) is found elsewhere in the NT where the question of Stoic influence does not arise (see Matt 6:27, 28, 31, 34; Phil 2:20; 4:6).

■ **34b-d** Attention now turns to the female gender. The text of v 32b is found in no fewer than eight forms in the Greek manuscripts. Metzger favors the reading that translates literally as "the unmarried woman and the virgin" (*TCGNT*, 490). However, there is also debate as to whether this reading refers to two persons: an unmarried woman and a betrothed virgin; or one: an unmarried woman—namely, a betrothed virgin. (For a full discussion of the textual and exegetical problems, see Guenther, *BBR*, 12.1 [2002], 33-45. For a brief treatment reaching a different conclusion, see Thiselton 2000b, 590.) The NIV can be understood either way.

Paul seems to be attempting to make a statement about females parallel to that which he has just made about males. However, his task is complicated by the theme to which this whole section is directed—betrothed virgins (v 25). Hence, when addressing the female side, he is compelled to include them specifically in his discussion. The compound expression "the unmarried woman and the betrothed virgin" does this very thing. As constituting a collective group, the same features can be attributed to both without distinction. Both being free from the responsibilities of marriage, can attend uninterruptedly to **the concerns of the Lord**. But whereas, regarding unmarried men, this was spelled out in terms of **pleasing the Lord**, here it is elaborated in terms of being **holy in both body and spirit**. Since Paul returns to the language of **pleasing** in the second half of the verse, he seems to have a particular reason for departing from it when speaking of betrothed virgins. His fear of sexual abstinence as leading to immorality expressed earlier in the chapter (e.g., vv 1-11) may well lie behind his choice of words here. Indeed, it is not impossible that being **holy in both body and spirit** may have been something of a slogan among ascetic women in Corinth. Paul is reminding them that he takes them at their word: they must mean what they say. (See Macdonald 1990.) In contrast to the betrothed virgin who has not yet assumed the responsibilities of married life, the married woman must give due place to the cares of the world: specifically, pleasing her husband. The pressures of the present crisis must not be forgotten in this context. The eschatological setting depicted in vv 29-31 has not been dismissed.

■ **35** Paul brings the argument of vv 25-34 to a conclusion by stating why he has said what he has. In particular, the use of the introductory formula **but this** (*touto de*) (NIV: **I am saying this**) in vv 29 and 35 serves to bind these verses together. He begins with a positive declaration: he has said what he has for their good. This is elaborated with a negative explanation: not to tie a noose (*brochon*) around their necks. This picks up the recurrent motif of these verses (and indeed of the whole chapter) that, while he thinks it best that they remain as they are, yet if they choose to do otherwise he does not forbid it (vv 21, 27-28). What he is concerned to ensure he expresses in three significant terms in the second half of the verse: "fitting" or "appropriate" (*euschēmon*), "constant" or "unfailing" (*euparedron*), and "undistracted" (*aperispastōs*).

All three qualify the words **to the Lord**: that is to say, they characterize the temper of the service that is pleasing to the Lord. F. F. Bruce does justice to them in rendering: "I do want you to live in a way that is seemly and devoted to the Lord, without distracting cares" (1965, 89).

d. Further Advice to the Engaged (7:36-38)

The difficulty of interpreting these verses is noted regularly by commentators (Fee 2014, 385-86; Thiselton 2000b, 593; Fitzmyer 2008, 322). It is illustrated dramatically by the NIV, which provides two totally different translations: one in the text, the other in the margin. The problems are basically two. The first is the meaning of the term "virgin": whether it refers to a virgin engaged to be married (as in the NIV text); or whether it refers to a virgin wife in a "spiritual" marriage; or whether it refers to a virgin daughter whose father holds the power of deciding whether or not she will marry (as in the NIV mg.). Reasons were given above as to why the first of these options is to be preferred (→ introduction to 7:25-38). This leads to the second problem: on what grounds can it be maintained that vv 36-38 continue the topic discussed in vv 25-28, rather than begin a new topic? From the point of view of content, vv 36-38 may be said to deal with an aspect of the problem implicit in vv 27-28 but not treated there; namely, what account is to be taken of the role of sexual attraction between engaged couples? Since the place of sex has been a recurrent theme in earlier parts of the chapter, it would be surprising if nothing were said of it regarding a relationship where it could be explosive. From the point of view of literary linkage there are clear indications that vv 36-38 belong with vv 25-35. The adversative particle "but" (*de* [omitted in the NIV]) has the effect of setting aside Paul's eschatological and practical reflections in vv 29-35, and resuming the advice to the betrothed in vv 27-28. "Anyone" (*tis*) is most naturally taken as masculine, given the rest of the clause. The play on words between "seemly" (*euschēmon* [v 35 NEB]) and "in a proper way" (*aschēmonein*) suggests a bond between the two sections, rather than an advance into a new theme.

■ **36** The thought appears to pick up from vv 26-28 where Paul's advice that engaged men remain in that state is followed by the contrasting declaration that marriage would be no sin. Paul now explores this tension from both sides. Remarkably for an age in which the male was the active party in making the decision to marry, the first consideration here is whether he is behaving considerately toward the woman betrothed to him. The matter in question is that of sexual arousal. The group of expressions used in the verse is best understood in this way. Not to act **honorably toward the virgin he is engaged to** means at the very least to arouse expectations of marriage only to dash them, all the while remaining engaged. The term meaning "to act in an unseemly or inappropriate way" (*aschēmonein*) frequently has sexual connotations (Winter 1998, 78-83). In this case it is unlikely to denote sexual relations. This would hardly be something an ascetic would conclude was improper only after mature consideration.

Attention now turns directly to the man. While the term translated **if his passions are too strong** (*hyperakmos*) could be feminine (in which case it would refer to the woman's having reached marriageable age), it is most probably masculine in keeping with the remainder of the verse. Again then, the reference is to the aroused sexual appetites of the man. In such conditions only one outcome is possible: **he should do as he wants. He is not sinning. They should get married.** Paul is thus repeating what he had said earlier: that marriage is a divine charism (v 7*b*) and as such is no sin (v 28).

■ **37** The above understanding of v 36 is confirmed by v 37 where Paul spells out the conditions for which a man may decide against marrying his betrothed. These are two, though the second is enclosed within a double statement of the first. First, he must stand fully convinced in his heart (v 37*a*), having reached this conviction in his inmost being (v 37*c*). Second, he must be free of any constraint or compulsion (*anangkē*): the reverse of being driven by sexual passion (a sense that is well attested: Winter 1998, 85-86). This is elaborated in the strong words that follow: he **has control over his own will.** Such a man may remain in a state of permanent betrothal. In doing so, *he is doing the right thing*.

■ **38** The conclusion Paul draws is that neither marrying one's betrothed nor not marrying her is a bad thing. But the case Paul has been debating throughout the chapter is not between good and bad, but between good and better (vv 1, 8-9). In the circumstances of the prevailing eschatological crisis described in vv 29-35, Paul is convinced that refraining from marriage is better.

4. The Question of Widows and Remarriage (7:39-40)

Why widows reappear in a tailpiece to the chapter is a question that has evoked many explanations. Has he not dealt with their case already in vv 8-9? Lightfoot thinks "it is impossible to say what led St. Paul to add these last two verses" (1895, 234). The suggestion that he addresses widows in order to preserve the balance observed thus far in the chapter of dealing alternately with male and then female issues can hardly in itself be considered conclusive. The answer may well lie in the overall context beginning with v 25 where the controlling theme is the treatment of those who may be described as "candidates" for marriage. The engaged man and the married woman are both bound to a partner and should not break that bond. Where a man has no such bond and a woman is freed by widowhood they are free to seek a partner, though Paul would not recommend it. It is possible that widows reappear in the chapter because the ascetics in the Corinthian church argued that, having been "delivered" from marriage, they should certainly not become enslaved in it again. Paul replies that the Christian view of marriage applies no less to them than to the unmarried. However, he couches his reply in the context of the current situation, not their jaundiced asceticism.

■ **39** Paul begins by stating the basic principle of Christian marriage that it is lifelong in God's purpose and intention (vv 10-11). However, should her husband die **she is free to marry anyone she wishes**. The only caveat Paul adds is that she marry **only in the Lord**. The NIV takes this to mean that **he must belong to the Lord**. It could mean that she marry only with due regard to her membership in the body of Christ (Lightfoot 1895, 235). But given Paul's earlier wrestling with the problems of mixed marriages (vv 12-16), it would be surprising if the broader interpretation did not include the narrower one.

■ **40** Paul now proceeds to give his own judgment. This is that she will be **happier** if she remains a widow. The use of the term **judgment** (*gnōmēn*), repeated from v 25, has the force of an inclusion, binding vv 25-40 as a unity. This confirms the suggestion made above that vv 39-40 are to be read in the light of the entire discussion in vv 25-38. This means that Paul's discouraging of remarriage for widows is not based on a principled opposition to marriage but rather on the hazards it entails in the present crisis. It is therefore Paul's advice, not a command. But as in v 25, this does not mean that Paul's view is to be treated lightly: "that is just Paul's opinion." The words are rather to be read as an expanded comment on his **judgment**: "and I also think I have the Spirit of God" (Robertson and Plummer 1914, 161). That is, they are a rejoinder to those who apparently thought they had the Spirit and Paul did not. (The NIV rendering, **I think that I too have the Spirit of God**, implies that Paul had the Spirit just as much as the Corinthian ascetics. It is doubtful that this was Paul's meaning—unless it was a sarcasm.)

FROM THE TEXT

1. The third main division of the chapter (7:25-40) must always be read in the light of the first two divisions (vv 1-16, 17-24). It is clear from these that Paul's fundamental view of sex and marriage is positive. Paul regards marriage as a divine gift or charism (v 7b) and the place of sex as being normal and nec-

essary (vv 4-5). Hence, it is natural and normal that spouses show concern and care for each other even if this takes time and energy that might otherwise be directed to the service of the Lord (vv 33-34).

2. Paul undoubtedly relativizes marriage (vv 32, 34). But he does so, not because of prudery or asceticism. It is because he is responding to "the present crisis" (v 26). The fact that he relativizes other aspects of life in addition to marriage (vv 29-31) confirms this. Accordingly, Paul's repeated advice that the engaged are to remain as they are has "'the character of a necessary emergency measure' rather than being his sober direction for all the churches" (Ciampa and Rosner 2010, 338). At the same time, Paul's expressed personal preference for celibacy (vv 7, 8, 40) indicates that it is as much a divine gift as marriage and is to be treated as such (see Matt 19:11-12).

3. The eschatological character of time since the coming of Christ conditions not only the attitude to marriage in Corinth with its "present crisis" (1 Cor 7:26) but the Christian attitude to life everywhere (vv 29-31). "Being eschatological people is to free us from the grip of the world and its values. We are to live 'as if not,' that is, as fully in the world, but not controlled by its systems or values" (Fee 2014, 384). Winter puts the point pungently in saying that

> much of contemporary Western Christian piety has "a future hope collapsed into the present" with a demand for fulfillment *now*, emphasizing "the feel-good factor." Alongside this there has grown a view of great deprivation, tragedy or spiritual disillusionment when the goals of success and happiness are not secured by Christians. (1997, 334)

Properly understood, 1 Cor 7 has much to say to today's church as it did to the church in Paul's Corinth.

B. Christian Freedom and Meat Offered to Idols (8:1—11:1)

Overview

There are good grounds for regarding 8:1—11:1 as a self-contained section. A new topic is plainly introduced by the stock expression "now about" (*peri de* [8:1]), while the content of the topic is indicated by the qualifying phrase "food sacrificed to idols." The substance of the discussion appears to be in what circumstances Christians were free to eat such food (v 9). This theme of freedom to exercise one's rights leads Paul to a personal application of his rights as an apostle (9:1-8, 15-19) and his refusal to claim them for the sake of avoiding offense to "the weak" (vv 20-23). His fear that this might lead to idolatry in the case of the Corinthians is illustrated by examples from the OT (10:1-13). The point is driven in even more sharply by a comparison between idol feasts and the Lord's Supper (vv 14-22). The section is rounded off with specific instructions about when idol meat might or might not be eaten (vv 23-30). It concludes with a repetition of Paul's guiding principle of avoiding creating traps for others (vv 31-33) and urging the Corinthians to follow his example (11:1). There has been much debate about exactly how the various sections are linked, as well as about the exact thrust of the argument (Fee 2014, 394-401; Garland 2003, 347-62; Fitzmyer 2008, 330-32).

The sociohistorical background. The question arises as to why a matter of this magnitude would not have presented itself during Paul's ministry in Corinth but only after he left. The evidence is clear that Corinth was awash with gods: "many 'gods' and many 'lords'" (8:5*b*). The corollary of this is that it was also awash with temples (Winter 1990, 210-15). Not only so, but the archaeological evidence shows that at least some temples were arranged so that special rooms were set aside for dining (Murphy-O'Connor 1983, 161-67 and Fig. 10). The assumption would be that any meat served would have been offered in sacrifice to the god whose temple it was. Such temple dining rooms would have had a combined religious and social function. It is improbable in the extreme that the question of idol worship had not arisen during Paul's ministry in Corinth. It was part of his standard proclamation throughout the Roman world (12:2; 1 Thess 1:9). The description of the Corinthian believers as "God's temple" (1 Cor 3:16-17; 6:19) points the same way.

What appears to have happened is that the question arose in an acute form because of changes in the religious-political situation following Paul's departure. There were two aspects to this. The first was the establishment of a federal (as opposed to local) cult of emperor worship in Corinth (Spawforth 1995, 161-63; Winter 1995, 170-72; 2001, 269-74). This involved feasts and celebrations at both the Isthmian Games and in Corinth. Roman citizens had a right to be invited to such events (Winter 1995, 170-72; 2001, 277-78). This may lie behind the language of "rights" in 8:9 (Winter 2001, 280-81). The second aspect had to do with the purchase of meat "sold in the meat market" (*en makellō* [10:25]). Judaism was a legally approved religion (*religio licita*) in the Roman Empire and it appears that, while most if not all meat sold in the meat market had been offered in sacrifice, provision was made for kosher meat to be available for Jews (Winter 2001, 293-95). Christians would have been able to take advantage of this. However, it is possible that the provision of kosher meat was discontinued following the ruling of Gallio against the Jews (Acts 18:12-17; Winter 2001, 298-301). Christians would then have had the choice between vegetarianism or eating meat offered to idols. First Corinthians 10:25 may well address that situation. The response of the Corinthians appears to have involved an application (or misapplication) of Paul's teaching that idols were "nothings." These chapters are Paul's corrective.

The precise form of the problem. From one point of view the answer to this question appears to be straightforward, being defined in the opening phrase, "Now about food sacrificed to idols" (8:1). It appears at first as though Paul saw nothing objectionable in this since idols were really "nothings" (→ vv 5-6). However, a new factor was injected in the persons of believers who were not convinced that idols were powerless and were in danger of falling under their spell again (v 7). These Paul describes as "weak" (*asthenēs* [v 9]). Their weakness is not to be despised by those who are strong (though Paul never uses this term).

At this point two other factors enter the argument. The first is the importance of the passing reference to "eating in an idol's temple" (v 10), which gives sharper definition to the opening phrase of ch 8, "Now about food sacrificed to idols" (v 1). The second is denoted by the term "right" (*exousia*), which becomes a synonym for the word "free" (*eleutheros*)—that is, the prerogative of the strong to exercise their freedom to behave in accordance with their superior understanding. This becomes the dominant theme of ch 9 in which the language of rights (9:4-6, 12, 15, 18) and freedom (vv 1, 19) is explored by Paul regarding his own apostolic ministry. He has deliberately forsworn his apostolic rights and freedom to claim material support in order to avoid giving offense to those he was seeking to win to Christ (8:13; 9:12, 18, 19).

Paul now returns to the theme of idolatry via two illustrations. The first is from the wilderness wanderings where the Israelites succumbed to it in the absence of Moses on the mount of God (10:1-10; see Exod 32:1-35). The second is from the Lord's Table where the believer participates in the body of Christ (1 Cor 10:14-17). In the same way participation in the table of the idol involves union with the idol. Participation in both is impossible; the two are incompatible (vv 14-22). It seems clear therefore that the precise form of the problem is participation in idol worship through the eating, in an idol temple, of meat offered there in sacrifice. That is to say, Paul's ultimate concern is idolatry: the appearance of patronizing it by the strong; and the danger of lapsing into it by the weak.

It is only after this issue has been settled that he takes up the subsidiary question of eating meat in the home of pagan friends or bought in the marketplace that might have been offered in sacrifice in a pagan temple (vv 25-27). His answer is to eat and ask no questions. But if told that it has been offered in sacrifice in an idol temple, then refuse it because of the damage it might do to those of weaker understanding (vv 28-29). However, if the overall theme is the danger of idolatry, its chosen instrument of accomplishment in Corinth was freedom: specifically, the freedom derived from knowledge. First Corinthians 8:1-13 and 10:31—11:1, which concentrate on this aspect, serve as inclusions for the entire section. Thus the section 8:1—11:1 has a dual focus. The central intent is soteriological: avoiding the sin of idolatry. But the way by which this end is attained is ethical: placing the needs of others before one's own rights.

The identity of the weak. It has been clear from the very first chapter of the letter that the Christians in Corinth were a mixed bag. A few came from the upper reaches of society, but not many (1:26-28). Moreover, there were divisions over Christian leaders (1:10-12; 3:4-7). As noted in the Introduction, there are also indications of social stratification in the letter (→ 11:17-22). It is doubtful, however, whether the contrast between the strong and the weak falls clearly into such categorization. For one thing, Paul never actually uses the term "the strong," nor does he give any specific definition. The only thing we know is that they exercised their right to eat idol meat. All we are told of the "weak" is that they were emboldened by the example of the strong to eat meat in idol temples. In their case, however, the weakness of their spiritual understanding exposed them to the danger of falling under the spell of the god in whose temple they dined. The question was one of "knowledge" (*gnōsis*) or understanding (8:1, 7) and the issue one of "conscience" (*suneidēsis*) (8:7, 10, 12) or conscious awareness. It is improbable that the strong or the weak were defined any more sharply than by their conduct in this particular regard.

The ethical dimension. Throughout 8:1—11:1 there runs an ongoing battle between knowing and doing, understanding and behavior. It is present in the very first verse where the Corinthian claim: "we all possess knowledge" is instantly countered by Paul's reply: "But knowledge puffs up while love builds up." The stroke-counterstroke pattern continues into ch 9 where Paul sets forth his rights as an apostle (vv 1-14), followed by an exposition of his refusal to claim them (vv 15-23). The sequence is rounded off by a replaying of the same theme (10:22-24, 31-33).

Paul thus injects into the discussion what has been conspicuously absent from the conduct of the Corinthian know-it-alls: that the Christian life requires more than understanding. It requires Christlike consideration for fellow believers whose understanding may not be equal to that of the strong. Indeed, Paul presses this point to the last degree when he brands the absence of such behavior as the means of destroying a **brother or sister, for whom Christ died** (8:11) and **sin against Christ** (v 12). Paul thus underlines what was conspicuously lacking in the Corinthians' understanding of Christianity: the ethical dimension of love (vv 1-3). It will emerge repeatedly throughout the rest of the letter, reaching eloquent expression in ch 13.

1. Meat Offered to Idols (8:1-13)

BEHIND THE TEXT

Apparently this topic represented a new departure in the exchange between Paul and the Corinthians. The subject of knowledge had, indeed, been mentioned previously as we have seen (→ the Overview to this section, above). Its application to idol meat, however, had not apparently been raised earlier. "Knowledge" was a theme on which the Corinthians abounded. Its application to idol meat was new, possibly since Paul's departure.

There is clearly a measure of quotation from the Corinthians' letter to Paul, followed by Paul's response. This is most evident in 8:1-3 where **we all possess knowledge** (at least) are the Corinthians' words, and vv 1*b*-3 are Paul's reply. Exactly how much is quotation has been debated. It is possible to interpret the chapter as a kind of dialogue (Willis 1985, 66).

IN THE TEXT

a. What the Corinthians Thought They Knew but Did Not Know (8:1-3)

■ 1 The section begins with the standard Pauline formula **Now about** (*peri de*), indicating the taking up of a new topic. That topic is **food sacrificed to idols**, more strictly translated as "meat sacrificed to idols." The Greek term in question (*eidōlothuta*) is very rare, reflecting a Jewish and Christian hostility to idol worship (Witherington 1993, 237-40). Its particular thrust, which is made clear in v 10, is that it refers not simply to eating idol food but also to eating it in an idol temple—that is, in the context of idol worship.

Paul now picks up a word that will dominate the rest of the chapter—**knowledge** (*gnōsis*). It was a watchword among the Corinthians and echoes the slogan from their letter: "We know that we all have knowledge." (Their original words may simply have been "we all have knowledge," and Paul, in keeping with his standard strategy, includes himself with them. "We know that we are all in-the-know.") The content of this knowledge will be spelled out in vv 4-6. However, no sooner does he concede their claim than he immediately explodes it. Knowledge can easily inflate the ego of the knower, without adding substance to him as a person. There is a moral dimension to the knowledge of which Paul is speaking—namely, love. Without it, knowledge is simply wind and adds nothing of moral substance—that is, does not build up (*oikodomei*).

■ 2 The unreality of such knowledge is indicated by the opening words: **if any think they know something**. The word **know** is expressed by the perfect infinitive, meaning "to have achieved final knowledge" (REB: "if anyone fancies that he has some kind of knowledge"). To imagine that one knows all there is to be known about the matter in hand merely indicates that one does not know what knowing means.

■ **3** The foregoing is particularly the case regarding knowing God. Paul emphasizes this both by inverting the order of the terms he uses and the mood of the term "know." One might have expected Paul to say: "whoever knows God loves God." Instead, he replaces the word "knows" with **loves** and "loves God" with **is known by God**. One does not know God by the act of knowing but by the relationship of loving. And in this relationship our loving God is a response to God's loving us. In Johannine idiom: "We love because he first loved us" (1 John 4:19). The knowledge of God is the gift of God, not the result of human exploration or discovery.

b. What the Corinthians Knew and Thought Everyone Knew (8:4-7)

■ **4** Following his interjection in vv 1*b*-3 Paul now returns to the announced theme of meat sacrificed to idols (*eidōlothuton*). The issue at stake is defined more specifically: it is the **eating** (*tēs brōseōs*) of such meat that is in mind. The setting in mind appears still to be that of eating in an idol temple. Paul now repeats the main verb from v 1: **we know** (*oidamen*). It is possible that, as in v 1, it refers to the Corinthians, but in view of the content of what is known it must also refer to Paul. What they know, they know because Paul taught them. The heart of this is that "there is no idol-god in the world and there is no God but one." The clauses are parallel and should be translated as such rather than taking **nothing** (*ouden*) predicatively as in the NIV: **an idol is nothing**. What is being emphatically affirmed is monotheism. It is a Christian affirmation of the Shema (Deut 6:4). Idol-gods are nonentities.

■ **5-6** The two opposing views are now developed in an explicit contrast. On the one hand are the **so-called gods, whether in heaven or on earth** (1 Cor 8:5). These are described further in the phrase "just as there are gods many and lords many." The question arises as to whether Paul is merely repeating his description of such gods and lords as **so-called** (which the NIV indicates by placing **gods** and **lords** in quotation marks); or whether he is conceding a degree of reality to them in the sense that, while they have no objective existence, yet for those who believe in them their power is very real. This is a dimension of knowledge that the Corinthians have overlooked. (Paul will identify it later as a demonic power. → 10:19-20.)

Against the commonly held view that there are many gods and many lords Paul now sets forth the Christian view, held by both himself and the Corinthians, but being pressed in this context by the latter in support of their eating in idol temples. The statement in 8:6 is emphatic, introduced by the strong adversative conjunction "but" (*alla* [KJV]). Picking up the terms **gods** and **lords** in v 5 Paul uses them for Christian purposes. In the Greek world of Paul's day, including Corinth, the two terms were synonymous, both being titles for gods and goddesses whose statues have been found in Corinth (Winter 1990, 214-15).

Against the background of Corinthian polytheism Paul proceeds to set forth Christian monotheism. **For us there is but one God, the Father** (v 6). The contrast is twofold: between **many** gods (v 5) and **one** God (v 6); and between faceless gods and a defined God—the Father. God is further defined as the source of all things, and the one **for whom we live**. Both our existence and our purpose for existence derive from him. Paul now proceeds spontaneously to affirm the deity of Christ: **there is but one Lord, Jesus Christ**. The fatherhood of God implies the lordship of Jesus, a connection that Paul makes repeatedly in the greeting with which many of his letters begin (1 Cor 1:3; 2 Cor 1:2; Gal 1:3; Phil 1:2; Rom 1:7). He sees no tension between affirming the two. This is clear from the functions that he proceeds to attribute to the Lord Jesus: first, a role in creation (**through whom all things came**). This passage not only attributes to Christ a mediating function in creation but also presupposes his preexistence.

A second function attributed to Christ is that he is the mediator of life. There has been much discussion as to whether the statements about Christ are cosmological or soteriological in intent. (See Murphy-O'Connor 2009, ch 6.) Attention is focused on **all things** (*ta panta*), a phrase that elsewhere in Paul is used to express Christ's saving work (1 Cor 2:10-13; 12:4-6; 2 Cor 4:14-15; 5:18; Rom 8:28, 31-32). However, it is doubtful whether the two are to be separated. It is precisely because of the lordship of Christ manifested in creation that he could become the Savior, that the Maker of all things could become their Redeemer.

Verses 5-6 stand out strikingly in many respects. For one thing, they represent a Christian recasting of the Shema: the classic Jewish declaration of the oneness of God (Deut 6:4). They do so, however, without discarding monotheism but rather by redefining it. Paul sees no tension between affirming the divinity of Christ and the uniqueness of God (Wright 2013, 663). The lordship of Christ expresses rather than replaces God's authority. What we are encountering here has been called christological monotheism arising from Christian experience and Jewish monotheism (Hurtado 1988, 123).

Another striking feature of 1 Cor 8:6 is its quasi-credal form. It has been suggested that this is the earliest formulation of christological monotheism (Wright 1993, 136). What is clear is that Paul had already instructed the

Corinthians in this view, and they are now quoting it back at him in defense of their patronizing idol temples.

■ **7** The Corinthians' defense had been that since idols were no-gods, it could do them no harm to eat meat sacrificed to "nothings" in godless temples. Paul agrees with this in principle but points out that this overlooks a significant aspect of the case: there are some who lack the strength of consciousness to shake off the old associations of their former modes of worship. Paul explicitly rejects the claim made in v 1 that "all possess knowledge." Knowledge is a deeper thing than correct information. It embraces the power to influence the affections, and in doing so, to drown the dictates of moral consciousness. For such people dining in a pagan temple on meat offered in sacrifice to the god exposes them to the dangers of idolatry. Paul will define such powers later as "demonic" (10:19-20). In inserting this objection Paul implicitly imports a significant ethical dimension into Christian behavior. Christian living involves more than conforming to Christian principles as one understands them; it involves living in a way that takes into account the effects of one's lifestyle on those who do not understand them. This, indeed, had been his own guiding principle in Corinth from the beginning (2:2; 9:22). It was the outworking of the theology of the cross.

c. What the Corinthians Did Not Know about the Effect of Their Knowledge on Others (8:8-13)

Just as 8:1a quotes the Corinthians followed by Paul's reply in vv 1b-3; and vv 4-6 constituted the Corinthians' case followed by Paul's rebuttal in v 7; so v 8 expresses a third Corinthian claim, followed by Paul's response in vv 9-13. The shift from the third-person plural in v 7 to the first-person plural in v 8 followed by the second-person plural in v 9 confirms this. It is sometimes claimed that v 8 is Paul's opinion, but v 9 stands in contrast with what precedes and clearly expresses a contrary view. Even if Paul agreed with the substance of v 8, that food neither commends us to nor distances us from God, that is not what he is arguing about here.

■ **8** The Corinthians now advance another argument against Paul's position. If idol-gods are no-gods, then food offered in sacrifice to them remains unchanged. Consequently, those who eat it remain unchanged too. So why not eat it? The order of the statements probably reflects the force with which the two sides have been pressing their case. Food would not affect their relationship with God. If they abstained, as Paul had been urging, they would not come up short; while if they indulged, as they had been doing, they would not particularly thrive. Eating does no harm, and not-eating does no particular good. It is spiritually neutral.

■ **9** Paul does not refute the substance of their argument. What he does is pick up the dimension missing from their case in the two earlier expositions: love (vv 1*b*-3) and concern for those with weaker consciences (v 7). A new factor comes into play at this point that will exercise a large role in the rest of this section (to 11:1): the factor of right (*exousia*). It carries the sense of "being at liberty with regard to a thing" (BDAG). "Right" and "liberty" become virtually interchangeable terms (9:1, 19; 10:23, 29). Paul's point here is that one person's "right" may mean another's restriction; one person's "liberty" may be another's limitation. In the Corinthian setting, this meant that the unrestrained freedom exercised by the "strong" became the means of tripping up **(stumbling block [*proskomma*]) of the weak**.

■ **10** Paul now brings his argument to its peak, both in its explicit and individual application. The verbs and pronouns are singular and personal: **someone, you, that person**. The picture is painted vividly: **you . . . eating in an idol's temple** seen by one with a weak conscience. The dominant motif of the chapter is drawn in to make the point still sharper: **you, with all your knowledge**. What outcome can be expected other than that the weak will follow the example of the strong? The verb translated **emboldened** (*oikodomēthēsetai*) means literally "be built up." This is the only negative use of this verb in Paul's writings. It is possible for people to be reinforced the wrong way, and this is what Paul sees happening in such cases as this.

■ **11** Paul spells out the implications still more sharply. The weak person is said to be **destroyed by your knowledge**. The knowledge, of which the strong are so assured (and proud?), proves to be the undoing of the weak. Paul uses a range of terms to describe the effect on the weak: "stumbling block" (*proskomma*), **destroyed** (*apollutai*), "wound" (*tuptontes* [BDAG]), "cause . . . to stumble" (*skandalizō* [NASB]). At the very least it means to sin in such a way as to cause the weak to sin. (For a review of the terminology, see *TDNT* 7:355-56.)

The gravamen of the offense is that it is against a **brother or sister, for whom Christ died**. The kinship language echoes the saying of Jesus against giving offense to the little ones who believe in him (Mark 9:42), intensified by the reference to his atoning death for them. Once again the matter is brought to the touchstone of the gospel. The common basis of their life in Christ is not "knowledge" or "rights" but the death of Christ.

■ **12** The point is elaborated still more keenly. Being the occasion of stumbling to the weak is branded flatly as **sin against them**. The singular "brother or sister" in 1 Cor 8:11 becomes the plural in v 12. This may mean no more than that more than one weak individual was involved. Inasmuch as Jesus affirmed that anything done to his people was done to him (Matt 25:40, 45; Mark 9:37, 41; Luke 10:16; John 13:20), sin of the kind in question was not only sin against the individuals concerned but also sin against himself. However, it is possible that the change to the plural indicates a reference to the church as a whole, the body of Christ. The use of the building metaphor in 1 Cor 8:10 (*oikodomēthēsetai*, lit. "be built up," obscured by the NIV's **emboldened**) may point this way, as may its earlier appearance in 3:9.

■ **13** The focus of the argument now changes dramatically from the behavior of the Corinthians ("you" in 8:9-12) to the behavior of Paul ("I" in v 13 and the whole of ch 9). The conjunction **therefore** (Gk. *dioper*), occurring only in 1 Corinthians in the NT (here and at 10:14 and in some manuscripts at 14:13), places emphatic stress on logical connection (Moule 1953, 164). Two word groups dominate his conclusion. The first is "food," expressed in two Greek words: the first (*brōma*) is a general term appropriately rendered as **what I eat** by the NIV; the second (*krea*) is rendered equally appropriately as **meat**.

This latter confirms that what is at issue is the eating of meat sacrificed to idols. The second word group is "cause . . . to stumble" (*skandalizō* [NASB]), which has already been identified as sin in the previous verse. This is something Paul will never countenance. To him, there is something more important than freedom of choice (which is the essential meaning of possessing knowledge in this context)—that is, the effect of one's choices upon others. Paul's personal choice is to avoid giving offense to weaker believers.

FROM THE TEXT

While the notes sounded in ch 8 will be both echoed and developed in chs 9 and 10, they are struck here from within a personal context that gives them particular force. If it be asked how the eating of meat offered to idols can have anything to say to today's world, the answer is that the principles underlying the practice are of permanent relevance.

- The absence of material idols from society as we know it does not mean the absence or impossibility of idolatry. Anything that takes first place in our lives usurps the place that belongs to God and thereby becomes a form of idolatry.
- The touchstone of Christian life and living is not knowledge but love. Specifically, it is by love that the knowledge of God is mediated: and by the knowledge of God Paul means not our knowing God but God's knowing us (8:3). In C. S Lewis' words: "St. Paul promises to those who love God not, as we should expect, that they will know Him, but that they will be known by Him (I Cor. 8:3)" (1980, 15). One is known by God as one loves him, not by the accumulation of theological information.
- By the same token, love is the guideline of Christian conscience and conduct. Those whose theological understanding is limited are not to

be swept aside as lesser breeds on that account. Their understanding may be limited and even mistaken, but they are not to be treated as unimportant for that reason. Their limitations are to be taken into account where ignoring them would lead to the damaging of their faith (vv 9-11).

- Sin is not merely an individualistic act with consequences only for the sinner. It is an offense against others whose faith is damaged by it, and an offense and affront to Christ (vv 11-12).
- For the Christian the right to freedom of choice can never be absolute, taking no regard of the effect of its exercise on others. This does not mean that the believer becomes the prisoner of the whims and susceptibilities of others. The issue Paul was addressing was one of clearly defined substance and spiritual import. His meaning is that, in matters having a direct bearing on the reality of faith, the believer is bound to take into serious account the effect of his or her choices upon those whose spiritual immaturity might expose them to spiritual damage and even destruction.

2. Paul's Rights as an Apostle and His Freedom in Using Them (9:1-27)

BEHIND THE TEXT

The argument now takes a highly personal turn, in which Paul applies to himself what he has been enjoining on the Corinthians. The shift from the second-person pronouns in 8:9-12 to the first person in v 13 is an advance warning of a major change of actor. In many respects 8:13 is a summary of the message of ch 9 and as such serves as a guideline in the interpretation of that chapter. Several matters that have a bearing on the understanding of the chapter as a whole are worth noting from the start.

The place of the chapter in the developing argument of the letter. It is not uncommon for the chapter to be described as a "digression" (Bruce 1976, 82; Fitzmyer 2008, 353) in which Paul steps aside from the question of eating idol meat to a vigorous defense of his apostleship (Fee 2014, 433-39; Fitzmyer 2008, 353-54). The distance between the two topics accounts for the description of the chapter as a digression. Against this it is argued that Paul is not intent on defending his apostleship at all. Rather, he is giving the Corinthians an example—his own practice—in subordinating his personal comfort for the sake of those with greater needs than his own. These are variously defined as providing the Corinthians with an example of self-sacrificial behavior (Witherington 1995, 203; and especially Garland 2003, 396-401) to demonstrating the priority of the gospel over one's personal rights (Ciampa and Rosner 2010, 396-97). Both positions seem to involve overstatement.

It is very difficult in the light of vv 1-3 to believe that Paul's apostleship was not being called into question in some way. At the same time, the purpose for which he cites his apostleship is not to prove it as a fact but to use it as an illustration of how to minister to the weak. But this obviously depends on the admission of his apostleship in the first place. In regard to the contending interpretations: it comes closer to the truth to say that it was not the *fact* of his apostleship but its *form* that was being queried; but it was in its form that its relevance to the problem of the weak is to be found. As participants in the new life in Christ, they were called upon to live the crucified life. Paul himself was the living embodiment of this as one commissioned as an apostle to the ministry of the gospel.

The cultural background. The particular form of Paul's apostolic practice that was giving offense to (at least) some in the Corinthian church was his refusal to accept money and material support for his preaching. In the Hellenistic world the prevailing practice was for philosophers to support themselves by becoming clients of wealthy patrons, or by charging students fees. This was not universally true. Some, particularly Stoic and Cynic philosophers, were self-supporting. Paul followed this last practice, which was evidently regarded as demeaning by some elements in the Corinthian church who queried his apostleship accordingly. Paul turns the tables on his critics by showing that its intent and effect are to further the proclamation of the gospel (Judge 1984, 12-15).

The distinctive vocabulary. Two words carry much of the weight of the argument in ch 9. The first is the word "free" (*eleutheros*), which occurs in the opening phrase. It is applied in the immediately following question in terms of Paul's apostleship. However, it is displaced for the next seventeen verses by the term "right" (*exousia* [vv 4, 5, 6, 12 (2x), 18]). His liberty to act as he did was not a casual option but an entrenched entitlement. The word "free" (*eleutheros*) emerges at the climax of the argument (v 19) where he concludes that, on the basis of his apostolic rights he possesses the liberty to make himself a servant (*edoulōsa*) so that he can "win as many as possible."

The intensity of the rhetoric. The argument of the chapter is expressed with a forcefulness that is notable in the letter. This indicates the importance of the issue at stake. A variety of rhetorical forms is employed. The chapter begins with a volley of rhetorical questions (v 1): a mode that is repeated at length (vv 4-12*a*, 13, 24). Their occurrence in groups of three (vv 1, 4-6, 7) interspersed with indications of the authority on which they are based—historical fact (v 1), apostolic precedent (vv 4-6), common practice (v 7), the Law (vv 8-12), temple regulations (v 13), and the authority of the Lord Jesus (v

14)—combine to create a powerful impact. Not least potent amid the multiple listings of his rights are his flat affirmations that he has refused to make use of them (vv 12*b*, 15*a*). (For a full analysis, see Fitzmyer 2008, 354-55.)

IN THE TEXT

a. Paul's Right as an Apostle to Receive Support (9:1-14)

Paul develops the case for his right to receive material support for his apostolic ministry.

■ 1 Paul begins his argument by placing himself on the same level as the Corinthians. They have claimed freedom to act in keeping with their superior knowledge (8:1, 4, 9-10). At the very least Paul can claim the wisdom they claim, and the right to act in accordance with it. The first question therefore expects a positive answer. **Am I not free?** means "Do not I have the liberty to act in keeping with my depth of understanding?" The second question drives more deeply still. Paul is more than simply "one of them." He is an apostle. In support of this he cites two pieces of evidence. The first—that he had seen Jesus the Lord—was the fundamental requirement for apostleship (Acts 1:21-22; 1 Cor 15:8). Again, the question is rhetorical. The second was that he had performed the work of an apostle. They themselves were the evidence of that (15:9-11). Once more a positive answer is expected as the Greek particle (*ouchi*) indicates.

■ 2 A caveat is now inserted. There are **others** who do not accept Paul's apostleship. Who these were is unknown. Many conjectures have been offered, ranging from some of the factions in the Corinthian church (→ 3:4; 9:6) to other churches outside of Corinth (e.g., Galatia). There is no clear evidence of their identity, but there is no doubt of their existence or that the Corinthians were aware of their existence. However, the Corinthians were unimpressed by it, and for a very good reason. They were **the seal of my apostleship in the Lord**. The seal was the stamp of authentication. Taken with the mention of his having "seen Jesus our Lord" (v 1), the implied argument seems to be that the establishment of the Corinthian church constituted the validation of his apostolic status. (The NIV's **surely I am to you** could carry an overtone of doubt. "I surely am to you" would avoid this. The emphatic conjunction "but" [*alla*] reinforced by the particle "at least" [*ge*; BDF, 439; Moule 1953, 164 n. 7] make clear that the Corinthians had no doubt on the matter.)

■ 3 Nevertheless, Paul's argument continues in a setting of contentiousness. This is indicated by the terms **defense** (*apologia*) and **those who sit in judgment on me** (*anakrinousin*). Both have legal overtones and suggest claims or charges that were currently being levelled against him. **This** (*hautē*), which stands as the first word in the NIV, stands last in the Greek—"my defense is this"—indicating that his response comes in the verses that follow.

■ **4-6** The first two questions (introduced by the double negative *mē ouk*) are even more emphatic than those in v 1. "Are we indeed without the right to food and drink?," and so forth. They clearly expect a negative answer. Paul's critics must have raised the issue: "he does not take support because he does not qualify"; that is, he is not really an apostle. He extends the argument in v 5 to include support for an accompanying wife, citing the parallel cases of **the other apostles and the Lord's brothers and Cephas**. We have no independent evidence of these, though the Eleven certainly received the commission (Matt 28:16-20). It would have been pointless to cite them to the Corinthians if they did not have some knowledge of their missionary activities. The mention of Barnabas (in 1 Cor 9:6) probably explains the shift from the first-person singular in vv 1-2 to the first-person plural in vv 4-6. The key word throughout is **right** (*exousia*), used forcefully in each of these verses. Paul now proceeds to spell out the bases on which his **right** to support rests.

■ **7** First, he draws upon analogies from accepted custom or common sense. The soldier did not pay for his own equipment or provisions (Thompson 2000, 993-94). The owner of the vineyard would naturally eat its grapes. The keeper of the flock would drink the milk that it yielded. These are not questions of wages. They are simply matters of subsistence within the chain of life.

■ **8-12** Paul's argument now advances beyond commonsense custom. It is grounded in the Law, which says the same thing. In illustration Paul quotes Deut 25:4, whose point is that the ox at the treadmill should not be muzzled and thereby deprived from eating the product of its own labor. Paul's argument has been criticized on contradictory grounds. On the one hand it has been argued that Paul attributes to God a demeaning attitude toward the animal creation (not least on the basis of the KJV: "Doth God take care for oxen? Or saith he it altogether for our sakes?" [1 Cor 9:9-10]). On the other hand, it has been maintained that Paul stretches the sense of the words by giving them an entirely human reference. Both seem to overlook that the context of Deut 25:4 deals largely with God's concern for human beings (e.g., 24:6-7, 10-22; 25:1-3), and Paul is interpreting it in keeping with its context. This appears to be confirmed by the conclusion of 1 Cor 9:10, stating that anyone who **plows and threshes** does so with the **hope** and expectation **of sharing in the harvest**.

But there is an even more striking note sounded in the first half of v 10 with the double affirmation that Deut 25:4 was given **for us** (*di' hēmas*). First Corinthians 9:11 makes clear that the phrase refers not to human beings in general but to Paul and Barnabas in particular, with specific reference to their apostolic ministry in bringing the gospel to Corinth. (The repeated **we** [*hēmeis*] in v 11 is emphatic.) He describes that ministry as **spiritual** (*ta pneumatika*), evidently as referring to the age of the Spirit that has already been launched (→ 1:7). In other words, Paul sees the Law as finding its eschatological fulfillment in the proclamation of the gospel. Hence the Law's provision for human material needs buttresses the right of material support in the cases of Paul and Barnabas.

The whole argument is summed up in 9:12*a*, where the **right** (*exousia*) to **support** of **others** (*alloi*)—evidently "the other apostles" (v 5)—clinches the similar right of Paul and Barnabas. Following this argumentative buildup one expects Paul to draw the irresistible conclusion that the Corinthians should pay up uncomplainingly. Instead, he draws precisely the opposite conclusion: that **we** [presumably himself and Barnabas] **did not use this right** (v 12*b*). The freedom that brought with it the right to material support also brought the freedom not to exercise that right. This they have opted to do, burdensome though it might be, in order to avoid placing any obstacle in the way of the gospel. This had been Paul's consistent practice from the earliest days of his ministry (1 Thess 2:9). He would not be seen as a freeloader, whatever conclusions some Corinthians might draw from it.

■ **13-14** Following this rather explosive interjection, Paul resumes the listing of reasons why the right of support is unequivocally his. First, he cites the precedent of the priests in the temple to whom the Law specifically allotted a share of the sacrificial offerings (Lev 6:16-18; 7:1-10, 28-36). It is, indeed, possible that a distinction is being made between the Levites who acted as temple assistants but without access to the altar (see Deut 18:8-32). In that case the point is being made even more pungently. How much stronger was the claim of the apostles to support if those serving in an ancillary role in the temple held such rights. However, Paul's climactic and conclusive argument is to be able to quote the teaching (indeed, the command) of Jesus himself (Matt 10:10; Luke 10:7). This is something Paul rarely does. This allusion at the climactic point of his argument indicates not only that Paul was more familiar with it than is sometimes supposed but also that he could assume that the Corinthians were familiar with it too.

b. Paul's Refusal to Use His Rights (9:15-18)

Throughout these verses Paul is playing with a paradox: that to be paid is to receive no pay; that to have his rights is not to use them; that to be free is to renounce his freedom—indeed, to be under compulsion; that he has the right to boast—yet lacks it.

■ **15** Having completed the list of his rights to material support, Paul resumes the note sounded so explosively in v 12*b* that he has not used any of them. It is significant that, whereas in v 12 he has used the first-person plural, here he makes emphatic use of the first-person singular (*egō*). Barnabas may have been his colleague (v 6), but Paul himself was the primary target of the critics. Much has been made of the fact that this refusal to use his rights would involve disobeying a command of the Lord (Horrell 1997). But had this been Paul's understanding there would have been no need for him to list the other supporting examples. Moreover, the verb "use" (*chrēsthai*) denotes "to avail oneself of" (as in v 12*b*), suggesting the freedom to use or not to use.

Paul now launches into a disavowal of any Corinthian notion that the reason for his writing was to stir them into a support-providing mode, as some of his critics might have alleged. The strength of his feeling is indicated in at least two ways. First, v 15 concludes with a breach in the syntax of the sentence (obscured in the NIV by being ironed out). Literally, the Greek text reads: "For it is better for me to die rather than—no one will deprive me of my boast!" This reveals the depth of Paul's opposition to accepting material support. The second mark of his intensity is the stringing together of a chain of reasons explaining the substance of **this boast** linked by the conjunction **for** (*gar*). There are five altogether (vv 15, 16 [3x], 17: three of which disappear from the NIV). They give a certain breathlessness to Paul's declamation.

■ **16** No sooner has Paul asserted that he will not be deprived of his right to boast than he declares that boasting is something he cannot do! Clearly, there is a shift of meaning. The right to which he lays claim and of which he rightly boasts is the right to the same support as the other apostles (vv 12*b*, 15*a*). But that is the self-same boast that he rejects since he preaches the gospel not by free personal choice but by divine appointment and compulsion. Boasting is inappropriate when one is acting under orders. There are overtones of two images here. First, that of the slave who acts under constraint (an image that he will develop in vv 19-23). Second, that of the prophet who feels the prophetic message like a fire in his inner being (Amos 3:8; Jer 20:9). Thus, he is a man with a sword suspended over his neck. Disaster awaits him if he does not preach.

■ **17** Once more Paul spells out his two options. If he preached the gospel of his own free choice, he would deserve to be paid since he had earned it. But if he preached as a slave under orders, he would deserve nothing. A slave is not paid for his work; unpaid labor is what slaves are for. At this point, however, Paul moves to another aspect of slavery. As noted above, slavery took many forms in the ancient world—from total servitude to positions of responsibility in the master's household. It is the latter that Paul appears to have in mind when he says that his forced labor takes the form of a **stewardship** (*oikonomia*) entrusted to him. Slavery to the gospel and the Christ of the gospel is what

Paul has been called to: not to please himself and satisfy his own interests. Anything more alien to the mentality of upscale Corinthians it would be difficult to imagine. Paul is thus coming close not only to justifying his own style of leadership but also to targeting the "freedom" of some Corinthians to eat idol meat regardless of the damage it did to those of weaker conscience.

■ **18** Paul now draws together the lines of his argument about payment and rights. His payment (which is to receive no payment) is that he is able to offer the gospel **free of charge**. He is thereby enabled to avoid making use of his rights: the perquisites that are rightfully his as a preacher of the gospel. Paul's overriding concern is to proclaim the gospel in such a way that the mode of presentation is in harmony with the message. We see yet again that Paul's unbroken preoccupation is with the gospel.

c. How Paul Uses His Freedom (9:19-23)

From the somewhat tense and involved argument of vv 15-18, Paul now moves into more open waters. The first word "though . . . free" (*eleutheros*) indicates that he is turning now to the first question posed in v 1: "Am I not free?" This suggests that we should expect an exposition of his view of the right use of freedom, which calls to mind earlier discussions of that topic (→ 6:12; 8:9-13). The macrostructure of the passage beginning with the phrase "to win as many as possible" (9:19) and ending with the purpose clause "so that by all possible means I might save some" (v 22) confirms this. Indeed, this point is reinforced by the repeated use of the phrase "so that I might win" (*kerdainō* [NRSV]) in each of vv 19-22: a total of five times. Another telling clue is the repeated use of the term "law" (*nomos*) and its compounds: a total of nine times in vv 20-21. These features seem to coalesce to provide a picture of how Paul used his freedom, and—by implication—how he thought the Corinthians should use theirs.

■ **19** As a self-supporting preacher Paul was not in anyone's pocket. This is the conclusion of his argument about his rights as an apostle. Yet paradoxically by the very act of forfeiting his rights he had made himself everyone's slave. His freedom was the freedom to serve everyone else. In Greco-Roman society taking a lower rung on the ladder was not regarded as a virtue. To Paul it was his vocation because it enabled him to win to Christ people across the whole range of society. This he now spells out in four specific examples. The dominant category throughout is that of law (*nomos*) even where the term itself is not used. The controlling theme is adaptation to the mentality and susceptibilities of others so as not to alienate them from the gospel. The first three examples concern Jewish-Gentile issues, while the fourth has regard specifically to "the weak" (v 22).

■ 20 (1) **To the Jews** Paul **became like a Jew**. The expression is striking, not to say stunning in view of Paul's sterling Jewish pedigree (see Phil 3:4-6). Yet being in Christ meant that he had been emancipated from the Jewish law with all of its ritualistic and cultural obligations. At the same time while no longer bound by the Law he chose to live by its requirements since to do otherwise would exclude him from the possibility of communing with Jews at meals, and particularly of being able to preach the gospel in synagogues. Perhaps the most radical illustration of this was his submission to the physical discipline imposed by the Jewish authorities (2 Cor 11:24). Yet he willingly accepted this since it left open the possibility of winning the Jews.

(2) Those **under the law** is sometimes taken to refer to Jews and therefore simply to repeat the first part of the verse (Thiselton 2000b, 702; Garland 2003, 430; Fitzmyer 2008, 369). However, if that is the case, it is odd that he should insert a reference to himself as **not under the law**, and also repeat the refrain about winning those in question. More probably **those under the law** are not Jews by national origin but those who have submitted to the Jewish law by choice—namely, converts to Judaism. Once again, Paul defines his own relationship to the Law in startling terms: he became **like** a law-keeper even though he is **not under the law**. He could hardly have described his view of the new creation in Christ in more thoroughgoing language. At the same time he has adopted the stance of living **like one under the law** for the specific purpose of winning **those under the law**.

■ 21 (3) **Those not having the law** are clearly the Gentiles who knew little and cared less about Jewish law. Here Paul makes the most astonishing declaration of all, that he has become like those he is referring to for the overriding purpose of winning them. Aware, however, that his affirmation might be misunderstood as a declaration of license, Paul adds the doubly significant parenthesis. First, it does not mean he is free from God's law and therefore to live a life of lawlessness. Second, he is—to render the Greek literalistically—"enlawed [*ennomos*] to Christ." This does not mean he has simply exchanged one law code for another. Christ's law is not a new legal code but a new pattern of living: life in keeping with the pattern of the example of Christ (11:1), expressed supremely in his self-giving on the cross (Gal 2:19-20; Phil 2:5-8, for a full discussion see Barrett 1968, 212-15).

■ 22 (4) The fourth, and in many respects the climactic, group is **the weak**. In a way, one could see this coming. It points back to vv 12*b*, 15*a*, and 19 where Paul is referring to his self-abasement in adopting a self-supporting lifestyle, which was despised among the Corinthians. But it also harks back to 8:9-13 and those weak in conscience. There is therefore both a sociological and a soteriological dimension to his action, and it is a mistake to separate the two.

Significantly, Paul does not say that he became *as* (*hōs*) weak (as in the three earlier examples) but that he **became weak.** ("As" [*hōs*] is missing from the oldest manuscripts.) He has used similar language earlier both of his person and his message (2:3-5). Thus his weakness on the social scale makes the same point as the message of the gospel: that God does not save by deploying the big battalions. It is for this reason that (to borrow Hock's phrase) Paul's "tentmaking was a constitutive part of his self-understanding as an apostle" (1980, 67).

Accordingly, his purpose in becoming **all things to all people** was that by any means he could lead them to salvation. This summarizing statement sheds light on all four applications in vv 19-22a. First, its replacement of the word **win** (*kerdainō*) by **save** (*sōzō*) shows that Paul's overriding concern was with the bringing to salvation in Christ of the different classes of persons named. Second, this gives definition to the expression **I have become all things to all people.** Paul was no chameleon, no unprincipled peddler prepared to take on the color of his surroundings if by so doing he could make a sale. This is made clear from the qualifying terms and phrases that he inserts in vv 20-21 (such as "like" and "though I am not"). The NIV aptly expresses this by inserting the word **possible** in v 22*b*. But in matters indifferent to the truth of the gospel Paul was ready to go to any length to gain a hearing. Nor was this merely a calculating tactic. Rather it was the underlying principle of the incarnation and the cross, in which Christ took human form, identifying himself with the whole range of human life in order to encompass its redemption (Phil 2:5-11).

■ **23** Paul now gathers up the entire range of his apostolic ministry with its distinctive characteristics of earning his own living and adapting himself to the status of his hearers by affirming that he has done it all (*panta*) on account of the gospel. He elaborates what he means by using the term **share** or "partner" (*synkoinōnos*). The NIV renders the clause **that I may share in its blessings.** But this strikes a jarring note in a context suffused with the idea of what Paul has given up in his apostolic ministry. It is much more probable that "partner" denotes sharing in the gospel in the active sense of sharing in the work of spreading it. The NEB is therefore to be preferred: "All this I do for the sake of the Gospel, to bear my part in proclaiming it."

d. The Need for Self-Discipline in the Exercise of Freedom (9:24-27)

Thus far in the chapter Paul has been addressing his own freedom, which, significantly, included the freedom not to exercise his freedom. He now expands that further, making use of an example well known to all citizens of Corinth. The Isthmian Games were one of the highlights of the city's life. Competition was intense. At the heart of it was the rigorous training undertaken freely by all who cherished any hope of winning. It was a perfect illustration of Paul's personal practice, as well as of the lifestyle he was urging upon the Corinthian believers.

■ **24** The passage begins with a sharp shift to the second-person pronoun: **Do you not know?** This defines not only the focus of the argument but also its subject. It resumes the theme of the Corinthians as those possessing superior knowledge, with which the section begins (8:1-2). This indicates that Paul is returning to the theme of eating meat in idol temples, which the know-it-alls indulged in without regard to its effects on the weak (8:9-12). The thrust of the illustration does not lie in the fact that only one competitor wins the prize while the rest get nothing. It lies rather in the fact that victory depends on subordinating one's freedom to the rigors of training. He therefore injects the imperative note: "Run so as to win."

■ **25** The guiding principle is now stated explicitly: those who enter the contest (*agōn*) submit themselves to **strict training**. Significantly, two of the areas in which Corinthian contestants deprived themselves were the very areas that had created problems in the Corinthian church: food and sex (Mitchell 1992, 248-49, esp. n. 346). The contrast between the prizes at stake in the two contests is now expressed vividly. In both cases it is a crown, but of very different kinds. At the Isthmian Games, the crown was made of celery, therefore perishable—perhaps already withered when it was awarded (Witherington 1995, 214 n. 35). By contrast, the crown awaiting the believer is imperishable: **will last forever**. With this an eschatological note is injected into the picture: not for the first time (see 3:12-15, 22). The crown is not just a thing, an object, an appendage. It is life in the eternity of God.

■ **26-27** The guideline that Paul is commending to the Corinthian believers is one that he follows himself. Continuing the games metaphor, he affirms that he does not run aimlessly (*adēlōs*): "not as one who has no fixed goal" (BDAG, 19). Extending the contest metaphor into the realm of boxing—which was part of the Isthmian Games—he declares that he is no shadowboxer, merely playing at boxing. Boxing was highly rated as a sport among Paul's contemporaries (Collins 1999, 362). The allusion to shadowboxing may be a dig at the Sophists whom Philo describes in such terms (Witherington 1995, 214 n. 37). On the contrary, Paul has bruises and blood to show for his exertions. Second Corinthians 11:23-28 serves as a powerful illustration of this. Just as Paul made himself a sociological slave to others (1 Cor 9:19), so he made his body a physical slave in pursuing his calling. This is an index of the seriousness of the issue both for Paul and—by implication—for the Corinthians.

What is at stake for Paul is not merely coming in second rather than first. The language of disqualification (*adokimos*) is linked directly with that of preaching the gospel (*kēruxas*) and forfeiting the crown, which symbolizes eternal life. As Garland puts it pungently:

> The immortal crown to be won (9:25) is not a good job-approval rating as an apostle, but salvation. The problem for many Corinthians is that they have disconnected their personal salvation from their calling to service and absolute allegiance to God. (2003, 444-45)

FROM THE TEXT

1. The dominant theme of the chapter—approached from opposite sides—is the renunciation of rights. Paul's title to material support was unimpeachable, yet he refused to claim it. In so doing he not only proclaimed the gospel free of charge, but by that very act he embodied it. Without question, rights—whether as a citizen or a believer—are fundamental in anything that can be called a society. Paul himself did not hesitate to use them (see Acts 16:35-40; 22:25-29; 25:9-12; 26:32). However, when the heart of the gospel was at stake, he readily accepted forfeiting his apostolic rights rather than distort the message. In so doing he was presenting a powerful example to the Corinthians. In an age such as ours when claims to one's rights are widely pressed, there may be times when forfeiting one's rights may be the best, and even the only, way of advancing the gospel.

2. In proclaiming the gospel there is a place, and in some settings a necessity for accommodation to the mindset of others if one is to win them to Christ (1 Cor 9:19-23). For Paul the great religious divide was between Jew and Gentile. To ignore this was to guarantee preaching to closed ears. Paul would do nothing that would betray the gospel. However, he was ready to countenance practices that were gospel-neutral where they built bridges to non-Christians, whether Jews or pagans.

3. There is a need for self-discipline in the Christian life to avoid forfeiting salvation. It is possible for salvation to be lost. Garland writes: "Any implication that one may forfeit one's salvation may cause theological dyspepsia for some [but] . . . the immortal crown to be won (9:25) is not a good job-approval rating as an apostle, but salvation" (2003, 444). The salvation that has been "worked in" by God is to be "worked out" by the believer (Phil 2:12-13), and a life of discipline and devotion is the means by which this is accomplished (1 Cor 9:24-27).

4. Paul stands out as a remarkable—and early—example of bivocational ministry. Not only so: he was bivocational by choice. His bivocational ministry was born not of financial necessity—the absence of support—but of pastoral example. Toiling at tentmaking was hard work, but it showed that he was not in ministry for the money. It demonstrated the sacrifices he was prepared to

make for the sake of the gospel: a point that some of the Corinthian believers had yet to grasp. In our day bivocational ministry is often regarded as a regrettable necessity. But it can also carry positive value.

3. Meat Offered to Idols and the Exercise of Christian Freedom (10:1—11:1)

BEHIND THE TEXT

In this section Paul brings together the themes of meat offered to idols and Christian freedom. He has already treated them successively in chs 8 and 9. Some of the Corinthians were more preoccupied with the freedom achieved through knowing that idols were nonentities, than with the danger of idolatry that their attendance at idol feasts created both for Christians of weaker understanding as well as for themselves.

In ch 10 he returns to both of these issues, exploring and applying them at greater depth. There can be no doubt where the primary emphasis lies: on the danger of idolatry (vv 7, 14). The Christian's freedom is real, and not to be negotiated away (vv 25-30). But it is to be practiced within the boundaries of love for others who might be endangered by its indiscriminate indulgence. Having expounded how he has employed his freedom as an apostle in ch 9, he now proceeds to apply it to the Corinthians in their very different context of pagan idolatry. While their spheres are different, the principles at work are the same.

IN THE TEXT

a. The Danger of Idolatry 10:1-22

While vv 1-22 stand together as being concerned with the same topic, there is a clear progression from the examples of idolatry in the history of Israel (vv 1-13) to their application to the situation of the Corinthians (vv 14-22).

(1) Warnings from Israel's History (10:1-13)

Verses 1-13 fall into three roughly distinct groups. Verses 1-5 list the blessings given by God to the Israelites at the exodus from Egypt and the journey through the wilderness. It is emphasized that while these blessings were given to "all" (*pantes* occurs five times in vv 1-4) yet the response of most of the Israelites was displeasing to God (v 5). Verses 6-10 consist of a generalized warning (v 6) followed by a sequence of four negative examples urging the Corinthians not to follow in the footsteps of the Israelites (vv 7-10). Verses 11-13 apply the examples to the Corinthians, mingling warning with encouragement.

■ 1 The opening clause is emphatic: The conjunction **for** (*gar*) links it firmly to 9:24-27, where Paul stresses his own self-discipline in the Christian life. This is something of which the Corinthian Christians dare not be ignorant. Still more, they must not be ignorant of the experience of their forefathers (Gk. "fathers"; NIV: **ancestors**). Since Paul has addressed the Corinthians as his **brothers and sisters** it follows that they had the same fathers. Paul has evidently instructed the Corinthian believers that, Gentiles as they were, they were grafted into Israel. This, indeed, was a fundamental part of Paul's understanding of the church (see Rom 11:17-24; Gal 6:16).

Accordingly, the assumption on which 1 Cor 10:1-13 rests is that Israel's story was the Corinthians' story, and he builds his argument on this basis without further justification. The particular part of their forefathers' story that Paul proceeds to interpret and apply to the Corinthian Christians was its most famous part: the Exodus from Egypt. Such transferred interpretation is known as midrash. Paul begins by depicting all the Israelites as having been **under the cloud** and **passed through the sea**. These expressions seem to be designed to denote that the Israelites were engulfed in the decisive moment of their deliverance. Whereas Exod 13:21-22 depicts the cloud as going before them, Ps 105:39 speaks of it as a "covering." Similarly, the reference to their having **passed through the sea** makes no mention of their having crossed "on dry ground" (Exod 14:16, 29; see v 21).

■ 2 The form of this deliverance is now interpreted in terms of having been **baptized into Moses in the cloud and in the sea**. Paul is not arguing that such baptism was sacramental and therefore Christian baptism is also sacramental. His argument runs in the opposite direction: that baptism **into Moses** was a partial parallel to baptism "into Christ" (see Rom 6:3; Gal 3:27), a point that will become more plain in 1 Cor 10:6, 11 where the Exodus events are described as types or "examples." Baptism **into Moses** was baptism into loyalty to and the leadership of Moses: the heart of this being the covenant community into which he was leading them (Exod 14:31; 19:4-6).

Again it is stressed that this experience was inclusive: it was shared by **all**. How much further the details of the Exodus event are to be pressed is a moot point; for example, that the cloud and the sea "correspond to Spirit and water in Christian baptism" (Hays 1997, 160). (Issues of this sort may also underlie the textual variant "baptized themselves," which would describe Jewish as opposed to Christian baptismal practice. See Garland [2003, 470].) The guiding point to be kept in mind is that the focus of Paul's argument is not how the Israelites and the Corinthians came to be the people of God but how they conducted themselves having become so.

■ **3-4** Two further elements of the Exodus experience are now invoked: the divine provision of food and drink (Exod 16:1—17:7). Two aspects of these are underlined. First, they were partaken by **all** (*pantes*)—used three times in these verses. The NIV omits the example in 1 Cor 10:4, presumably for stylistic reasons. And second, they were **spiritual** (*pneumatikon*)—used three times in vv 3-4—in character. Just as "baptized" is used in a figurative sense in v 2, **food** and **drink** are used figuratively to refer to the bread and wine of the Lord's Supper (v 16). They were spiritual not in the sense that they transmitted magical power, but in the sense that they were gifts prompted by God's grace (Exod 16:15). (For a brief survey of interpretations, see Willis 1985, 130-32.) The spiritual character of the drink is underlined by the explanation (**for** [*gar*]) that its source was **the spiritual rock that accompanied them**, which in turn is identified with Christ (1 Cor 10:4).

There is no mention in the OT of the rock that followed the Israelites. It is recorded, however, that God provided the Israelites with water from a rock both at the beginning and the end of the wilderness wanderings (Exod 17:1-7; Num 20:2-13; note also Num 21:16-18 where God is said to have provided them with water from a well). Later Jewish tradition spoke in literalistic terms of the following rock (Fee 2014, 494 nn. 468, 469), though how literally it was taken by the rabbis or by Paul is uncertain (for discussion, see Enns 1996, 23-38).

For Paul, the focal point of the illustration is that **that rock was Christ**. In the OT God is frequently spoken of as a Rock (Exod 32:4, 30-31; Pss 19:14; 78:35; 89:26; Isa 30:29; 44:8; 48:21; Hab 1:12), including terms such as Savior and Redeemer, which transferred readily to Christ. Paul is thus expressing the same view of Christ as is seen in 1 Cor 8:6: the names and functions of God are applied to Christ. "Paul is not saying that Christ is now the rock, but that in the rock he was somehow actually present in Israel" (Fee 2014, 495 n. 471). What we have here is another example of christological monotheism (→ 8:6).

It is also to be noted that Paul describes Christ as **the spiritual rock** (10:4). Garland comments: "He is not thinking of a material rock following them, or a moveable well, but of the divine source of water that journeyed with them. He understands the replenishing rock in a spiritual sense, not a physical sense" (2003, 456-57). The crucial implication of the conclusion that **that rock was Christ** is that it builds a bridge between the experience of the Israelites in the wilderness and that of the Corinthian Christians. It is on the parallel and continuity between the two that Paul's argument proceeds.

■ **5** Regarding the Israelites it is stated that **God was not pleased with most of them**—not a blanket condemnation but a careful distinction from the repeated reference to "all" in vv 1-4, which implicitly carries over to the Corinthians. The depth of God's displeasure with the Israelites is indicated by the fact that

their bodies were scattered in the wilderness. The word rendered **not pleased** (*ouk . . . eudokēsen*) denotes much more than simply mild disapproval. Used positively it denotes God's act of election, and used negatively of rejection (G. Schrenk in *TDNT* 2:740-41). This explains the severity of their fate, and by implication, the depth of the danger to the Corinthians.

■ **6** This verse becomes the explicit bridge over which the experience of the Israelites is transferred to the Corinthians. The argument is developed in two stages. First, the conduct of the Israelites is described as **examples** (*typoi*) to the Corinthians. While the form of the Greek word suggests a kind of typology, it is not intended in a futuristic sense in which what *will* happen can be inferred from what *has* happened. At the same time, the language implies a foreshadowing of the spiritual response to God's redemptive activity (→ v 11, and Ciampa and Rosner in Beale and Carson 2007, 724-25). The examples referred to in vv 1-5 are described as examples "for us" (*hēmōn* [omitted in the NIV]).

Second, the focus of the verse (as of the Israelites' response) falls on the word *epithumeō* ("desires" [NEB]; *covets*; NIV: **setting our hearts on evil things**), which occurs twice within the verse. More particularly the same term is used in Num 11:4 of the Israelites' craving for meat, having seen all they wanted to see of manna (Num 11:31-34). The thrust at the Corinthians is pointed. First, they were consumed with a hunger that amounted to covetousness, which Paul elsewhere describes as the quintessential sin (Rom 7:7-8). Second, that which the Corinthians craved was the self-same thing that the Israelites craved: meat.

■ **7-10** Paul now proceeds to cite four specific instances of sin from the wilderness wanderings, together with the judgment that they entailed. All are expressed in the form of negative warnings, introduced by the negative particle *mēde* (**and do not**). It is also significant that Paul does not deliver a blanket condemnation, but states in each case that the sin in question was committed by **some** (*tines*), not all. Presumably, this was also the case at Corinth.

The first sin Paul warns against is idolatry (1 Cor 10:7). This has been Paul's target since 8:1, 7. However, the proof text that Paul quotes (Exod 32:6 LXX) with its mention of eating, drinking, and immoral revelry—all of them components of the Corinthian problem (1 Cor 8:13; 10:20-21)—gives this first warning a comprehensive aspect. All of the items listed could be features of idol feasts.

The second sin referred to—**sexual immorality** (v 8)—picks up the mention of **revelry** in v 7. The incident in mind concerns the Israelites' worship of the Moabite god, the Baal of Peor, and their immoral behavior with Moabite women (Num 25:1-3). As 1 Cor 10:7 has suggested, the two items could readily go together. Numbers 25:4-5 records the Lord's anger and judgment, the latter taking the form of the death penalty against the offenders. Paul telescopes the account of the Israelite man and the Midianite woman (Num 25:6-8), concluding with the judgment in the form of plague in which twenty-four thousand people died (Num 25:9). Paul gives the number of the dead as **twenty-three thousand**. No conclusive solution of the divergence has been found. As probable as any is that Paul deliberately combined the three thousand of the slain in Exod 32:28 with the twenty thousand (*eikosi*) of Num 25:9. Since he has just quoted Exod 32:6 in 1 Cor 10:7 as a kind of banner headline, he could well have been linking the two episodes by this means (Garland 2003, 462-63).

The third sin cited is that of putting God to the **test** (v 9), by complaining about the lack of water and the limited menu (Num 21:4-5). The narrative context and the use of the present subjunctive of the intensive form of the verb (*ekpeirazōmen*) may mean that a continuous state of complaining is in mind (Thistleton 2000, 740-41). Just as Christ was identified as the following rock (1 Cor 10:4), he is also identified as the object of the testing by both the Israelites and the Corinthians (so NIV). (For a discussion of the textual problem, see Garland 2003, 470-71.) As with the fornicators in v 8, the judgment of God fell on the complainers: this time in the form of an infestation of snakes, resulting in many deaths (Num 21:6). (Paul makes no mention of the saving gift of the bronze snake [Num 21:7-9].)

The fourth sin Paul uses in illustration is that of grumbling (1 Cor 10:10). Paul now returns to the second-person plural (*gogguzete*), after using the hortatory subjunctive ("let us not") in vv 8 and 9. This means he is addressing the Corinthians directly. The natural inference is that they did their share of complaining. Criticism of his apostleship (see ch 9) may have been one of the stock topics of their complaining. While many OT contexts document the grumbling of the Israelites (Num 14:2-4; 16:41; 17:5, 10; Ps 106), Num 14:2 may have particular relevance in that it speaks of the Israelites grumbling against Moses and Aaron. To complain of being *victims* of deliverance shows not simply ingratitude but an inversion of moral values. As such it evoked the judgment of God: they "were destroyed by the destroyer" (KJV, NRSV). "The destroyer"—a rare term in Scripture—was God's agent of death on the night of the deliverance from Egypt (Exod 12:23 LXX). Paul understands him to have continued this mission of judgment on the complaining Israelites.

■ **11** This verse serves as a summary statement of the purpose of the examples listed in 1 Cor 10:7-10, just as v 6 did of the examples listed in vv 1-5. The language of vv 6*a* and 11*a* is closely parallel. The added note in v 11 is that the events in vv 7-10 are said to have been **written down as warnings for us**. (This clarifies the meaning of the terms *typoi* and *typikōs* in vv 6 and 11: both translated as **examples** in the NIV.) The surpassing significance of this for the Corinthians is that they are living at **the culmination** [lit. "ends"] **of the ages**. This sets everything in an eschatological perspective. The exact meaning of the clause is debated (Willis 1985, 154-55). Since Paul continues by warning his readers against the possibility of failing amid temptation (v 12), his meaning may be that to fall when God's saving revelation has reached its fullness is of the utmost seriousness since it involves a rejection of God's grace in its ultimate measure. He uses plural language elsewhere to describe the climax of salvation history (see 2 Cor 5:17). *The ends of the ages* may carry the same force.

■ 12 The note of warning now becomes explicit. The Corinthians (or at least some of them) had become famous for what they thought they knew (→ 1 Cor 8:1-3). Paul had news for those who thought their standing was firm: they should **be careful that you don't fall!** This marks the climax of 10:1-11: **So** [*hōste*], **if you think you are standing firm**. The fate of the refractory Israelites in the wilderness (vv 5, 8-10) transferred into the Corinthian context indicates that their danger was the loss of their salvation. A false sense of spiritual security arises from a superficial understanding of sin. The Corinthians should wake up to this fact.

■ 13 However, it is not as though God is hovering like a bird of prey waiting to pounce on its victim. It is rather that, when we test God (v 9) we are exposing ourselves to temptation. It is not that God tempts us to do evil (Jas 1:13-14). Testing is part of the human condition in a fallen world—something that overtakes us. In every and all temptation we can count on the faithfulness of God, who has made covenant to save his people (see Deut 7:9; 1 Cor 1:6-9). God, not Satan, holds ultimate control over good and evil and prevents temptation from inevitably being destructive (see Job 1:6-12). Temptation is not eliminated, but there is always **a way out so that you can endure it**. Thus in a section dominated by examples of people putting God to the test with disastrous results for most of them, Paul recognizes that there is another side to the story in which the people of God are tested. He reassures them that God is on their side in their temptation as is shown by the fact that not all succumbed to it.

(2) The Incompatibility of the Lord's Table and the Table of Idols (10:14-22)

The thought now advances from Israelite idolatry to Corinthian idolatry (1 Cor 10:14). Paul illustrates the latter by reference to the Lord's Supper, in which all the Corinthian believers had participated (v 16). It affirmed both their faith in Christ and their unity in Christ. The key words in vv 14-22 are "participate" (*koinonia* [4x]: vv 16 [2x], 18, 20) and "share in" (*metechō* [2x]: vv 17, 21). By participation in the body and blood of Christ they became one body or community (v 17). To participate in idol sacrifices was to give allegiance to a "no-god" who was really a demon-god (v 20). This not only breached the body but evoked the righteous anger of God who demands our exclusive allegiance (vv 21-22).

■ **14** The verse is a remarkable example of what may be called strong-armed affection. The conjunction **therefore** (*dioper*) is emphatic, carrying the sense "so then." It is followed by an equally emphatic prepositional phrase: ***take flight from*** [*apo*] ***idolatry***. This has been his message from v 1 (and, indeed, from 8:1). If God helps us in times of temptation (10:13), his help is not to be traded on. Taking risks with idol feasts is folly. At the same time, Paul has not lost his affection for his converts and addresses them as "my dear ones."

■ **15** Paul has already used the term translated **sensible** (*phronimoi*) ironically in reference to the Corinthians (see 4:10), and it is taken by some to carry that overtone here (Hays 1997, 166; Witherington 1995, 224). More probably it is to be taken at its face value, but modified by the adverb "as" (*hōs* [omitted by the NIV]): ***I am speaking to you as to sensible people***. He is appealing to them to use their better judgment.

Paul now proceeds to compare sacred meals of three different belief systems, all of which have at their core the same central element: communal participation (*koinōnia*) or sharing (*metechō*). These have both a vertical and a horizontal aspect, involving both God (or the god) and one's fellow worshippers.

■ **16-17** The Lord's Supper. Paul begins with the Lord's Supper because it is the meal in which all the Corinthian believers have taken part, and that exhibits best the point he is making. In reversal of the order of the rite, he mentions the cup first (→ 11:23-26) probably because he wishes to lay emphasis on the significance of the bread. "The cup of blessing" (10:16 NRSV) was a Jewish technical term for the cup of wine for which a blessing (i.e., thanksgiving) was given to God. It was used in reference to the cup of wine drunk at the end of a meal and, in the Passover meal, of the third of the four that had to be drunk (→ 11:25). To indicate that he is referring to the cup of the Lord's Table, Paul adds the words **for which we give thanks** (10:16). (It has nothing to do with blessing the cup, which was alien to Jewish practice. See I. Howard Marshall 1980, 119-20.) To partake of the cup is to participate in the covenant sealed by the blood of Christ—in Charles Wesley's words to "gain an interest in the Savior's blood."

To partake of the broken bread is likewise to participate in the body of Christ broken for our redemption. But whereas partaking of the cup may be said to express primarily communion with God, partaking of the bread carries the further overtone of expressing communion with one's fellow participants. This is because the expression **the body of Christ** has a wider sphere of reference. The **one loaf** (v 17), of which we all partake, constitutes the many partakers as **one body**—namely, **the body of Christ** (v 16). "The Lord's Supper is rooted in the concept of the community as a body (I Cor 10:16-17). What stands in the center is not the elements of bread and wine as such, but the reality of fellowship in the body of Christ" (*NIDNTTE* 4:441). The emphatic use of the word **all** (*pantes* [v 17]) shows which way Paul's mind is going. Any action that threatens the unity of the body contradicts the intent of the Lord's Supper and the reality that it expresses: fellowship with fellow believers and fellowship with God.

■ **18** Jewish sacrificial meals. Paul advances his argument that participation in a sacrificial meal means partaking of the reality that it embodies by reference to OT sacrifices. The priests had the right to eat portions of the sacrifices that they had offered (Lev 10:12-15). The same right was accorded to nonpriestly worshippers (Deut 14:22-29; 1 Sam 9:10-24). The implied meaning is that to partake of the altar was to enter into fellowship with God. This brings Paul to the threshold of the destination he has been moving toward from the start. (It is pressing the language too far to take the Greek underlying **the people of Israel** literally, "Israel according to the flesh" [*ton Israel kata sarka*] in the sense of the life in sin as in Rom 8:3-8 as agreed by Garland [2003, 478-79]. More probably Paul is simply referring to "the earthly Israel, still observing the Levitical ritual" [Bruce 1976, 95].)

■ **19** Meals at the table of a pagan god have been Paul's target from as far back as 8:1, 4-6, 9-10. He now addresses them directly. Paul resumes the warning of 8:7 that the weak will be damaged by the eating within the temple premises of meat sacrificed to idols (*eidōlothuton*—a rare Greek word, possibly a Pauline coinage [Witherington 1993, 239]). Since, however, he conceded there that pagan sacrificial offerings were nothing because the gods to whom they were offered were no-gods (8:4-6) his argument is in danger of total collapse.

■ **20** Paul avoids this collapse of his case by recourse to a parallel line of interpretation: ***Rather, (what I am saying is) that the things they sacrifice they sacrifice to demons and not to God***. This is a virtual quotation of Deut 32:17 (LXX). For Paul demons "were probably not personal beings but impersonal forces which exerted a powerful influence over unregenerate men" (Bruce 1976, 96). They may not have had objective reality, but they had subjective reality for those who believed in them. To treat them as having reality was the first step toward falling under their sway. That was a kind of *koinōnia* or fellowship that Paul wanted the Corinthians to avoid.

■ **21** This is spelled out in terms of the two elements of the Lord's Supper of which he has just spoken: the cup and the bread. (The latter is indicated by the use of the verb "share" in v 17 or **have a part in** [*metechein*] in v 21.) It is impossible logically and spiritually to participate in both the cup and table of the Lord, and the cup and table of demons. The wine of the Lord's Supper speaks of the blood of the covenant; the bread, of the body of Christ. Together, they exclude any other religious loyalty.

■ **22** The issue confronting the Corinthians is not a matter of taste or individual preference. They face stark alternatives, highlighted by the simple adverb "or" ($ē$) (omitted in the NIV, which also takes the verb conatively: **Are we trying to arouse the Lord's jealousy?**). In the biblical tradition the Lord's jealousy is repeatedly associated with idol worship (Exod 20:5; 34:14; Deut 5:9; Ezek 8:3; etc.). There may be a particular reflection of Deut 32:21 (LXX) where the language of jealousy is found and where there is also emphasis on the strength of the Lord and the weakness of Israel (vv 36-38). A sideswipe at the "strong" in Corinth may well be implied. Do they imagine they are stronger than God? These questions bring to a conclusion the argument already begun in 1 Cor 8:1 and taken up again in 10:1.

b. The Touchstones of Freedom: The Good of One's Neighbor and the Glory of God (10:23—11:1)

The difficulties of this passage have often been noted (see Fee 2014, 525-28). It seems clearly to bring to a conclusion the discussion of idol meat begun in 8:1. At the same time there is a marked difference not merely in tone but in substance between the earlier and later treatments. In 8:12-13 and as recently as 10:20-22 Paul flatly forbids participation in pagan meals, yet in vv 25-27 he permits it and in vv 29b-30 forcefully defends his right to do so. Part of the explanation lies in the fact that in vv 25-28 he is dealing with meat purchased in the marketplace (v 25) and eaten in a home rather than in a temple (v 27). But part of it also arises from applying the principle of freedom (which he strongly affirms [see vv 29b-30]) in a context in which it might damage believers who were less mature and more vulnerable. It was a tension between "absolutes and nonessentials" (Fee 2014, 526) or absolutes and gray areas: "a moral halfway house" (Wright 2004, 136). In such circumstances Paul's assertion of his own rights must give way to the dangers that it created for the weak (8:9-13; 10:24, 28, 32-33).

■ **23-24** The thought of these verses echoes that of ch 8, suggesting that the argument begun there is now reaching its conclusion. The claim to possessing "rights" may be true, but the exercising of them does not always lead to the upbuilding of others in the faith (8:9; 10:23). The guiding principle is therefore that nothing should be done—one's rights notwithstanding—that would militate against the good of others (8:13; 10:24).

■ **25-26** The first concrete situation to which these principles are applied is that of eating meat bought in the meat market. The underlying assumption is that meat sold in the meat market (*en makellō*) could have been offered in sacrifice in an idol temple. Hence, Paul's directive that the believer should eat it **without raising questions of conscience** (v 25). This stands in a degree of tension with his earlier declarations and prohibitions against eating meat sacrificed to idols (8:10, 13; 10:20-21).

The commentators have struggled with this. Fee speaks of "some difficult jumps in the logic of the argument" (2014, 527) and finds the solution in the alternation between the two concerns of the good of others (vv 23-24, 28-29*a*, 31-33) and personal freedom (vv 25-27, 29*b*-30). Collins argues that Paul, as before, "interrupts the flow of his more theoretical discourse so as to address a variety of real situations that the Corinthians might face" (1999, 383). Garland sees a move "from an absolute prohibition based on general arguments . . . to conditional liberty" (2003, 486). Earlier, Willis found an expansion from specific cases to broader issues, making the section look uneven (1985, 223-24, 262-63).

It is possible that Paul is taking into account the changed sociohistorical situation (noted in the introduction to 8:1—11:1) in Corinth since his departure. If kosher food was no longer available, were Christians to avoid meat altogether in view of the strong possibility that it had been sacrificed to idols? His reply was an emphatic *no*. They were not to look for trouble. This shows how emancipated Paul was from the food obligations of Judaism and the Jerusalem decree (Bruce 1976, 98). The basis on which he grounds his position is Ps 24:1—the biblical basis for the rabbinic command of blessing meals. But Paul is going further than the rabbis, since they investigated the purity of the food before eating. (The tractate *Hullin* in the Mishnah is devoted to regulations for "Animals killed for food" [Danby 1938, 513-29].) Paul takes the passage to mean that everything created by God is good (see 1 Tim 4:4). Paul's argument in these verses has the interesting consequence of aligning him in principle with the strong as depicted in 1 Cor 8:1-4, 8.

■ **27-29*a*** The second concrete situation to which the principles of vv 24-25 are applied is that of eating as a guest in the home of an unbeliever. It is assumed that such invitations might be received and that believers might want to accept them. Social isolationism was not envisaged as a Christian virtue. (The verbs and pronouns in v 27 are plural.) Following from this the believer was not to look for occasions of offense and so should eat whatever was served, asking no questions. The situation was changed, however, if someone else disclosed information about the origin of the meat. The identity of the informant is not clear. It is unlikely to have been the pagan host, who would presumably have considered the matter of no consequence. A fellow believer would probably have determined that the culinary coast would be clear before accepting the invitation. The most probable candidate is a pagan fellow guest concerned to spare embarrassment to a Christian believer. The term in v 28 translated **offered in sacrifice** (*hierothuton*) would be more naturally used by a pagan than "sacrificed to an idol" (*eidōlothuton* [v 19]).

In such a mixed setting it would be preferable for a believer to avoid sending signals that might be regarded as approval of idol worship. This is confirmed by the explanation that the abstinence would be **for the sake of conscience** (v 28). Here, as in 8:7, 10-12 and 10:25, **conscience** denotes not moral arbitration (as in "a good or bad conscience") but moral awareness or judgment: the ability to distinguish right from wrong. Hence the explanation that the abstinence would be for **the other person's conscience**, not yours (v 29a).

■ **29b-30** The crucial problem here is determining who is protesting about the limiting of their freedom. There is an apparent contradiction between the regard for "the other person's conscience" in v 29a and the protest against being **judged by another's conscience** in v 29b. It is probable that in thought v 29b follows v 27. In that case Paul is the protestor. Verse 30 confirms this, resuming the thought of v 26 that every created thing is the Lord's, and when received with thanksgiving is fit for food. The rhetorical tone of vv 29b-30 suggests that Paul is responding to sniping comments on his own behavior. This further reinforces the conclusion that Paul accepted the view of the strong—but with the significant addition that he would not follow his view in practice if it constituted a snare for the weak.

■ **31—11:1** These verses sum up Paul's counsel regarding the whole question of food offered to idols discussed in 8:1—10:30. A blanket statement of options (**whether you eat or drink or whatever you do** [v 31]) is governed by a blanket principle (**do it all for the glory of God**). But acting for the glory of God means taking into account the needs of others (including the weak). The idea of living for the glory of God has already appeared in 6:20 and is frequent in other Pauline writings. Of particular significance are Rom 15:6-7 and Phil 2:11, both of which stand in contexts concerned with caring for the good of others (Rom 15:1-5; Phil 2:1-4). Romans 14 is concerned specifically with the scruples of others about diet. (For a comprehensive treatment, see Willis 1985, 250-57.)

Eating is listed first in 1 Cor 10:31 presumably as the prime problem under consideration, but the list rapidly expands to include everything: Jews, Greeks, the church of God. Offense against the church has already been censured in 3:16-17. In many respects 10:32 is a summary of 9:19-23. Paul reinforces his directive to the Corinthians by citing his own example. The NIV renders this as: **I try to please everyone in every way** (10:33). Quite apart from the feasibility of such a strategy, it does not sit comfortably with Paul's declaration a few verses earlier of his freedom in regard to eating meat (vv 25-27, 29b-30). Thiselton's paraphrase captures Paul's meaning better: "I on my part strive to take account of all the interests of everyone" (2000b, 795). The remainder of the verse confirms this with the declaration that he is seeking not his own good but that of others: specifically, **that they may be saved**.

The note sounded throughout the section is expressed at the end with forceful simplicity: idolatry or salvation. This section is clearly concluded (despite its being placed in a new chapter) by **Follow my example** (11:1), which suggests that Paul's pattern of living is in mind. The reference would then be to his adoption of the crucified lifestyle, subordinating his personal interests to those whose salvation he seeks. This seems clearly to be in mind. However, the same language appears in 4:16, where it is expounded in terms of following the teaching (lit. "ways" [*hodoi*]) that he gives in the whole church. It would seem to be a mistake, therefore, to separate the two by selecting one over the other. Paul imitates Christ by both teaching the message of the cross and living the crucified life.

FROM THE TEXT

In many respects the notes sounded in 10:1—11:1 are those that recur throughout the whole section (8:1—11:1). At the same time, there is a dimension of application not found in chs 8—9. Several points come into particular focus.

The reality of the power of evil. The examples drawn from Israel's history are cited "to keep us from setting our hearts on evil things" (10:6). The specific form of evil that Paul emphasizes is idolatry (v 14) because it is the ultimate means of dethroning God from his solitary supremacy in the universe. The biblical faith is radically monotheistic, and anything that detracts from the divine supremacy—whether it be collusion with horoscopes, St. Christopher's, or any other superstitious impedimenta—opens the door to the power of evil (v 20).

The need for spiritual self-discipline. There are two sides to this. The first is that the danger of falling is a hard fact. Paul has already recognized it as a possibility for himself (9:27). He now affirms it as a possibility for the Corinthian believers (10:12). The other side to it is the supporting grace of God (v 13). God, not the devil, has the last word in the strength of temptation, and overcoming it is always possible. There is always "a way out" (v 13).

You become one with what you worship. Participation or sharing in the object of worship is both the presupposition and consequence of worship. To partake of the cup and the bread of the Lord's Table are acts of participation (v 16), demonstrating that we are part of the one body of Christ. Hence to partake of "the cup of the Lord and the cup of demons" is not merely a contradiction but an impossibility (v 21). It is an either/or.

The right use of freedom and the responsibilities of privilege. The question concerns whether the use of good things can become a bad thing: specifically, whether the use of God's good creation should be foresworn because it could become a snare for others (vv 25-26). Paul affirmed the principle of freedom but curbed it in practice, the touchstone being not narrow-mindedness but the danger posed to the faith of weak believers.

The believer as an example to others. Paul's readiness in pointing to himself as an example to be copied is striking. As noted in the exegesis, it is to be understood as following his teaching as well as his mode of life. It stands in contrast to the "Don't do as I do—do as I say" advice that one often hears. Paul did not hesitate to confess his faults (15:9). At the same time he expected the marks of the likeness of Christ to be visible in himself (11:1; Gal 6:17; Phil 3:17). Indeed, his example was to be followed because he himself followed the example of Christ.

The overarching principle in regard to all others is to be that of love. This applies to unbelievers (1 Cor 10:27), those of any state or condition whose salvation might be in doubt (vv 28-29a), those of varying ethical traditions as well as those within the church (vv 32-33). There can only be one guideline for those who follow the crucified Christ: the guideline of self-giving love.

V. THE GOSPEL AND PROPRIETY IN CHRISTIAN WORSHIP: I CORINTHIANS 11:2—14:40

Overview

These chapters appear to be held together by the common thread of propriety in Christian worship. Formally ch 11 lacks the standard introductory expression "now about" (*peri de*) found last at 8:1 and next at 12:1. As we have seen, this introduces issues that the Corinthians had raised with Paul (see 7:1). Its absence at 11:2 may indicate that Paul is raising issues with the Corinthians that had been reported to him other than in their letter. The use of the verb "I praise" (*epainō*) at 11:2, 17 is consistent with this. At the same time, the topic of orderliness in worship, which dominates ch 11, emerges also in chs 12 and 14. The note of rebuke in 14:36 picks up that of 11:16, while 14:40 serves as a succinct summary of the emphasis of chs 11—14.

A. Covering the Head in Worship (11:2-16)

BEHIND THE TEXT

Few biblical passages have given rise to more competing interpretations than this. It has been taken to teach the subordination of women to men and on the other hand the equality of male and female. Again, it has been taken to deal with head coverings on the one hand or hairstyles on the other. Or again, it has been held to base its argument on either theological principle (the order of creation) or prevailing social custom. For a brief survey, see Gorman 2017, 315-18. A fuller introduction may be found in Fee 2014, 542-50. It may serve to clear the ground to set down facts or factors that lie on the surface of the text and may provide a framework within which the details of interpretation may be sought. A further guideline may be found in the sociohistorical situation in which the problem arose.

Data on the surface of the text. It is assumed that women and men alike have the right to participate publicly in Christian worship (11:4-5). The point at issue is the appropriate headgear to be worn or not worn and why female headgear differs from male (vv 4-7). The matter was important as involving questions of honor and shame. See the language of shame (*aischron* [vv 4, 5, 6]; *atimia* [v 14]; NIV: "disgrace") and honor (*doxa* [vv 7, 15]). Hence, the good name of the church was at stake (vv 13, 14). In addition to damaging the image of the church in the eyes of outsiders, the differences regarding headgear were a source of conflict and contention within the church (v 16). It would appear that this much must be conceded, even if the specifics behind these data are contested. (The details will be treated below.)

The sociohistorical background. However theological Paul's argument may be (see below), it is directed to a particular historical situation. The sociohistorical question is: why would head presentation be an occasion of dispute in first-century Corinth? The language of v 16*b* implies that it was an issue throughout the Roman world. The Romans were fastidious when it came to matters of dress since dress was taken to indicate status. The evidence is clear that anyone offering sacrifice to the gods—whether male or female, up to and including the emperor—could do so only with covered head. By this was meant an article of clothing. The toga pulled up over the ears served the purpose, though a covering of the crown of the head is also attested (Oster 1988, 493-502). A further factor in the situation is that it was taken for granted in the Corinthian culture that no respectable woman would appear in public without a head covering (Conzelmann 1975, 185).

The problem Paul was addressing. Apparently some Corinthian Christians were conducting themselves in worship in ways that conflicted with Pauline teaching. Men (assuming that they were part of the problem) were engaging in worship in ways that owed more to paganism than to Christ, covering their heads as Roman practice dictated (Gill 1993, 331-32). Women, on the other hand, were leading worship with uncovered heads, which conflicted not only with Roman practice but with Corinthian culture. Their exact reasons for doing so are not made clear and can only be inferred. It may be that they had concluded that with the coming of Christ the distinctions between the sexes no longer held (2 Cor 5:17; Gal 3:28). Paul's task was to affirm the theological truths of the reality of the change that the coming of Christ had brought while holding to the reality of the order of creation in which man and woman were created as distinct beings (1 Cor 11:7-9, 12). Both realities were preserved in worship by the differing head décor of male and female (vv 4-5). Observance of both also had the effect of avoiding confusion and conflict with contemporary cultural understandings (vv 5*b*-6) as well as with the practice of the universal church (v 16).

It appears, therefore, that Paul's purpose was to formulate a theological argument that, while affirming the right of women to exercise a leadership role in corporate worship, provided guidelines about the appropriate headgear to be worn by men and women in the prevailing culture.

IN THE TEXT

■ **2** Paul begins with a word of praise for the Corinthians. The statement that they remember him **in everything** is probably elaborated in the second clause: they are **holding to the traditions just as I passed them on to you**. To remember Paul was to remember what he had taught. The language of "passing on the traditions" (*paredōka . . . tas paradoseis*) is technical language for the transmission of Christian teaching regarding salvation, ethics, and worship (see 11:23; 15:1-3; 2 Thess 2:15; and *TDNT* 2:172). As before, Paul brought everything to the touchstone of the gospel. Typically, Paul begins by commending his readers even if, or especially if, other features were present that were not particularly commendable.

■ **3** He now sets down the matter in which their understanding was defective (the language is emphatic). This was the idea of headship and (as the later verses will make clear) its implications for the conduct of worship. The pivotal term is **head** (*kephalē*). Its precise import here has been strongly debated. This is partly because it has a wide field of meaning (*TDNT* 3:673-76), as is also the case in English. At least three interpretations of it in this verse have been advanced:

(1) It has been taken to denote the authority of a superior. This has been the traditional understanding. The covered head of the woman in worship as opposed to the uncovered head of the man indicates her subordinate status. However, it has been questioned whether the term **head** denotes "authority over" (Thiselton 2000b, 815-16). It is also questionable whether the idea of subordination rather than empowerment is the controlling thought in the ensuing verses (see v 10).

(2) A second view takes **head** to mean "source." Woman was made from man (Gen 2:18-23; 1 Cor 11:12), and thereby holds a derivative status that must be acknowledged in worship. However, the use of **head** to mean "source" is difficult (some would say impossible: Perriman 1994, 612-14) to document elsewhere and does not lead naturally to Paul's statements in vv 11-12.

(3) A third view takes **head** to denote that which is foremost or prominent, like the physical head (to which Paul will immediately refer in v 4). As such it denotes the place of order in the scheme of things (as in the English expression that he or she "stood at the head of the line" [Garland 2003, 514-16]). The point is made particularly forcefully by the christological reference: Christ is both a head and has a head—God. That is to say, the holding of a head position does not exclude but rather requires respect for the position of others. Accordingly, the thrust of v 3 is that there is an orderliness in God's creation. This prepares the way for the argument of the rest of the passage that there must also be an orderliness in God's church, specifically in its worship. Verse 3 constitutes the premise on which the rest of the argument is constructed.

■ **4** The specific problem in the Corinthian church is now addressed: respect for the order of things in worship. This took the form of the wearing of appropriate headgear. He begins with men, not merely to balance out the argument, but presumably because at least some men were following the Roman custom of covering their head while praying or prophesying. Verse 4 reads as though it is a statement of fact, not merely hypothetical (v 5 reads the same way). Prophesying was probably not ecstatic utterance, but the exposition and application of Christian truth.

The wearing of a head covering would have had a multiple effect. Socially, their dress would have stressed their superior status; religiously, it would not only have imported pagan practices into the church but also have brought shame upon Christ, their head. The word **head** is thus being used in a double sense. To have their physical head covered by material headgear (lit. "having down the head" [*kata kephalēs echōn*]) implied that the head was shameful and could not be shown openly in the presence of God. By that selfsame act it also repudiated the God-given dignity bestowed on man as God's creation (see v 7a).

■ **5-6** The right of women to engage in worship in prayer or prophesying is assumed. What is disallowed is their doing so bareheaded. This would bring a double dishonor: first upon man, woman's head as standing before her in the order of creation (see v 8); and second upon her physical head by uncovered exposure in a society where this was the mark of the whore or libertine. Cropped hair or shaved head told their own story in that culture.

■ **7-16** Paul now seeks to validate the position he has defined by three main arguments. In vv 7-12 he appeals to creation as known in Scripture but as interpreted from a Christian perspective. In vv 13-15 he appeals to their own sense of what is proper and appropriate based on the nature of things. In v 16 his final source of authority is his own practice and that of the churches.

■ **7-12** First Paul grounds his ruling in creation. He advances three considerations (introduced by **for** [*gar*]) in support of the ruling he has just laid down in vv 4-6. The first is the argument from **glory** (*doxa* [v 7]). The creation narrative is in the background. As created in the image of God (Gen 1:27) man is the glory of God—the expression of God's likeness. This is not to be concealed by any kind of covering. The second consideration is that woman, on the other hand, in consequence of having been created from man (Gen 2:22), is the glory of man (1 Cor 11:8). Man's glory is not to be displayed in worship in the presence of God, therefore women should cover their heads. The third consideration is that woman was created as a support and help for man (v 9; see Gen 2:19-22) without whom man would be incomplete (Gen 2:23-24). In yet another aspect, therefore, she constitutes man's glory, and so is to cover her head in the presence of God.

First Corinthians 11:10-12 both expands and explains the meaning of the preceding verses. A further reason for women to cover their heads is given in v 10. There is much uncertainty as to its import. At best only a probable interpretation is possible. The problematic phrase is **authority over** [on] **her own head** (*exousian echein epi tēs kephalēs*). There seem to be two major options (among many suggested).

> (1) The woman acknowledges her place in the line of creation and shows her authority over her head by covering it. This is the understanding reflected in the NIV. It is the most natural meaning of the Greek phrase. If the introductory expression **it is for this reason** (*dia touto*) refers back to vv 7-9, then this interpretation follows well from the emphasis of those verses on the role of woman as being created later than man and as his helper.

(2) The phrase may be taken to mean that the head covering was itself the authorization of women's right to public involvement in worship—that is, the sign of her authority to do so. This is the sense of the NIV margin. However, this is an unusual (and unprecedented) use of the word **authority**, though it is arguable that it is a Pauline coinage, struck to meet the Corinthian situation. Whichever interpretation be preferred, the result is the same: women were enabled or empowered to exercise an active role in worship by wearing a head covering.

No less problematic is the final phrase: **because of the angels** (*dia tous angelous*). The introductory words **for this reason** may point forward as well as back, and probably do both here. Angels appear elsewhere in the epistle (4:9; 6:3; 13:1). Their presence in worship is taken for granted. In Judaism they were regarded as guardians of the created order (*2 En.* 19:1-5). If this is the background, then the freedom of women to participate in worship was accompanied by the recognition that the created order was not overthrown. The wearing of a head covering by women was thus a two-sided phenomenon: it bespoke both the emancipation of women in worship and a recognition that the old order had not passed away completely.

A qualification is now inserted: **nevertheless** (*plēn* [1 Cor 11:11]). What Paul has just said in vv 7-10 regarding the woman's creation from and therefore after the man does not imply that she is inferior or subordinate. "Neither (is) woman (anything) apart from man, nor man from woman" (BDAG 1095). The setting in which this is so is **in the Lord** (*en kuriō*): an expression denoting the sphere of their existence in the new age (→ 7:22, 39; 9:1, 2). The point is reinforced in 11:12a, which is a reversal of v 8. At creation woman came from man's side; ever since, man (and woman) have been woman-born. All of this is God's doing. That is, on Christian terms there is a fundamental equality between men and women.

■ **13-15** The exposition now advances beyond the argument from creation to an argument from nature or what is **proper** (v 13). Paul appeals to their own sense of what is fitting. Social convention of the day indicated that it was improper for a woman to pray publicly with her head uncovered. By the same token (i.e., according to what society thought was natural), long hair was a disgrace to a man but a glory to a woman, because her hair was given to her as a covering. (It is a mistake on the basis of this verse to assume that hair is the head covering referred to earlier in the passage.) The use of the terms **disgrace** (*atimia* [v 14]) and **glory** (*doxa* [v 15]) shows that what is natural (*phusis* [v 14]) is measured in terms reflecting an honor-and-shame culture typical of the first-century Mediterranean world.

■ **16** Paul's third argument in support of his ruling in vv 4-5a is his own **practice** and that of the **churches** elsewhere (v 16). The underlying assumption is that the Corinthians he was addressing might not have found his first two arguments convincing. In this he sees Corinthian factionalism and contentiousness. His reply to this is his own practice (assuming that **we** means "I" and is not a reference to his fellow apostles) and that of the churches elsewhere. Apparently the Corinthian believers were famous for doing things their own way. Paul will have occasion to call them to account later on the same score even more sharply (→ 14:36-37).

FROM THE TEXT

The principles underlying these verses are as important as the specific applications.

The openness to women of ministry in worship. It is striking that this issue—which may well have been the most visible, even if not the only, form of the problem in Corinth—is never once questioned. It is accepted, and even assumed, by Paul that women are as free as men to exercise an active role in worship. This is evidently based on the belief in the fundamental equality of the sexes. Any suggestion to the contrary in 11:7-9 is removed in vv 10-12. It has already been anticipated in 7:3.

The cultural conditioning of Paul's teaching on dress in worship. The wearing or nonwearing of headgear in worship could only have become a problem in a culture where such forms had meaning. Paul was prepared to bow to cultural norms where ignoring them would lead to misunderstanding (vv 5-6). However, he was also prepared to ignore them (as in the case of head coverings for men) where they conflicted with Christian understandings (v 4).

There is a place for the mind of the church at large (v 16). In an age when large (and sometimes less than large) congregations assume an individualistic identity, it is salutary to remember that the church is the church everywhere. Where local individualisms obscure the relation to the body of Christ as a whole, the question arises as to their true identity. Of course this is a vastly more difficult issue today than it was in Paul's day, given the fragmented state of Christendom. Even so, the question is still worth asking.

B. Conduct at the Lord's Supper: Worship That Makes Things Worse (11:17-34)

BEHIND THE TEXT

The problem addressed is unintelligible apart from two realities: (*a*) the place of cultic meals in pagan worship; and (*b*) the fact that the Lord's Supper in the NT church, like the Last Supper before it, was eaten in conjunction with such a meal. The words "after supper he took the cup" (v 25) seem clearly to indicate this. It was the conjunction of these two realities that made the problem possible.

The problem arose from sociological differences within the Christian community. Even in pagan settings, where groups meeting for social and religious meals were socially homogeneous, it was not uncommon to hear complaints of discrimination at the inferior quality of the food served to less favored members. The problem would be accentuated where—as in Corinth—there was a considerable social divide. A further factor may have been the holding of such events in a wealthy house whose design may have consisted of an inner room for the host and his intimates and an outer room for more distant acquaintances. Yet another factor may have been the working conditions of poorer members, which caused them to arrive later than wealthier members. Taken together these factors help to explain the existence of a divide between the haves and the have-nots (vv 20-22).

IN THE TEXT

While Paul is dealing with a problem rooted in sociological differences, he does not address it in sociological or even ethical terms, such as the evil of inequality. His response is framed in theological categories. Thus the humiliation of the have-nots is, indeed, just that. But it is more than that. It is an attitude showing contempt for the church of God (v 22). Similarly, partaking of the Lord's Supper while at the same time facilitating social divisions is an offense against the body of Christ (v 7).

The passage is distinguished by a strength of language and expression that bespeaks the depth of Paul's concern. His refusal to use the language of praise is repeated and emphatic (vv 17, 22). His characterization of the situation in terms of sharp contrast: "more harm than good" (v 17); "the Lord's Supper . . . your own private suppers" (vv 20-21); his multiple use of the language of judgment (vv 29, 31, 32); the use of irony in accepting the necessity of divisions (v 19)—these underscore the urgency and seriousness of Paul's concern.

The unit as a whole is held together by the verb "you come together" (*sunerchēsthe*) in vv 17-34 (the NIV translates it here as "your meetings"). Within the unit, vv 17-22 (held together by the verb "praise") describe the problem; vv 23-26 recount the institution of the Lord's Supper and its significance; vv 27-32 spell out the consequences of observing the Lord's Supper in an unfitting way; and vv 33-34 give Paul's summarizing directions for correcting the Corinthians' missteps.

■ **17** Paul's focus in vv 17-22 is on their conduct when they meet together for worship. The verb meaning "meet together" (*sunerchomai*) is used three times (vv 17, 18, 20). In contrast with v 2, in v 17 Paul flatly refuses to praise them. Their gatherings rather receive a blanket condemnation. What purported to be Christian worship was no such thing. If anything, it was anti-Christian—surely a serious charge.

■ **18** The first aspect of this was that when they came together as a church they were not together! They were divided into different cliques. Paul has learned this, not from their letter (→ 7:1), but by report perhaps from members of Chloe's household (→ 1:10). Paul adds that he is inclined to believe this: a statement that probably has a tinge of irony.

■ **19** Paul, who deplores divisions, appears now to reverse himself and find a useful and even necessary purpose for them: they show who the truly trustworthy people are. The ironical tone may thus continue. However, there may also be an allusion to the final judgment in which tribulation and persecution sort out the genuine from the rest (see Mark 4:14-20; 13:9-13).

■ **20-21** The heart of the problem is now named specifically: when they gather together to eat the Lord's Supper it is not the Lord's Supper that they eat at all. What makes this so is that each goes ahead and eats their own supper. This is all very well for those—the wealthy—who have a supper to eat. For those who do not—the poor—it is hard luck. The one goes hungry and another gets drunk. So the sacrament that fundamentally denotes unity—a common table and a common Lord—is degraded into an instrument of division.

■ **22** Paul now demolishes their practice with a series of rhetorical questions (implying that they should have had the wit to know what he was saying without having to be told). If satisfying their appetites was their prime concern, they could—and should—do that at home. To do so in a church gathering was to despise the church of God and humiliate the have-nots. What do they expect Paul to say? Do they expect him to praise them? In no way will he praise them for this.

■ **23** Paul now sets down the tradition of the institution of the Lord's Supper as indicating the pattern to be followed. Paul rarely quotes the words of Jesus in his letters, but it is clear that the tradition about Jesus was well-known in the Corinthian church (see 2:2). The Last Supper (which was the prototype of the Lord's Supper) was a Passover meal reinterpreted by Jesus in terms of his own life and mission.

The language **I received** (*parelabon*) and **passed on** (*paredideto*) is the standard terminology for the transmission of tradition. The ultimate source of that tradition was **the Lord**. The tradition was rooted in a specific historical situation: **on the night he was betrayed** (*paredideto*).

The Greek term may carry a further overtone: it is used in Rom 4:25 and 8:32 of Jesus' being "handed over" by God for our trespasses, which in turn may reflect Isa 53:12 (LXX).

■ **24** At some point in the meal (see Mark 14:22; Matt 26:26; Luke 22:19) Jesus "took a loaf of bread" (1 Cor 11:23 NRSV), gave **thanks** for it and **broke it**. Two interpretative statements followed. First, whereas the unleavened bread of the Passover represented and reminded them of the haste in which their forefathers left Egypt (Deut 16:3), Jesus reinterpreted it as his body broken for them. Second, he commanded them to keep doing this in remembrance of himself, rather than of the deliverance from Egypt, as the Passover ritual decreed (Exod 12:14; Deut 16:1).

■ **25** The Passover meal was followed (and concluded) by the drinking of several cups. One of these Jesus reinterpreted as his blood sealing the new covenant (Jer 31:31-34) just as the blood of the sacrificed animals sealed the old covenant (Exod 24:3-8). The command to **do this . . . in remembrance** of himself **whenever you drink it** is repeated (1 Cor 11:25). For Paul's understanding of the meaning of Christ's sacrificial blood, see Rom 3:25; Eph 1:7; Col 1:20.

■ **26** The text now passes from the tradition "from the Lord" (1 Cor 11:23) to Paul's interpretative comment (as the phrase **the Lord's death** makes clear). The heart of this is that whenever the Lord's Supper is observed the Lord's death is proclaimed. The action is also a proclamation, a "visible word." The word and the sacrament are inseparable. A final note in Paul's interpretation is that the proclamation of the Lord's death is a feature of the interim: **until he comes**. Remembrance and proclamation are the aspects underlined: the first in the imperative, the second in the indicative. But taken together they still speak only of the absence of the Lord. The eschatological note transforms what would otherwise be a memorial act into an act of anticipation.

■ **27** The thought now returns to the theme of the caricature of the Lord's Supper as practiced in Corinth (vv 17-22). Here, however, it is viewed through the lens of the Last Supper.

It is possible to eat the bread and drink the cup **in an unworthy manner**. The context makes clear that this is precisely what the Corinthians had been doing. Their conduct contradicted the meaning of Christ's death as being for others. As such it constituted a sin against the body and blood of Christ by nullifying the message of the Supper as a proclamation of the Lord's death (v 26). In so doing they were placing themselves on the side of those who were guilty of his death.

■ **28-29** The cure for eating and drinking "in an unworthy manner" (v 27) is self-examination. The verb **examine** (*dokimazeto* [v 28]) is from the same root as "genuine" (*dokimoi*) in v 19 (NRSV). To eat and drink without self-examination is to eat and drink without recognizing the true meaning of **the body of Christ** (v 29). Consequently, the supper becomes an instrument of judgment—a note that will control the remaining verses of the chapter. It is argued by some interpreters that **the body of Christ** includes the church (Bruce 1976, 115; Fee 2014, 622-24). There can be no doubt that this is the practical implication of Paul's words. However, the primary reference is to **the body of Christ** understood as his body and blood (as in v 27). (The NIV gives a true interpretation, even though **of Christ** has no equivalent in the Greek text.) The **judgment** (*krima*) referred to is not the final judgment but the present penalty, as vv 30-32 make clear.

■ **30** The form taken by the penalty is weakness, sickness, and falling **asleep**—a metaphor for death. An impressive case can be made for understanding these in a spiritual sense (see Ramelli 2011). At the same time there are indications that Paul saw a connection between some physical debilities and the judgment of God (see 5:5). Uncontrolled indulgence in food and drink could well have had such consequences. **Many** were affected.

■ **31** There is a play on words meaning **judgment** (*krima*) and "judge" or "discern" (*diakrinō*) and their cognates in vv 29-34, which can only be partially reproduced in English (see the NIV; compare the NRSV: "But if we judged ourselves, we would not be judged"). The theme of self-examination is picked up from v 28. Self-judgment is the way to avoid judgment.

■ **32 Nevertheless**, the judgment in question is not the final judgment. It is rather the judgment of discipline such as is meted out to children, and its very purpose is to avoid being condemned with the world.

■ **33** Paul summarizes the main instructions he has given (vv 33-34). These relate to the times when they meet together (*sunerchomai*) as in v 17. Paul has used blunt language earlier (vv 17-22). Now he addresses them as **my brothers and sisters**, indicating his underlying affection. His directive to them is that when they gather to eat they should wait for each other (hence the NIV's **you should all eat together**) or receive each other (the Greek verb *ekdechomai* is ambiguous).

■ **34** Those for whom satisfying hunger rather than sharing fellowship was the primary concern should eat at home. In this way falling under judgment will be avoided (→ v 29). Evidently there were other matters that needed to be put in order, but these could await Paul's next visit.

FROM THE TEXT

The Lord's Supper focuses the church's memory on the death of Jesus. The Christ whom the church remembers in its central sacrament is the Christ of the cross. At the same time there is a double personal focus: "for you . . .

in remembrance of me" (11:24). The Christ whom Jesus wished his church to remember was the Christ who gave himself for them.

The Lord's Table expresses the community's unity as the new covenant people of God (v 25). As such it is never a purely individual event: it can never be a self-service event for one. It is always a community event, even if the community present numbers only two.

The Lord's Supper is not only an act of recollection but also an act of proclamation. The center of that proclamation is the redeeming death of Jesus. At the same time it is a temporary proclamation. One day the return of Jesus will remove the need for recollection as well as proclamation, for they will be replaced by his immediate presence.

The Lord's Supper brings with it the possibility of divine judgment (vv 27-29). Gifts necessarily come with strings attached, even when (perhaps particularly when) they are totally free. They carry with them the test of our valuation of them. To treat them as cheap because they are free brings its own condemnation.

It is possible for Christian observances to make things worse rather than better (v 17). An observance in itself is no guarantee of moral quality. Attitudes, social customs must all come under the scrutiny of the message that the observance conveys.

C. Spiritual Gifts and Their Place in Worship (12:1—14:40)

BEHIND THE TEXT

While 11:2—14:40 shares a common concern with propriety in worship, chs 12—14 have an individual bond in that they focus specifically on the place in worship of spiritual gifts. The use of the prepositional phrase "Now about" (*peri de* [12:1]) found already in contexts where Paul begins to address matters raised in the Corinthians' letter to him (see 7:1, 25; 8:1) indicates that he is moving to a distinct, even if not unrelated, topic. Moreover, chs 12—14 show an internal structure whereby Paul sets forth successively (1) the common purpose of spiritual gifts, notwithstanding their varied character (ch 12); (2) love as the grace surpassing and outlasting all gifts (ch 13); and (3) the exercise of spiritual gifts in worship in a way that is consistent with good order and the edification of the church (ch 14). Love is thus given the central and loftiest place in the whole matter of the exercise of spiritual gifts.

IN THE TEXT

1. The Lordship of Christ as the Touchstone of the Gifts (12:1-3)

These verses are a shrewdly calculated introduction to the topic of spiritual gifts. The Corinthians evidently thought they were authorities on the subject. Paul had his doubts about this and his use of a verb denoting some form of "knowing" in each verse makes this clear.

■ 1 The opening phrase (*tōn pneumatikōn*) may be neuter (**the gifts of the Spirit**) or masculine (the spiritual people). Paul has already used it twice in a personal sense (2:15; 3:1) and will do so once more (14:37). It is not impossible that at Corinth those exercising the gifts may have been known (or referred to themselves) as "the spirituals." If so there would be a touch of irony in Paul's language. There may be a further ironical note in Paul's statement that he does not want them to be uninformed. They are not the experts they thought they were.

■ 2 One thing on which they were experts was their experience as pagans. (Apparently the problems created by the exercise of the spiritual gifts were concentrated among the Gentile rather than the Jewish elements in the church.) That experience made clear to them (**you know**) what it meant to be **led** (forms of the Greek word "led" are used twice) by the spirit of the god, even when it involved being led to idols incapable of speech.

■ 3 Paul now turns to the Christian experience of **speaking by the Spirit of God**. This is a matter that he emphatically wants them to know. It is an experience of being led, like their experience as pagans. However, the touchstone is not *how* things are said (as in some kind of ecstatic compulsion), but rather *what* is said. It is impossible that anyone led by the Spirit of God would say: **Jesus be cursed**. Indeed, it is unimaginable that such an utterance was ever heard in Christian worship. More probably it was an exclamation heard among Jews (see Gal 3:13). On the other side the confession **Jesus is Lord** can only be made under the influence of the Spirit of God. This is the basic Christian confession of faith (see Rom 10:9). Paul is thus affirming that all Christians are spiritual, not just those who exercise a pneumatic gift.

2. The Varied Gifts as Given by the One Spirit (12:4-11)

The stress in these verses falls on the Spirit as the Giver of the varied gifts, the emphatic expression "the same Spirit" or its equivalent being used seven times. While the diversity of the gifts is acknowledged, it is affirmed clearly that all are gifts of one and the same Spirit (see vv 4, 11). Nor is it to be forgotten that this same Spirit is the Spirit who inspires the confession of the Lordship of Jesus (v 3).

a. The Fundamental Principle (12:4-6)

These verses exhibit a clear degree of parallelism. The first member of each verse states the general nature of the gifts, the second member the God at work in them. A single emphasis runs through them—namely, that notwithstanding differences between the three categories of phenomena mentioned (**kinds of gifts . . . kinds of service . . . kinds of working** [vv 4-6])—**the same God** is **at work** in all (v 6). The Corinthians discerned God at work only, or certainly chiefly, in the dramatic gifts. Paul thinks otherwise.

■ **4** Paul does not use the same word for spiritual gifts as that favored by the Corinthians (*pneumatika*), preferring instead *charismata* (meaning "grace-gifts"). This appears to be a deliberate attempt on Paul's part to shift the emphasis from a subjectivist understanding resulting in spiritual exhibitionism to an objectivist view in which the gifts are the product of God's grace. The use of the plural **different kinds** may also be a corrective of the Corinthian mindset in which the only gifts that mattered were speaking gifts—tongues and prophecy (14:27-33). The point is underscored by the declaration that **the same Spirit distributes them.**

■ **5** Alongside grace-gifts are placed **different kinds of service**, thus elevating everyday acts of help to a place among supernatural phenomena. **The same Lord** is at work in both.

■ **6 Different kinds of working** (*energēmatōn*) seems to refer to the exercise of miraculous powers (→ 12:10, the only other example of the term in the NT). It is the same God who is at work in all such manifestations and those who do them. It is significant that Paul traces all such operations to "the same Spirit" (12:4), "the same Lord" (v 5), and **the same God**—a piece of implied but uncontrived Trinitarianism.

b. Some Individual Gifts (12:7-11)

The gifts named in these verses (as well as in vv 28-29) do not constitute a complete list (compare Rom 12:6-8). They are chosen because of their relevance to the situation in Corinth, where the more sensational gifts were prized above all others.

■ **7** The principles underlying the gifts and their use are now spelled out. First, it is affirmed that each person has a gift (1 Cor 12:11). Second, the Spirit is the source of the gifts. The substitution of the expression **manifestation of the Spirit** (*hē phanerōsis tōn pneumatōn*) indicates that Paul's immediate focus is on the external signs of the working of the Spirit (Fitzmyer 2008, 466). At the same time, the repetition of Spirit-language in vv 8, 9, and 11 for gift-language (vv 1, 4) shows that the overriding emphasis is on the Giver rather than the gifts. Third, the full range of grace-gifts referred to in vv 4-6 are given, not for the satisfaction of the individual recipient but for the good of the whole community. All three points are clearly targeted to the Corinthian situation.

■ **8-10** These principles are now unpacked in specific terms in vv 8-10, where nine forms of manifestation are listed. Almost certainly the particular grace-gifts named are chosen with the Corinthian situation in mind. (For Paul's preferred ranking of the gifts, see vv 27-28.) The use of a different Greek word for **another** in vv 9 and 10 (*heterō* for *allō*) may mark off the gifts into three groups—all prized in the church in Corinth. First, in v 8 are gifts that involve the intellect. Second, in vv 9-10*a* are gifts of supernatural power. Third, in v 10*b-c* are gifts of supernatural communication. The exact meaning of some is not completely clear. What is clear is that a corrective note runs through Paul's treatment. This has been evident from v 7 (→) and continues through v 11.

The prizing of certain gifts (and their practitioners) at the expense of others is repudiated by Paul as the listing of the gifts of tongues and interpretation last makes clear. The mention of **distinguishing between spirits** (v 10*c*) points the same way. The references to **wisdom** (v 8*a*) and **knowledge** (v 8*b*) could not fail to remind his readers of earlier discussions of these topics (1:17—2:16; 3:18-20). **Prophecy** was likewise a familiar phenomenon (12:10*b*). We may not know enough to catch the overtones of the references to other gifts. The emphasis on the Spirit as the Giver of the gifts underscores the point that the gifts were not up for sale.

■ **8** First, Paul deals with gifts that involve the intellect. The expressions used to describe these are literally "a word of wisdom" (*logos sophias*) and "a word of knowledge" (*logos gnōseōs*). The NIV translates these as **a message of wisdom . . . a message of knowledge** (v 8). The NRSV renders "the utterance of wisdom . . . the utterance of knowledge." The former stresses content; the latter mode of delivery. Together they suggest practical teaching rather than doctrinal theology. The Corinthians probably had their own definition of **a message of wisdom**. Paul has been at pains to redefine it (→ 1:1—2:4, 13-17). At the very least, it must denote a message in harmony with the message of the cross. **Knowledge** was also prized among the Corinthians: often in a sense that damaged less-instructed believers (→ ch 8). The **message of knowledge** truly inspired by the Spirit would take this into account.

■ **9-10*a*** The second group of gifts is characterized by supernatural power. The **faith** (12:9) in question is not the faith that brings salvation (Rom 10:9) and thus is the perquisite of all believers; it is rather the special endowment that makes possible the working of miracles (1 Cor 13:2). Next are **grace-gifts** [*charismata*] **of healings**—the plural possibly suggesting that the gift is given for the individual situation and is not a permanent endowment. **Miraculous powers** (12:10a) are presumably other supernatural powers than healing. In Gal 3:5 Paul speaks of such happenings as matters of course.

■ **10b-e** The third group of gifts finds its focus in supernatural communication. **Prophecy** (of which he will say much more in 1 Cor 14) is not simply preaching (for a review of suggested possibilities, see Thiselton 2000b, 956-65). Standing as it does among other gifts characterized by supernatural power, it is much more probably concerned with the application of the gospel to new situations and problems (→ 14:3). Delivered under the evident impress of the Spirit, it was neither to be dismissed cynically nor accepted uncritically (see 1 Thess 5:20-21). Hence, the next named gift: **distinguishing between spirits**. High-pressure delivery was no necessary guarantee of divine inspiration. The messages of the prophets must be tested for their conformity with the message of the gospel (→ 1 Cor 14:29). The two remaining gifts mentioned are **speaking in different kinds of tongues** and **the interpretation of tongues**. The precise terms used in both cases are significant. **Kinds of tongues** (*genē glōssōn*) implies that Paul envisages not so much the *gift* of tongues as the *gifts* of tongues. The use of the term **interpretation** may have a wider reference than the term "translation." We may expect these points to become clearer as Paul's discussion continues.

■ **11** The gift list is now concluded as it began (12:7) with a summary statement of the principles underlying the grace-gifts. First, all of the gifts mentioned, not just those favored by the "spiritual" elite, are products of the Spirit's power, not the effort of the recipients. The language is emphatic in its reference to **all** (*panta*) the gifts, as also to **one and the same Spirit** as the Giver. Second, **each one** receives a gift. Third, the gifts are given at the Spirit's choice and determination, not the preference of the individual recipient.

3. The Varied Gifts for the One Body (12:12-31)

Just as vv 8-11 have elaborated the varied manifestations of the Spirit (→ v 7), so vv 12-31 now demonstrate that these are given not for the satisfaction of the individual recipients but "for the common good" (v 7). The controlling image Paul uses to make his point is that of the body. (He has used it already in 10:16-17.)

Paul's Use of the Image of the Body to Refer to the Church

Much has been written about the use Paul makes of the image of the body and where he got it. (For surveys of scholarship, see Dunn 1998, 548-52; Fitzmyer 2008, 475-76.) The body in the sense of the "body politic" was a widely used figure in contemporary Greek thought. A well-known form was the fable of the Belly and the Members recorded by the Roman historian Livy (*Historia* 2.32). This describes how the Plebs refused to work for their masters who exploited them. The fable points out that, in depriving the apparently nonproductive belly of food, the members were in reality damaging themselves since the belly in fact supported the whole body. Here the image of the body is being used to suppress the members.

Paul's use is quite the reverse. His emphasis falls on the fact that the body, although one, is composed of many members (12:12) from multiple races and classes. The unity is grounded in the theological truth that all believers have partaken of the same Spirit (v 13). This leads to the repeated point that the body, though one, is made of many members (v 14)—a truth that the Corinthians with their exaggerated view of some gifts were in danger of denying.

As to where Paul got the idea of the body, many suggestions have been made. It is claimed that it may be rooted in the OT idea of corporate personality. This is connected with the idea grounded in Paul's conversion that in persecuting Christians he was persecuting Christ (Acts 9:4-5; 22:7-8; 26:14-15). Again, it is claimed that he borrowed it from current Greek ways of thinking of the body politic (*TDNT* 7:1067-71). Dunn regards this as the most likely source of Paul's usage (1998, 550-51; see also Fitzmyer 2008, 475-76). F. F. Bruce thinks Paul may have developed the usage independently, though he does not regard determining how Paul reached it as particularly helpful (1976, 120). What is clear is that Paul uses the image in a carefully crafted way to address the contentions among the Corinthians.

The idea of some members repudiating their membership of the body because others were more important (vv 15-20); or more visible members disclaiming their need for humbler members (vv 21-26) seem clearly to reflect adaptation and application to the Corinthian situation in which some gifts were prized above others.

The fact that the body is one does not exclude the reality that it is composed of many parts. Indeed, the diversity ministers to the unity inasmuch as the various members are interdependent. The argument is now developed in four stages.

a. Diversity and Unity in the Human Body and the Body of Christ (12:12-14)

■ **12** The body is at one and the same time a unity and a multi-membered entity. All the members, while being many (*polla onta*) constitute one body. By definition there cannot be either without the other. Hence the conclusion: the same is true of the body of Christ. (Strictly speaking, Paul says **so it is with Christ**, but presumably he means "the body of Christ" as the context suggests.) This does not mean that diversity in unity and unity in diversity are equal. In Christ unity is the primary reality that gives meaning to diversity (Soards 1999, 263; Fitzmyer 2008, 474).

■ **13** The claim made in v 12 is now explained theologically. The introductory expression *for indeed* (*kai gar*) suggests that what is about to be said is undeniably true, even though the Corinthians were acting otherwise. The argument consists of at least three elements.

(1) The motif of "one and all" controls the thought of the verse. The overriding emphasis is on diversity based on unity. The diversity is expressed in the emphatic phrase **we . . . all** (*hēmeis pantes*), the unity by the repeated expressions **by one Spirit** (*en heni pneumati*), **form one body** (*eis hen sōma*), and **one Spirit** (*hen pneuma*). The experimental reality was common to all the Corinthians as well as to Paul himself (**we . . . all**). Whereas some Corinthians—the pneumatics or spiritual persons as they saw themselves—imagined they were superspiritual because they had more dramatic gifts than others, Paul insists that all believers, himself included, stand on common ground. The universal note is spelled out more specifically in the interjection in the middle of the verse of the reference to the two great divides in the ancient world between Jews and Greeks, slaves and free. These are the very divisions Paul has already used to expound the gospel (1:22-24; 7:21-23; 10:32).

(2) The substance of this event or experience was their incorporation into the body of Christ. It was the work of the one Spirit. The idea that Christian life begins with the Spirit is fundamental in Pauline thought (Rom 8:9; 1 Cor 6:17, 19; Gal 3:3). Accordingly, Paul uses baptismal language. However, such language does not always refer to the rite itself but to what the rite means. This is the case here (Dunn 1975, 261). The Greek text is ambiguous in expressing the manner of the Spirit's work. The preposition **by** (*en*) may denote the agent (**baptized by one Spirit** as in NIV, NASB) or the element ("in the one Spirit we were all baptized" [as NRSV; see REB]).

Some interpreters claim that Paul typically speaks of the Spirit as the medium into which one is baptized rather than the agent who baptizes (Carson 1987, 46-47). However, Paul can use varying images to describe the relation between the believer and the Spirit, such as being joined to the Lord (1 Cor 6:17) or receiving the Spirit or beginning with the Spirit (Gal 3:2-3). The emphasis in 1 Cor 12:7-11 falls on the Spirit as the agent of the distribution of gifts, and it probably continues in v 13 (Thiselton 2000b, 997).

(3) The argument that diversity does not destroy the unity of the body is further confirmed by the declaration that **we were all given the one Spirit to drink**. The verb *potizō* regularly means to give someone something to drink (Matt 25:35, 37; Mark 15:36; Rom 12:20). The form used here means "made to drink" (of one Spirit) or "given (the

one Spirit) to drink" (BDAG). The image of the Spirit as water to be drunk is found in Isa 44:3. The point Paul is making, however, is that *all* without exception partook of *one* Spirit. Accordingly, the diversity of gifts given to the Corinthians does not militate against their unity in the body of Christ. This affirmation is now expressed in theological terms. The meaning of baptism is the incorporation of all by one Spirit into one body, and the partaking by all of one Spirit. The boundaries of race (**Jews or Gentiles**) and political status (**slave or free**) are swept aside by this act that is common to all.

■ **14** The reason for this is that the body by definition is multi-membered and cannot function on any other basis. Where there is no plurality of members there is no body. Paul now proceeds to apply this to the Corinthian situation. He addresses two aspects, both of which were evidently present in the Corinthian church. His method in each case is to show the absurdity of the position involved.

b. The Need of the Body for a Variety of Members (12:15-20)

■ **15-17** The problem presupposed is apparently that some Corinthian Christians regarded themselves as being inferior because they did not possess the more dramatic, public gifts of some of their fellow believers. The foot was less visible than the hand and the ear than the eye. Consequently they felt that they were unimportant. But this is self-evidently absurd, assuming—as it does—that the body would be better off without feet and ears. To push the argument to the last degree: if the prominent member should—*per impossibile*—take over as the whole body, then many basic functions would be eliminated.

■ **18** This is not simply a fact of life: it is part of the divine order and design. God has willed that the body should be multi-membered.

■ **19-20** The argument is now pressed to its absurd conclusion: if all the members were one part, there would be no body—just a monstrous eye or ear or foot. In fact, there are many parts, hence one body. This stage of the argument thus ends on the need for diversity as a guarantee of unity.

c. The Need of Each Member for All the Others (12:21-26)

A reverse aspect of the problem of inferiority felt by some members (vv 15-20) was the superior attitude toward them shown by those with more visible gifts.

■ **21** The eye and the head are more prominent than the hand or the feet, but it is absurd for the former to treat the latter as dispensable.

■ **22-24a** In terms of the physical body, appearances are no sure index of importance. The weaker and less presentable bodily members are treated with greater care. What this amounts to is that the body is a unity in which all the members have an indispensable function so that the whole idea of a hierarchy of importance has no place. Significantly, the language used of appearances (*dokounta*), weakness (*asthenestera*), and honor (*atimotera*) is the same language used to describe the cross (1:25, 27) and Paul as its messenger (2:3; 4:9-13). The church as the body of Christ shares the cruciform character of its founder.

■ **24b-26** It is affirmed again (→ 12:18) that God is the designer of the body, and the purpose of the varying distribution of gifts is not to produce dissension but for mutual recognition and regard. A right understanding shows that the unity of the body is the point and purpose of the plurality of members. **Division** (*schisma* [v 25]) such as was occurring among the Corinthian Christians (→ 1:10-11) was the exact opposite of this. Significantly, the truth of the unity of the body is developed in terms of two pointed ideas: weakness versus strength, and unpresentability versus honor. The weaker members of the body are functionally indispensable (12:21-22); and the less presentable members are given special care (vv 23-25). It is difficult not to see this as directed to the condescending attitude of the pneumatics toward their less demonstrative fellow believers. Paul now presses beyond the strict limits of the body image to insist that the task of the various members is to show concern for each other, so that the suffering or rejoicing of one member is shared by all members (vv 25-26).

d. The Varied Gifts and Their Various Recipients (12:27-31)

There is a double emphasis in these verses. First, there is a repetition of the point that each of them, with their differing gifts, is equally a member of the body of Christ (vv 27, 29-30). Second, it is emphasized no less that some gifted persons contribute in a particularly substantive and singular way to the upbuilding of the church (v 28). Michael Gorman puts it finely, saying that Paul describes the church as a paradoxical combination of equality and hierarchy (2017, 323). As Paul will go on to say: some gifts are greater than others (v 31). But their greatness consists not in superiority of status but in their capacity and opportunity for service (4:9-13).

■ **27** The note struck in 12:12—that there is one body and many members—is resumed here, with this difference—that it is emphatically (**Now you**) applied to the Corinthians. Indeed, it is applied to each of them individually (NIV, NRSV). Paul is thus applying to the local church what applies also to the universal church. The former is **the body of Christ** just as much as the latter.

■ **28** The gifts are now listed a second time. The contrast with the first listing (vv 8-10) is striking. Only four gifts from the earlier list are repeated: healing, miracles, prophecy, and tongues. Even more striking is the emphatic ranking of the first three gifts: first of all **apostles**, second **prophets**, third **teachers**. The earlier list appears to be intent on correcting the Corinthian notion that some gifts—the more dramatic—were more spiritual than others. The exaggerated Corinthian preference for the gift of **tongues** is put in perspective by listing it last. The second list asserts positively that some gifts hold a precedence and priority over others. The first three gifts are named in personal form and numerical order. Paul has already identified himself as the one who laid the foundation of the church in Corinth (3:10). More specifically, he has identified himself as an apostle—one who has seen the risen Lord (9:1-2). He will repeat this double claim in 15:8-11 and exercise the authority implicit in it in 14:37.

The form of ministry listed second is that of the prophet. This seems to have involved the inspired disclosure of instruction and direction that would build up the church (→ 14:3, 29-32; → sidebar "The Gift of Prophecy in 1 Corinthians" at From the Text for 14:1-40). The role of teacher, which is listed third, presumably involved giving instruction in the significance of the faith tradition in general (compare Acts 13:1-3; Eph 4:11-16). These three gifts stand apart in the fundamental sense that without them there would be no church. Fee argues they refer primarily to function rather than status (2014, 685-87). Their ranking hardly agrees with this. In particular it does not sit comfortably with the meaning of "apostle" elsewhere in the letter (1:1; 9:1-2; 15:7-10).

The remaining five gifts are stated in functional rather than personal terms, perhaps implying that they are detachable from specific individuals and therefore anyone may have them. The first two—**miracles** and **gifts of healing**—are introduced by the adverb **then**, the remainder without any formula. This suggests that the order of listing is without significance. Taken with the last three gifts—**helping, guidance,** and **different kinds of tongues**—the overall impression given is of the diverse range of the gifts, with the gift of tongues ranked with the gifts of healing and guidance, which may not have entered into the reckoning of many Corinthians as gifts at all.

■ **29-30** The gift list (with the exception of "helping" and "guidance" [v 28]) is now cast into the form of rhetorical questions. In contrast with v 28, the gifts are all expressed in personal form (though "helping" and "guidance" are omitted). The argument is essentially that of vv 17-20: if all the members were the same thing, there would be no body—just a useless monstrosity. In short, diversity is indispensable for the body to be a functioning entity.

■ **31** This is a bridge verse, the first part forming Paul's conclusion to ch 12, the second part pointing forward to ch 13 (as in the NIV). As to the first part: the verb form **eagerly desire** (*zēloute*) may be imperative (as in the NIV) or present indicative ("you are desiring"). The latter hardly fits the Corinthian situation. Desiring the grace-gifts (*charismata*) as opposed to the pneumatic gifts (*pneumatica*) was precisely what the Corinthians had not been doing.

Accordingly, the imperative is to be preferred as expressing what Paul had been consistently urging them to do: set their hearts on the gifts that build up the body. There is thus an ironic overtone to Paul's injunction. The Corinthians had indeed been hungering for greater gifts—but in the wrong place. The second part of the verse forms the link with ch 13. Paul is about to show them "a way beyond measure" (BDAG) that leads beyond spiritual gifts. As Conzelmann rightly puts it, love is itself the way (1975, 216). Over and above the character of the gifts—any and all of them—is the way in which they are exercised. The criterion by which they are to be evaluated is not whether they had worth to the practitioner but whether they had worth to the observer. This is more than a gift; it is a way of living.

FROM THE TEXT

1. There is a wide variety in the character of the gifts, ranging from the spectacular to the commonplace. However, all are part of God's beneficence and have a significant and necessary role in the functioning of the body. Hence, no one is to be acclaimed because they are gifted in performing a public role, nor are any to be treated dismissively because they discharge an inconspicuous role. The language of weakness and honor (12:22-23) is the same language used earlier of Christ and the cross (1:25-27; 4:10; 8:9-10; 9:19-23; 11:14) and is here applied to the church. In the weakness of the church lies its strength.

2. No one gift is said to be given to everyone or to be sought by everyone. To focus on any one gift as being supremely desirable, let alone necessary, is to damage both in principle and practice the diversity that is necessary for the proper functioning of the body of Christ (12:29-30). Implicit in this is the truth that the grace-gifts are not soteriologically necessary in the strict sense; they function rather in the sphere of Christian life and service.

3. The overriding factor in the whole matter is that the gifts are what the term says they are: graces given by God (see the emphatic language of vv 18 and 28). Accordingly, it is not our task to covet gifts but rather to accept them. For this reason, gifts such as apostleship—which Paul claimed both as a witness to the resurrected Christ (15:8) and as the founder of the church in Corinth (3:10; 4:15)—were not to be denied their place in the providential ordering of God, although by definition they were unrepeatable. The same would apply to prophets and teachers who are grouped with apostles as associated with their apostolic ministry. A similar role may be intended by the term "guidance" (*kubernēseis*) rendered by Keener as "forms of leadership" (2005, 102), which he takes to suggest some form of supervision or oversight (104; Keener cites 16:15-16 as a possible example; see also 1 Thess 5:12-13). The

inspiration of the Spirit does not exclude the leadership of those whom the Spirit has gifted in this way.

4. Love as the Controlling Principle of the Use of the Gifts (13:1-13)

BEHIND THE TEXT

1. First Corinthians 13 stands out in chs 12—14 (and indeed, in the letter as a whole) for its literary eloquence and style. For this reason it has sometimes been regarded as an independent composition (a poem or encomium) written by Paul on another occasion but called into service here. However, the contents of the chapter fit the Corinthian situation so well: the prior place given to the gifts of tongues and prophecy (13:1-2, 8), not to mention the overriding need for love, that it would be remarkable if a casual or occasional piece of writing could address the need so perfectly. The suggestion that if ch 13 was composed previously it was with the Corinthian situation in mind (Thiselton 2000b, 1029) comes close to being a distinction without a difference. Paul had thought long and deeply about love before (1 Thess 1:3; 3:6, 12). It would not strain his powers as a writer to express himself with the elevation and incisiveness exhibited here.

In some degree Paul may have been influenced by the rhetorical style of contemporary orators (Witherington 1995, 264-65). At the same time, his argument with the Corinthians is continued. The primary aim of the chapter is the evaluation of spiritual gifts, but it does this by extolling the surpassing value of love. Moreover, the argument thus far has led only to a debate about which were the greatest gifts (12:31a): a debate resumed in 14:1b-c. But this is entirely unsatisfactory for Paul's purposes. What is needed is something that transcends the debate completely. The moral superiority of love is such a thing.

2. In keeping with the foregoing, the aspect of love that is emphasized is the ethical. The contentiousness stirred by the exaggerated display of the gifts is to be eliminated by the solvent of love. Without love the exercise of the gifts is empty exhibitionism. Love does not merely embody every positive moral quality: it enacts them in the pressures and stresses of daily life. It is no surprise, therefore, that love will survive after even the most impressive gifts and powers have withered and vanished. These carry within themselves the seeds of their own decay; love will remain as belonging to the eternal order.

3. The exposition of love follows a readily discernible structure. It comes in three movements. First is a movement expressing the relative worthlessness of all gifts and activities apart from love (13:1-3). Second is a character sketch

of love, describing not merely what love is and what it is not, but how it behaves and refrains from behaving. It is a concrete characterization, rather than an abstract description of love (vv 4-7). The third movement affirms the permanence of love in contrast with the transience of the gifts of tongues and prophecy and even knowledge itself (vv 8-13). Accordingly, love stands out as the greatest of the trinity of the graces cherished by Paul: faith, hope, and love (v 13).

4. While love becomes the dominant theme at this point, it is by no means a novel idea in the epistle. It has received earlier mention as the essence of the relationship with God (2:9; 8:3). First Corinthians 8:1-3 is particularly notable in its anticipation of terms and ideas that will receive fuller treatment in ch 13. "Knowledge" (v 2), being "puffed up" (v 4 KJV; obscured in the NIV, which is rendered "is not proud"), being "known" by God (v 12*b*) all make an earlier appearance in 8:1-3. Love has also been the essence of Paul's relationship with the Corinthians (16:24), and he addresses them as his "beloved [*agapēta*] children" (4:14 NASB, NRSV). At the same time misguided (and egotistical) views must be labeled for what they are. Love has principles, and that which is unloving must be called by its proper name (4:21). So far, love has been the background of Paul's message; now it moves onto center stage.

Paul now embarks, therefore, not on his own preferred ranking of the gifts in contrast to that of the gift-enthused Corinthians, but on the way in which any and all of them are to be exercised. The touchstone is the ethical aspect, not the dramatic.

IN THE TEXT

a. The Worthlessness of the Gifts without Love (13:1-3)

The use of the verb "have" (*echō*) five times in these verses is significant. The enthusiasts in Corinth apparently divided the church into two groups—the *haves* (themselves) and the *have-nots* (the rest: those not blessed with supernatural demonstrative gifts). The three contrasts spelled out in vv 1-3 refer to excesses generated by zeal for Spirit manifestations. Paul's response is that however many gifts one may have, if one does not have love one has nothing. The use of the first personal pronoun throughout these verses is generic: he is not claiming to possess all of the gifts mentioned. The "I" referred to is anyone.

■ 1 The first gift mentioned is that of tongues. In all of the treatments of the gifts in the letter this is the only one in which tongues is listed first (compare 12:8-10, 28-29). Undoubtedly this was because it was the gift causing most of the trouble in the Corinthian church (→ 12:30). The exercise of the gift of tongues was not unknown in Judaism where it was also seen as a form of angelic speech (*T. Job* 48-50). But without love even such lofty effusions amount to no more than the clashing of tin cans and noisy cymbals. These images are probably borrowings from the bronze jars used in Greek theaters to amplify the natural voice or the booming of echoing cymbals (for a review and evaluation of the options, see Thiselton 2000b, 1035-39). Significantly, the loveless enthusiast is said not only to sound *like* the gong or the cymbal but to have *become* the instrument named.

■ **2** Paul's next examples were also hot favorites at Corinth: inspired prophetic speech unlocking **all mysteries and all knowledge**, and the faith capable of moving mountains. Without in any way denying the validity of these gifts (12:8-10*b*) Paul affirms that notwithstanding their spectacular power, without love they amount to nothing (compare 1:21-22; 2:1, 4-5). The point is made emphatically by the threefold repetition of **all**. Equally significant is the threefold repetition of the first personal pronoun "I." The problem and, by implication, its solution finds its fundamental form in the personal dimension.

■ **3** The final examples Paul cites are those of self-giving or self-sacrifice. The first is disposing of his possessions for the sake of the poor, probably to provide them with food. The second is surrendering his body. The meaning of this is debated. Translations vary between those that take the verb of the purpose clause as a form of the verb "to burn" (*kauthēsomai*: so KJV, NIV[84], REB, RSV); and those taking it as a form of the verb "to **boast**" (*kauchēsōmai*: so NIV, NRSV). The manuscript evidence is divided (*TCGNT*, 497). That some sort of hardship is in mind is clear. While Paul deplores human boasting that detracts from the glory of God (1 Cor 1:28-31; 9:16), he also affirms it when it redounds to that glory (Rom 5:2-3; 2 Cor 1:11). The point here then is that even self-surrender that advances the gospel and of which one may legitimately boast (2 Cor 11:16-18, 21-30; 12:1-10) brings no gain when it is unaccompanied by love. Taken together then, 1 Cor 13:1-3 says that without love there is no meaning (v 1), no reality (v 2), no accomplishment (v 3).

b. How Love Acts and Does Not Act (13:4-7)

The verses are basically a collection of verbs: two positive (v 4*a*) followed by seven negative (vv 4*b*-5). Then comes an eighth negative verb balanced by its positive counterpart (v 6). The sequence concludes with four more positive verbs, each governing the object "all things" (*panta* [v 7 KJV, NASB, NRSV]). The verbs are not chosen haphazardly but mirror the situation in the Corinthian church. It is no surprise therefore that the greater number reflect what love does not do. The exclusive use of verbs rather than nouns to describe or define love makes the further point that love is not an abstract entity but an activity, seen through what it does. Most translations obscure this by renderings that state what love "is." The KJV and MSG are most successful in preserving the active aspect of the verbs.

■ **4-6** The first two terms express the love that "bears up under provocation without complaint" (BDAG 612: *makrothumei*) and radiates goodwill (*chrēsteuetai*). They are used rarely in the NT and (in one form or another) always together. They bespeak the unending compassion of God toward the sinner (Rom 2:4) exhibited in the cross and expressed in the gospel proclamation (2 Cor 6:6). These positive qualities are followed by a series of terms that denote what love does not do. It does not burn with envy—an emotion not unknown in the Corinthian church (1 Cor 3:3). It does not brag (*perpereuetai*), another familiar attitude among the Corinthians (3:3-4, even though the term is not used). Nor does love have an inflated sense of its own importance (*phusioutai*) as had some Corinthian believers (4:6, 18-19; 5:2). Love does not seek to put others to shame or pursue its own interests. It does not fly into a rage (*paroxunetai*) or keep score of hurts—a very penetrating statement expressing the depth of evil and the depth of love. Doing evil is one thing; rejoicing in it is quite another. Love takes no pleasure in evil of any kind. It finds its joy (the verb is intensive: *sunchairei*) rather in the truth that here is a synonym for holiness (Eph 4:23-24 and BDAG 42). It takes no pleasure in the evildoing of others (*adikia* [i]); rather it finds its pleasure in goodness.

■ **7** Following the statements in vv 4*b*-6, which are negative in form describing what love does *not* do, v 7 expresses positively what love does. The first and emphatic term in each of the four phrases is "all things" (*panta* [NASB, NRSV]) or **always**. Either expresses the unchanging constancy of love. The first verb (*stegei*) is most probably to be rendered "bears" (KJV, NRSV), meaning "bears up under difficulties" (BDAG 942). The second verb, "believes" (*pisteuei* [NASB, NRSV]), denotes not simple acceptance of all that is said but rather that it never loses faith (Barrett 1968, 305). The third verb, "hopes all things" (*elpizei* [NASB, NRSV]), denotes more than "hoping for the best": it denotes rather trust in God and the fulfillment of his purposes. Hence, it holds out (*hupomenei*) in confidence.

c. The Permanence of Love (13:8-13)

The focus now shifts from how love acts to how it lasts. The superiority of love is demonstrated by underlining its eternal dimension. The accent falls on the imperfect character of knowledge—even knowledge that is revealed under the Spirit's inspiration. Derivatives of "to know" (*ginōskō*) are used five times (vv 8, 9, 12). The contrasting term "love" (*agapē*) appears in the first and last verses (vv 8, 13): the control points of the argument. The style of the argument places love and the charismata in opposition (Conzelmann 1975, 225).

■ **8** The keynote of the argument is struck in the opening phrase. To say that **love never fails**—"never collapses" (BDAG 815)—is to say that, in contrast to the gifts mentioned, love belongs to the eternal order (this is the only example of the term "never" [*oudepote*] in all of Paul's writings [BDAG 735]). The three gifts named in this verse—prophecy, **tongues**, and **knowledge**—are all attempts to penetrate and master eternal knowledge. This was their attraction in the Corinthian setting. But all are doomed in their quest. The language deployed is definitive. The gifts of prophecy and knowledge will be destroyed; the gift of tongues will cease. In the fine phrase of Garland: "the spiritual gifts have a built-in obsolescence" (2003, 621). Love, on the other hand, will endure into the eschaton as the abiding quality of the relationship between and among God and his people.

■ **9-12** The argument now assumes a personal dimension, as the personal pronouns indicate. The use of the first-person plural in vv 9 and 12*a* appeals to the experience of the Corinthians, while the use of the first-person singular in vv 11 and 12*b* associates Paul's experience with theirs. Two reasons are now given (note the conjunction **for** [*gar*] in vv 9 and 12*a*) for the superseding of the gifts.

First, our present knowledge—including that yielded by prophecy—is partial and incomplete. But when the complete (*to teleion*) comes the partial will be abolished (the same strong term, *katargeō*, is used twice in v 8). "The complete" refers to the eschaton (v 10 NRSV; Fitzmyer 2008, 498). Paul cites human development as an analogy (v 11). The speaking, thinking, and reasoning of a child are adequate for the years of childhood, but when maturity comes they no longer suffice and are destroyed. This is universally true, as the first-person singular indicates.

The second reason given for the superseding of the gifts is that the knowledge they yield is indirect and temporary (v 12). The point is elaborated by a double contrast between **now** (*arti*) and **then** (*tote*), **then** denoting the age to come. The first contrast is expressed in terms of sight. In the present age sight is not that of direct perception but rather that of a reflected image in a mirror. In the age to come our sight will be **face to face** like that of Moses' direct (and unique) vision of God (Deut 34:10). The second contrast is expressed in terms of knowledge. Present knowledge is partial. In the age to come Paul will **know** as **fully** as God knows him now (the verb **know** is an intensive form: *epiginōskō*).

■ **13** This verse has been described as the most difficult in the chapter (Fee 2014, 719-20). Thiselton lists five different interpretations (2000b, 1071-74). A double contrast seems to be intended. First, faith, hope, and love are contrasted with the gifts of prophecy, tongues, and knowledge, which are passing (vv 8-11). Second, our understanding **now** (*arti*) is contrasted with our understanding in the future: "then" (*tote* [v 12]). In this conflicted situation faith, hope, and love remain—they have lasting meaning and relevance. Faith and hope have been mentioned earlier in the chapter as characteristics of love at work (v 7).

The trio of faith, hope, and love is familiar in Paul's thought as denoting the indispensable constituents of present life in Christ (Rom 5:1-5; Gal 5:5-6; 1 Thess 1:3; 5:18; this is the intended sense in this verse [1 Cor 13:3] rather than the gift of faith in v 2). Interpreters are divided as to whether Paul means that all three will last into eternity or that only love will do so. Proponents of the former view argue that there will be a place in eternity for faith in the sense of thankful trust in God and hope as the confident expectation of God's eternal grace (Carson 1987, 72-75). Proponents of the latter view hold that there is no meaningful sense that faith and hope can have in the eternal sphere (Hays 1997, 230-31; Fitzmyer 2008, 502; Fee 2014, 721). Hence, faith and hope—basic to salvation as they are—will yield the stage to love, which will be eternally relevant as the relationship among the people of God and between them and their Redeemer. Accordingly, the greatest of these is love.

FROM THE TEXT

1. Love, not the gifts of the Spirit, is the fundamental touchstone of authentic Christianity. It is shaped and defined by the self-surrender of Christ (1:17; 2:1-5). Hence, true knowledge consists not in understanding spiritual mysteries but in loving God and one's neighbor. Indeed, to love God is more than to know God; it is to be known by God (8:3). Love is thus the Christian way (12:31*b*; 14:1*a*). Every moral virtue comes with it. No capacity has meaning without it. It is heaven come down to earth—part of the age to come fulfilled in the present. As Wesley put it: "The heaven of heavens is love. There is nothing higher in religion—there is, in effect, nothing else; if you look for anything but more love, you are looking wide of the mark, you are getting out of the royal way" (1978, 11:430).

2. Paul never directs his readers to seek all of the gifts (12:11). He encourages seeking "the greater gifts" (12:31*a*), "especially prophecy" (14:1). He rates this so highly because it is given not for the benefit of the recipient but for those who are edified by the message conveyed (14:1-5). In a word: love is embodied in the form of the gift. The Corinthian misuse of it was a perversion of its very nature.

3. Love is not simply an emotional reaction to be switched on and off again. It is a bent or inclination of the heart. It is possible to abandon oneself to evil. Lady Macbeth's bloodcurdling prayer as she plots to murder Duncan is that she may be filled "from crown to the toe top full of direst cruelty." It

is also possible to abandon oneself to goodness. Hence, Paul's description of love as a *way* of life: "the most excellent way" (12:31*b*). It is by "being rooted and established in love" that one comes to know "how wide and long and high and deep is the love of Christ" (Eph 3:17-18). To know this is to know what surpasses knowledge: to "be filled to the measure of all the fullness of God" (v 19).

4. The life of love is a realizable possibility. The shift to the first-person singular in 1 Cor 13:1-3 is very striking. It suggests that Paul expects to be judged by the standard he is laying down for the Corinthians. N. T. Wright observes that no one could have written ch 13 to a community unless he knew that they knew that this was the kind of person he was (2004, 171). In the ambiguities of human life it may from time to time be obscured. Nevertheless, it can remain as the abiding and controlling undertone of heart and mind.

5. In Worship Intelligibility and Order Are Preferable to Unintelligibility and Disorder (14:1-40)

BEHIND THE TEXT

The problem of worship in the Corinthian church. The treatment of worship and its attendant problems begun in 11:2 continues, with a particular focus on the place of the gifts of tongues and prophecy. Apparently the exercise of the gift of tongues in Corinth was characterized by the lack of intelligible meaning (14:2, 6, 9, 16) and therefore power to build up the church (vv 4, 17, 19, 26). In practice it had reduced worship to a scene of confusion (vv 16, 27-28, 33, 40). Paul replies by arguing that the gift of tongues had been significantly overrated (→ 12:10). If it emerged in worship at all its employment must be strictly controlled and limited (14:27-28). Further, a preferred place should be accorded to the gift of prophecy, which had the capacity to convince and convert unbelievers (vv 24-25) as well as to build up believers (vv 3, 4, 12, 26). However, the gift of prophecy apparently was also being abused, and strict conditions are laid down for its employment. Two criteria are laid down for its use. The first is that the content of the prophecy is to be evaluated by the hearers (v 29). The second is that the number of prophecies should be limited (vv 29-32).

The significance of the gift of tongues in the Corinthian church. Paul has already spoken at some length of the gifts of the Spirit in ch 12. Several points mentioned there apparently in passing may well play a larger role than the space given to them might suggest. First, there is the reference to their pagan days and the influence this had on the form of their participation in Christian worship (12.2-3). Second, there is the note that manifestations of the Spirit are intended not for the glorification of the gifted individual but for the common good (12:7). Third, there appears to be an attempt to diminish the place of the gift of tongues. On the one hand, it is placed last in every list of gifts (12:10, 28-30; 14:26); again, it is named first as demonstrating that gifts are worthless apart from love (13:1-2). It appears therefore that the exercise of these gifts in the Corinthian church may have represented a new development that Paul viewed with distinct caution.

Paul was familiar with the gift of tongues as described in Acts (see 19:1-6). He would certainly have been familiar with the narrative of Pentecost. Each time he writes a statement suggesting acceptance of tongues he follows it immediately with a statement commending an alternative (14:5, 6-7, 12-13, 15, 18-19, 26). Further, while Spirit-language is entirely acceptable to Paul (12:1-12), its apparent use by some of the Corinthians to denote an otherworldly level of spiritual attainment (14:37) led Paul to prefer the term "grace-gifts" (*charismata*) to denote the gifts God had given to his people (12:30-31; Witherington 1995, 255).

The character of Corinthian Christianity. While the factors mentioned may account for the form of the gift of tongues, they hardly provide a rationale for the emergence of this kind of religious expression. The disorder in worship most probably arose from theological confusion. This has already been in evidence from the beginning of ch 11. It had led to the valuing of some gifts over others (12:11-14, 21-22), particularly those that could be understood to open the door into an exalted spiritual realm where the language of angels was spoken (13:1). It has been variously characterized as "over-realized eschatology" (Barrett 1968, 109, 347-48; Thiselton 2000b, 1173), or "over-realized spirituality" (Fee 2014, 696).

The tone of the argument in ch 14. Paul's language shows every sign of being carefully chosen. While he does not wish to alienate, he is not afraid to confront. Irony appears to be notably at work as one of Paul's weapons. It was a common tool in Hellenistic rhetoric (Forbes 1986, 10-13; Smit 1993, 250-53). It is not too much to say that it is a recurrent if not pervasive element in this chapter. (Gardner finds an "ironic feel" in much of what Paul has said since 8:1 [2018, 552]). **Eagerly desire spirit-things** (*ta pneumatika* [14:1]) contrasts strikingly with his earlier phrase **eagerly strive for the greater gifts of grace** (*ta charismata* [12:31])—Paul's preferred term. Again, it is a moot point how literally 14:5a and 18-19 (→) are to be taken. Wry humor may also be at work in vv 5a, 12, and 18-19 (Findlay 1912, 905; Robertson and Plummer 1914, 311; Fitzmyer 2008, 509-10, 518-20). At the same time he does not shrink from forthright evaluation of how mass tongues-speaking would appear to an outsider (v 23). Nor is he afraid to assert his authority as the Lord's inspired spokesman (vv 36-38).

IN THE TEXT

a. Prophecy as Being of Greater Value than Tongues (14:1-5)

■ 1 This is a carefully calculated summary of Paul's overall position. In keeping with his characterization of love as the best way (12:31*b*) and greater than all the gifts (13:13) Paul places it first as the quality to be not merely desired but pursued. **Love** has the definite article in Greek (*tēn agapēn*), most probably meaning "the love just described" (i.e., in ch 13). The next phrase: **eagerly desire gifts of the Spirit** probably carries an overtone of irony: "keep up your chase after 'spirit-things.'" (Paul uses a similar expression in 14:12, possibly quoting and certainly describing the attitude of the Corinthians to "spiritual things.") Paul has already shown his own preference for the term "gifts of grace" (*charismata*: 12:4, 9, 28, 30, 31) over "gifts of the spirit" (*pneumatika*: which appears after ch 12 only here [14:1] and at v 37; in both cases it refers to the Corinthians). They hunger for the dramatic. Rather than seeking a stage for themselves they should seek to benefit others, which the gift of prophecy would do.

■ 2-3 The reasoning behind Paul's directive is now spelled out. The intended audience of glossolalia is not human but divine, shown by the fact that no one understands what is being said. This does not mean the utterance is meaningless: only that God alone is able to understand it. The things spoken are Spirit-inspired mysteries (2 Cor 12:2-4 may provide a parallel). In contrast with one speaking in tongues, the one who prophesies is speaking to fellow creatures. Such prophesying ministers to the strengthening, encouraging, and reassuring of the hearers.

■ 4 The contrasting outcomes of glossolalia and prophecy are now brought into defined focus. The one produces self-edification, the other the edification of the church. Concern for the upbuilding of the church is a recurrent note throughout the epistle (1 Cor 10:32; 11:22; 12:27-28; 14:26-28; compare 3:10; 4:17).

■ 5 The ironical note found in 14:1 emerges again in the rhetorical overstatement that he wishes they would all speak in tongues. Indeed, God has already excluded this possibility (12:30). Prophecy is preferable to tongues because, being intelligible, it can edify the church. The one exception is when the utterance in tongues is interpreted. The phrase rendered **unless someone interprets** may be translated "unless he interprets," implying that the speaker in tongues may also serve as his or her interpreter (Brookings and Longenecker 2016, 103).

b. Meaning as More Important than Mode of Delivery (14:6-12)

Paul now proceeds to set out his reasons for holding that meaning, as represented by prophecy, has a prior claim in worship over tongues, which as practiced in the Corinthian church had no meaning. There is a notable personal overtone in these verses. Paul begins by addressing the Corinthians as "brothers and sisters" (v 6). He refers to their practice in personal terms (v 9) as well as his own (vv 6, 11). He also picks up his ironical description of them as **zealous for spirit-things** (v 12). He thereby contrives to make this issue one of his personal authority without either disfellowshipping the Corinthian "spiritists" or muting his criticism of them. He spells out his case in terms of three distinguishable yet related analogies.

■ **6** *The argument from his personal practice.* Paul has already indicated his intention to visit them (4:18-21). They should not expect any speaking in tongues from him when he comes. This implies that Paul did not engage in glossolalia during his first visit to Corinth. Presumably, he had come under criticism from the "spiritists" for not being as spiritual as they were. A further implication is that the Corinthians did not learn about speaking in tongues from Paul. If not from Paul, from whom? That question is left unanswered. What is clear is that Paul's involvement was in terms of curbing and correcting. For him to come to them only to offer words without meaning would be a mockery. But apparently the Corinthians would have welcomed this. What they should expect when he comes is what would be of benefit to them—namely, speech with meaning. This determines the sense of the items he lists as being objective rather than functional: **revelation** as content that is disclosed, **knowledge** as that which is made known, **prophecy** as what is declared rather than the process of declaration, "teaching" (NASB, NRSV) as what is taught rather than the activity. The examples given were highly valued at Corinth, but more for the means by which they were conveyed rather than the substance transmitted.

■ **7-9** *The analogy of musical instruments.* The **pipe** and the **harp** are the examples given (14:7). Tune depends on the distinction of notes. Where it is absent only a jumble of sound is possible. Clarity is crucially important with the trumpet call giving the summons to **battle** (v 8). The same is true of the gift of tongues at Corinth, which consisted of meaningless words cast into the wind (v 9).

■ **10-12** *The argument from human languages.* Verse 10 is best taken to refer to the many languages in the world (a phenomenon well known in Corinth), none of which lacks its individual meaning. But unless the hearer understands the language spoken, he and the speaker remain strangers to each other. This was precisely the situation created by the Corinthians in their **zeal for spirits**. As Paul ironically describes them, they had become **coveters of spirits**, "enthusiasts after spirits" (Findlay 1912, 905). The word rendered **eager** (v 12) is the Greek noun *zēlōtai* ("zealots"), commonly used to describe fanatical supporters of a school or party (ibid., 906). Paul's counsel to them therefore is: "If you are going to be zealots, be zealots for what will build the church, not damage it." Rather than seeking the dramatic **spirit-gifts** (*pneumatōn*) that inflate their own personae, they should seek the **grace-gifts** (*charismata*) that build up the church—namely, those that convey meaning clearly. The assumption on which Paul's argument has proceeded to this point is that this has not been the case in Corinth thus far.

c. The Place of the Mind in Worship and Its Implications (14:13-25)

The focus of the argument now shifts from the general issue of intelligibility to the specific concern for intelligibility in the setting of corporate worship. This, indeed, has been Paul's target from the beginning of the chapter. The first person is resumed from v 6 and culminates in Paul's personal declarations in vv 18-19, but the implied context throughout is the worship of the church. The section is bound together by concern for "an inquirer" (vv 16, 23-24).

■ **13-17** The thrust of v 13 is the commending of meaningful speech. This controls the interpretation of vv 14-15 (which is much debated). Verse 14 describes speech in which the mind is dormant—the reverse of what Paul is recommending. This in turn determines the import of v 15, which is the uniting of spirit and mind in the act of meaningful prayer or praise. The practical consequences of the failure to do so are spelled out in vv 16-17.

■ **13** The prime concern of any who speak in tongues should be that their utterances will be interpreted. The interpreter may be either the tongues-speaker (which is probably the meaning of the NIV) or some other (vv 28-29). The note of irony surfaces again. The prayer of the tongues-speaker should include the petition that his prayer will be interpreted.

■ **14-15** The mention of praying in v 13 is continued in vv 14-15, together with singing in v 15. Praying and singing in tongues are merely different aspects of speaking in tongues rather than different gifts. Since tongues are fundamentally addressed to God (v 2), prayer and praise are entirely fitting aspects or applications of it. Praying in tongues involves a tension between the spirit and the mind of the one who prays (lit. **my spirit** [vv 14, 15] and **my mind** [v 14]). **My spirit** (*to pneuma mou*) denotes the inward aspect of human personality and is open to the influence of the divine Spirit. **Mind** (*ho nous*) denotes the faculty of reason and makes possible rational communication with God. The weakness of praying in tongues is that it engages only the spirit but excludes the mind, which is "unproductive" (NRSV).

The resolving of the tension is found in the engagement of both the spirit and the mind in prayer. The meaning is not that Paul will sometimes pray with his spirit and sometimes with his mind but rather that both will be engaged together. Being spiritual does not depend on the mind being in suspense; it is perfectly possible when both the spirit and the mind are open to and led by the Holy Spirit. (The same principle is applied to singing.) This will result in the building up of the church. Accordingly, it should be the norm in congregational worship.

■ **16** The issue is now brought to bear sharply, indicated by the shift from the third person: **the one who speaks in a tongue** (*ho lalōn* [v 13]) to the second person: **when you are praising** (*eulogēs* [v 16]). The Corinthians are being addressed directly as responsible individuals. The spirit referred to in v 16 is taken by the NIV to be the Holy **Spirit** since it lacks the definite article in Greek. In contrast, all the other references to the spirit in vv 14-15 have the article since they refer to the spirit of the worshipper.

The specific objection is stated vividly to be the inability to say **Amen** at appropriate points, because the utterance was not interpreted. This would seem to imply that the individuals affected were more than outsiders (see NRSV). (They are distinguished from unbelievers in vv 23-24.) The NIV takes a mediating view, characterizing the uncomprehending individual as **put in the position of an inquirer**. However, Paul's meaning is more specific. The ability to know points at which saying **Amen** was appropriate, as well as to be **edified** (v 17)—that is, built up in faith—implies a positive Christian status. "New convert" perhaps captures the meaning. It is not clear whether they occupied a separate space in church gatherings. What is clear is that they did not understand what was being said.

■ **17** The sharp contrast between the ***spiritual one*** (***you on your part***: *su men gar*) and ***the other*** (*ho heteros*) continues. The note of irony emerges again. The ***spirit-lovers*** on their part were giving thanks **well enough** (*kalōs*) for their own satisfaction and fulfillment, but the rest were out in the cold, uncomprehending and unedified.

■ **18-19** Interpreters have taken v 18 in at least two ways. It has been taken literally. In this case Paul is now disclosing to the Corinthians what they did not know previously (→ v 6): that he not only practiced the gift of tongues but did so on a scale greater than any of them. The reason they did not know was that he practiced the gift privately (v 19). Thus Paul himself is the greatest example of the view he is commending to the Corinthians. This is the majority view (see Fitzmyer 2008, 518).

On the other hand, the verse has been understood rhetorically—as yet another example of Pauline irony. His thanksgiving is in the same satirical vein as in 1:14. He proceeds immediately to cite the language of the Assyrians as an example of tongues (14:20-22). Paul's thrust is therefore that, while he could have dazzled them with learning and rhetoric he would—and did—speak to them in language that conveyed the meaning of his message (2:1-5; Fitzmyer 2008, 518-19; Perkins 2012, 160-61).

The irony continues with Paul's expressed preference for five intelligible words over ten thousand words conveying nothing to anyone. The touchstone is the ability to convey meaningful instruction. This carries the further implication that the employment of tongues in church is a matter of decision and choice, not of submission to an irresistible power. Paul had no doubt as to what the choice should be.

■ **20-25** Paul now restates and develops the argument of 14:13-19. The argument is prefaced with a personal albeit double-edged appeal. Paul begins with a term of affection: **brothers and sisters** (v 20). However, it is followed immediately by a robust command to them to stop behaving **like children**. If they want to behave like **infants**, then let them be infants in evil. In their thinking, let them be mature. This is clearly a comment on their behavior described in vv 16-17, in which they were perfectly ready to leave the uninstructed in the dark while they themselves soared on the lofty heights of glossolalia. This defines the situation addressed in vv 21-22 and is the basic guide to their interpretation. What we should expect therefore, is an argument demonstrating why tongues is not a practice in which a mature believer would engage in public worship and conversely, why prophecy is an apt medium for believers.

These verses are difficult to exegete as most commentators admit. Not surprisingly, interpretations vary. (For summaries, see Thiselton 2000b, 1123-26; Garland 2003, 648-51.) The core of the problem is that what Paul says in v 22 about tongues being a sign not for believers but for unbelievers and prophecy being a sign not for unbelievers but for believers he seems to reverse in vv 23-25 (not to mention what he has already said in vv 16-17). His argument seems to turn on the Corinthians' childish mindset (v 20), and the significance of the term **sign** (v 22).

■ **21** Paul now proceeds to interpret the Corinthian situation on the basis of the situation in Isaiah's day. The quotation of Isa 28:11-12 (described as part of **the Law**, meaning the OT) is inexact and seems to combine text and interpretation. The immediate link is the use of the expression **other tongues** (*heteroglōssois*). It is evidently an explanatory comment on the childish failure of the Corinthians to understand Paul's message, which has been like a foreign language to them. (This explains why he says in v 18 that he speaks **in tongues more than all of** them.)

Paul is apparently using Isaiah's words to refer to both the Corinthians' attitude to him and the effect of his ministry on them. Isaiah was ridiculed as talking down to his hearers: "Who is he trying to teach? To whom is he explaining his message? . . . those just taken from the breast? For it is: Do this, do that, a rule for this, a rule for that" (Isa 28:9-10). The Corinthians seemingly ridiculed Paul in the same way. Similarly, just as Isaiah's hearers failed to grasp the significance of the tongues of the Assyrians, so the Corinthians failed to grasp the message of Paul. He might just as well have been speaking in tongues for all that his message got through (or failed to get through) to them.

■ 22 In keeping with the objective implied in 1 Cor 14:20, Paul now states his own view on the respective roles of tongues and prophecy. A crucial phrase is that **tongues . . . are a sign** (*eis semeion* [v 22]). It is possible, perhaps even likely, that the viewing of tongues as a sign of divine favor was a Corinthian idea. Paul seizes it and brings it to the touchstone of Scripture. The expression "as a sign" (REB) may have positive or negative significance (Dunn 1975, 231-32). The Corinthian tongues-speakers supposed that glossolalia as such was a sign of divine approval. On the contrary, says Paul, tongues not understood were a sign to unbelievers—of divine judgment as in Isaiah's day. It was prophecy rather than tongues that was a sign to believers inasmuch as it made them instruments of God's saving message to unbelievers. Paul has thus, in a sentence dripping with irony, stood the Corinthians' evaluation of tongues and prophecy on its head. The conclusion thus follows, **tongues . . . are a sign . . . for unbelievers**, that is to say, they do not lead people to become believers—quite the opposite. Prophecy, on the other hand, is a sign for believers; that is to say, it leads unbelievers to become believers. In vv 23-25 Paul will now show how this works out in practice.

■ 23 The scene depicted is that of a meeting of **the whole church** (v 23). This intensive expression may refer to a gathering of all the house churches in a wider area. The term **everyone** may not be intended literally, though it certainly gives the impression of speaking in tongues on a congregation-wide scale. There was evidently enough continuous participation that outsiders might justifiably conclude that the participants had lost their minds. The two terms used previously to refer to such outsiders (*idiotai* [v 16]; *apistoi* [v 22]) are here brought together. They are probably not synonymous, but refer respectively to new converts (→ v 16) and those who had not yet come to faith. The thrust of the verse is that just as the other tongues in Isaiah's day resulted in alienation and not conversion, so will glossolalia in church.

■ 24-25 Prophecy will yield a different result. Its scale is the same as glossolalia (**all** [v 24]) as are its hearers (**unbeliever or . . . inquirer**). However, the results are different: conviction and **judgment**. The unanimity of the prophetic message reinforces its positive impact just as the meaninglessness of the utterances in tongues results in a negative impact. The consequences for the hearers are the revelation of their true condition of heart and the recognition of the presence of God among his people (Isa 45:14; Zech 8:23). In this way prophecy, while a medium of salvation to unbelievers, is also a sign to believers.

d. Practical Guidelines (14:26-35)

Paul now proceeds to draw together the guidelines for worship embodied in what he has said. **What then shall we say?** implies as much. It is probable that these verses apply to only one side of Corinthian worship: that involving the exercise of the spiritual gifts. In the forms of ministry listed in v 26 there is no mention of the Lord's Supper, though its established place is made clear in 11:17-26. A place for the ministry of the Word seems also to be implied in 3:1-2 and 4:17. Hays suggests that the setting for the use of the gifts was "a prayer and praise meeting" (1997, 241). The verses are bound together by a common idea: the appropriate limitations on speaking in worship. The verb "be silent" (*sigaō* [NRSV]) is used in reference to each of the topics addressed: the gift of tongues (v 28), the gift of prophecy (v 30), and the participation of women (v 34). Apparently being silent was not something the Corinthian Christians were good at.

(1) Regarding the Exercise of the Gift of Tongues (14:26-28)

■ **26** Other gifts besides tongues figured in Corinthian worship. It is not clear whether all of those listed were the product of immediate inspiration. **A hymn** (*psalmon*) could have been either (but see v 15), likewise **a word of instruction** (*didache*, but see 12:28 where teaching is listed among the *pneumatika*); **a revelation** is the work of a prophet; finally (as always) **a tongue or an interpretation**. It is not implied that everyone has a gift each time there is a meeting: only that those who have should conduct themselves in conformity to the overriding principle that everything should be done with a view to building up the church.

■ **27** The focus is now turned on tongues. Three conditions are laid down for its exercise. First, there must be only **two—or at the most three** expressions: it is not to take over the meeting. Second, the speakers should **speak, one at a time**: it is not to degenerate into a babble. Third, one person (*heis*) **must interpret**: a requirement excluding multiple interpretations while at the same time requiring interpretation. The interpreter may be the glossolalist in person or someone else.

■ **28** It appears to be assumed that those possessing the gift of interpretation were known. For Paul their absence foreclosed the exercise of glossolalia since it foreclosed the possibility of the edification of the worshippers as a whole. In this situation the tongues-speakers should be silent in church and exercise their gift privately for their own edification (v 4a) and communion with God (v 2).

(2) Regarding the Exercise of the Gift of Prophecy (14:29-33)

For all that Paul has repeatedly expressed a preference for prophecy over tongues (vv 1, 3-5, 24-25) he is aware that it too may be misused. The essential problem with the Corinthian use of the gift was that, in a variety of ways, it was uncontrolled. Paul proceeds to spell out the controls needed.

■ **29** Prophets must not take over the service as though they were the only item that mattered: **two or three** would be enough. Further, their prophecies were not to be accepted without evaluation merely because they were delivered in prophetic mode. The weighing of the prophecies could have been the work of the other prophets. However, in 12:10 this gift is given to others than prophets; it may mean the hearers in general. The important point is that the prophets were accountable to other members of the congregation; they were not a law unto themselves.

■ **30** Prophets apparently stood to prophesy. If a seated prophet received a revelation, the speaking prophet must give way to him. It seems that the identity of those with the prophetic gift was known (12:29). How the reception of a revelation was known is not clear. What is clear is that the gift of prophecy in Corinth was of a very different character from OT prophecy.

■ **31** The word **all** (*pantes*) appears three times (the NIV obscures this by rendering the second example as **everyone** and omitting the third). The first refers to all the prophets (11:4 and 12:29 make it clear that the gift is not universal). The second and third examples refer to the congregation as a whole. The purpose of prophecy is the instruction and encouragement of the hearers. This gives an important insight into the content of prophetic speeches. The phrase **in turn** (*kath hena*) underscores the emphasis on orderliness in 14:30.

■ **32-33** The reality underlying the stress on order is twofold. First, stirrings animating the prophets are in the control of the prophets. No prophet *has* to speak. The gift of prophecy is subject to rational control. Second, the reason behind this is that God is a God of order and reason: not of disorder and confusion. The target here may be the frenzy that characterized Hellenistic prophecy and made its mark on prophetic ministry among the Corinthians.

Translations differ in taking v 33b with v 33a (as NIV) or v 34 (as NRSV). The former avoids the cumbersome repetition of "in the churches" (NRSV; obscured in the NIV by rendering v 33b as **in the congregations of the Lord's people**). The paragraph thus concludes with the statement that what Paul is enjoining is, in fact, common practice in Christian congregations everywhere. Evidently, the problems Paul has been addressing were unique to the church in Corinth. Paul has appealed earlier in the letter to the practice of the church or churches of God as a factor to be treated with respect (4:17; 7:17; 10:32; 11:16). To be out of step with fellow believers was not something to be undertaken lightly.

The above interpretation assumes that 14:33b is to be taken with v 33a, which clearly concludes the treatment of tongues and prophecy begun in v 26 (so NIV and NASB; note the conjunction **for** in v 33a). Some interpreters, however, take v 33b with v 34, making the practice refer to the silence of women in worship (so NRSV and REB; for a summary of scholars on both sides see Fitzmyer 2008, 527-28). This is not impossible though it creates an overweight sentence: "as in all the churches . . . women should be silent in the churches" (NRSV). In addition, v 36 follows awkwardly from vv 34-35. Some textual traditions (notably the Western text) place v 36 immediately after v 33, followed by vv 34-35. This gives a smooth connection. However, it is not completely clear whether this rearrangement was itself a scribal attempt to solve the problem.

(3) Regarding the Conduct of Women in Worship (14:34-35)

The authenticity of vv 34-35 has been rejected by some scholars on at least two grounds. First, in some manuscripts they stand after 40 and so are judged to be an interpolation by later scribes (Fee 2014, 782). Second, they flatly contradict 11:2-16 where women are assumed to be participants in worship (Hays 1997, 246). More probably, what is in mind here is conversational speech possibly weighing prophetic utterances (v 29). This could involve exchanging opinions with men other than their husbands (v 35). Such conversation would have been regarded as shameful in Corinthian society and Paul therefore excludes it (Paige 2002, 219-25, 240-42).

■ **34** The women in question were married as becomes clear in v 35. The submission enjoined is what was deemed appropriate in Corinthian society. **The law** is not that of the OT, which does not address this point. The reference is rather to what was the rule in Corinth.

■ **35** The involvement of married women in such matters as weighing the messages of the prophets led to their receiving instructions from husbands other than their own. This was shameful in Corinthian culture. Paul therefore directs that they should take their questions home where they could discuss the issues with their own husbands. The command that women keep silent is therefore occasion-specific, not general. (→ 11:2-16.)

e. Summary Conclusions and Advices (14:36-40)

Paul now moves into summarizing mode, drawing together the issues that have occupied him since 12:1, but with particular focus on the exercise of the gifts of prophecy and tongues.

■ **36** The assertiveness of the Corinthians in insisting that their view was the only possible view is now met with a pair of devastating rhetorical questions. Did they seriously believe that the word of God originated with them? Or did they think they were the only people it had reached? The use of the masculine adjective (*monous*) indicates that Paul is now addressing the church as a whole. This in turn makes clear that the problems discussed were Corinth-specific.

■ **37-38** The note of irony appears again, directed against those who thought (*dokei*) they were prophets or pneumatics (*pneumatikos*—shown again to be a Corinthian catchword). Paul now asserts his own authority as the Lord's spokesperson. A truly inspired prophet or pneumatic would recognize that Paul's word did not need to be weighed like those of the Corinthian prophets. It is the command of the Lord and therefore self-attesting. Those who know the Lord will recognize his voice. If anyone is ignorant of this, let him be ignorant.

■ **39-40** This is Paul's summary conclusion of the argument begun in 14:1 but which also picks up on 12:31 and 12:1. The tone of irony is not far away as the verb **be eager** (*zēloute* [14:39]) suggests (→ 12:31; 14:1). If the Corinthians are to covet any gift, let it be the gift of prophecy. The gift of tongues is neither to be sought nor excluded. This tends to confirm that earlier statements speaking approvingly of the gift of tongues (vv 5, 18, 19) are to be read in the same sense. The overriding principle is that everything be done in a fitting and orderly way.

FROM THE TEXT

The place of the mind in worship. In many respects this is the controlling theme of the entire chapter. Paul repeatedly brings the practice of the Corinthians to this touchstone (14:15). The ultimate test is whether the gospel is proclaimed, unbelievers are converted, and the people of God are built up in the faith. Worship that makes no great demands on the mind contributes little to the edification of the hearers. The trap the Corinthians fell into was associating the operation of the Holy Spirit more closely with noncognitive, spontaneous phenomena than with reflection on the Word, which addresses the understanding and transforms the heart.

Allied to the foregoing is *the place of order in worship.* When freedom borders on disorder and threatens meaning it stands at variance with God's created order. God's work in creation was to bring order out of chaos. Worship is to reflect that purpose which it does not do when it is defaced by clamor (vv 22-25) and confusion (vv 33, 40). However, this does not mean that free congregational participation in worship is prohibited (v 26). It is in order if it is in order!

The primacy of the word in worship. The preferred place given to prophecy by Paul is precisely because it is the vehicle of the word in its power to beget and strengthen faith (vv 24-26). There is a clear overlap between the gift of prophecy described here and the ministry of preaching as practiced throughout most of the history of the church. Prophetic preaching in important measure is part of the continuum of the prophetic gift described in this chapter.

The place of community in worship. The setting presupposed in ch 14 is the worshipping community. Of the twenty-two examples of the word "church" (*ekklēsia*) in the letter, nine occur in this chapter. The focus is on what takes place "in church" (vv 19, 23, 28, 33-35). Individual experience has, indeed, a place, but in corporate worship it should have meaning for more than the individual. Corporate worship by definition is not simply about "God and me" but rather about "God and all of us" (Thiselton 2000b, 1116-17).

The Gift of Tongues at Corinth

The character of the gift of tongues at Corinth appears to have been distinctive. In Acts glossolalia took the form of the ability to speak in unlearned languages (Acts 2:4) that were immediately understood by the hearers without the need for interpreters (vv 6-8). Its purpose was to facilitate and authenticate the spread of the gospel in cross-cultural settings at crucial moments in salvation history (10:44-48; 19:1-6). Only at such unique and historic turning points is it found. This understanding of tongues prevails throughout Acts (Keener 2003, 155; Schreiner 2008, 722; Levison 2009b, 627). In Corinth, on the other hand, the setting of tongues was the meetings of believers for worship (though outsiders might be present), and the utterances spoken required interpretation if anyone (including the speaker) was to understand (Collins 1999, 456). The difference between the two has given rise to perplexity and debate among Pentecostals (Ahn 2013, ch 2).

Apparently what was happening in the church at Corinth was unique among the churches (1 Cor 14:33, 36-40). In the other two gift lists in the Pauline writings (Rom 12:3-8; Eph 4:7-16), both concerned with the growth of the body, no mention of speaking in tongues or interpretation of tongues is made. This is particularly significant since the gift of prophecy is named in Rom 12:6, while the emphasis falls on building up the body of Christ in Eph 4:11-12. The distinctiveness of the Corinthian practice consisted in recurrent, unrestrained, congregation-wide glossolalia in languages understood by no one (1 Cor 14:9-11, 23).

The idea of a gift of tongues as a supernatural endowment had something of a history. It emerged from time to time in a variety of forms. The sect of the Dead Sea Scrolls, while not using the image of tongues-speaking in a literal sense, believed that its worship was caught up with that of the angels (4Q400-407, Wise, Abegg, and Cook 1996, 365-77; for a fuller statement see Deasley 2000b, 238-40). It is possible that some of the Corinthians may have claimed to be speaking the tongues of angels (13:1). A more literal form of tongues-speaking is found in the Testament of Job, a Jewish work roughly contemporary with Paul. In it Job's three daughters, deprived of any inheritance from their father, are given instead costly necklaces that will save them not only in this world but in the next. Hearing this, they are gifted with the angelic dialect (T. Job 48-50).

It is also worth noting that at the beginning of his treatment of spiritual gifts Paul makes mention of the influence of pagan religion on the Corinthians (12:2-3). The specific item he refers to is speaking: the absence of it in the case of idols; and its presence in the form of blasphemy ("Jesus be cursed") or confession ("Jesus is Lord"). The origin of the gift of tongues at Corinth is obscure (Forbes 1986, 257-69). The most famous oracle in ancient Greece was that of Apollo at Delphi. There the priestess, the Pythia, responded to questions put to her by the priests who also conveyed her responses to the inquirers.

It cannot be shown that the *form* of the gift of tongues in the Corinthian church owed anything to the practice of communication with the spirit world in Greek religion. But the *idea* of divine communication through human media was evidently present, as 12:3 clearly implies. The gift of tongues was one form of this as the expression "speaking in different kinds of tongues" (*genē glōssōn* [12:10]) suggests. The word "tongue" (*glōssa*) by itself denotes a known language (Rom 14:11; Phil 2:11). "Different kinds of tongues" suggests tongues of a different character: unknown languages. "Tongues . . . of angels" (1 Cor 13:1) is an example of this. Since they were unknown they required interpretation.

The picture of glossolalia that thus emerges is of an overwhelming though not irresistible rush of unintelligible speech (14:27). But the activity itself conveyed nothing since the language or tongue spoken was unknown. Its utility could be validated only by being interpreted. If there was no interpreter, the speaker should remain silent. Max Turner therefore characterizes the phenomenon aptly when he says that "Christian glossolalia was thus something of a religious novum" (1996, 237).

If as appears to be the case, the glossolalia at Corinth was one of a kind, then its significance for the church at other times and places becomes a large question. This is especially so in the light of Paul's distinctly reserved evaluation of it. It belongs to the ways of childhood (13:11; 14:20). It is inferior to the language of communication (14:6, 13-14). It does not merit positive recommendation (14:39). As R. P. Martin puts it, "Glossolalia was a Corinthian phenomenon with which Paul identified himself only with extreme caution and circumspection" (1984, vi).

After a lengthy review of the data Thiselton (2000b, 972-88) concludes that "to define the nature of 'tongues' with any degree of certainty is not . . . straightforward" (1077). Pentecostal scholars agree. Max Turner concedes that tongues at Corinth are "analogous to but different from modern tongues" (in Cartledge 2006, 1 n. 1). Gordon Fee writes, "The question as to whether the 'speaking in tongues' in contemporary Pentecostal and charismatic communities is the same in kind as that in the Pauline churches is moot. . . . There is simply no way to know" (2005, 170). Craig Keener holds that some modern forms of glossolalia are not what Paul understood by it (or, he adds, by what some other moderns understand by it [2012, 816]). Yongnan Jeon Ahn concludes, "Paul's view on tongues is still an uneasy one for Pentecostals" (2013, 145).

What this amounts to is that current practice of glossolalia cannot be used to interpret the gift of tongues in 1 Corinthians, and the gift of tongues in 1 Corinthians cannot be used to interpret or validate the gift of tongues as practiced today.

The Gift of Prophecy in 1 Corinthians

Prophecy is the only gift mentioned in all of the gift lists in Paul's writings (Rom 12:6-8; 1 Cor 12:8-10, 28-29; 14:6-8, 26-32; 1 Thess 5:19-22; Eph 4:11). He places prophecy first in order of importance among the gifts (1 Cor 14:1). In the two passages where he speaks of "prophets" (as distinct from "prophecy") they are placed second only after apostles (1 Cor 12:28; Eph 2:20; 4:11).

The nature of prophecy must be inferred from the various functions attributed to it. First, and emphatically, it was a means of building up the church (1 Cor 14:1-5). This is defined as strengthening, encouraging, and comforting the hearers (v 3). It is also associated with revelation and instruction (vv 29-31). Furthermore, it was a means of bringing unbelievers to repentance and faith (vv 23-25). While it took place at the urging and inspiration of the Spirit, such urgings were controllable and should be controlled by the prophet to avoid more than one prophet prophesying at a time, which would create confusion in worship (vv 29-32). Women receive the gift of prophecy as well as men (11:4-5). Prophecies are not to be accepted merely because they are delivered in prophetic mode, but should be evaluated carefully (14:29). Indeed, prophecy in its very nature is partial and transient (13:9-10).

How then is the gift of prophecy to be characterized? A variety of answers has been proposed (for an extended review, see Thiselton 2000b, 956-65).

1. Some place it on the same level as OT prophecy. T. R. Schreiner argues that just as the OT prophets spoke the word of God directly and authoritatively so did the NT prophets (2001, 360-64; 2018, 105-6). It is for this reason that prophets are linked with apostles as the foundation of the church (1 Cor 12:28; Eph 2:20; 3:5; 4:11). On this basis Schreiner argues that the gift of prophecy is no longer active today since its task was completed in the founding of the church (2018, 159-62).

2. Others find the evidence pointing to pastoral proclamation and instruction. The comprehensive term used to denote this is the upbuilding or edification of the church (1 Cor 12:7; 14:4-5, 19). Accordingly, prophecy is taken by R. P. Martin to be a charismatic gift of hortatory preaching in the context of pastoral ministry (1984, 14). Fee rejects any specific connection with pastoral ministry, stressing rather spontaneous Spirit-inspired messages designed to edify (2014, 660).

3. A broader definition is favored by some in view of the wide range of factors at work in prophecy (see above). Thus Thiselton includes pastoral insight into personal needs addressed in prepared or unprepared responses giving support and edification (2000b, 964).

It would seem that the data require a wider rather than a narrower definition. In particular the significance of the listing of prophets second only to apostles (12:28-29) needs to be taken into account. It is notable that Paul states repeatedly that it is the church that is built up by prophecy (12:7; 14:4, 5, 12, 19).

This coheres with Eph 2:20 where, following a lengthy exposition of how Gentiles and Jews alike have been reconciled through the cross (vv 11-18), he now affirms that God's new temple is "built on the foundation of the apostles and prophets" (v 20). The same language appears again in Eph 4:11-13, where the aim and purpose of the apostles and prophets is to build up the body of Christ "in the faith and in the knowledge of the Son of God" (v 13). This is defined even more precisely as the mystery "now . . . revealed by the Spirit to God's holy apostles and prophets" (3:5). This suggests that prophecy involved the interpretation of the faith: a point also implied in Rom 12:6, where the faith referred to is the faith believed rather than the act of believing (Wright 2002, 10:711). It is therefore understandable how such prophecy should demand careful evaluation by other persons of insight (1 Cor 14:29; 1 Thess 5:19-21; Rom 12:6).

VI. THE GOSPEL AND THE CHRISTIAN FUTURE: THE MESSAGE OF THE RESURRECTION: I CORINTHIANS 15:1-58

BEHIND THE TEXT

1. The place of the resurrection in the argument of the epistle as a whole as well as its position at the end of the epistle have been variously explained. On the one hand, it is pointed out that the section is not introduced by the formula indicating matters the Corinthians raised in their letter to Paul (7:1, 25; 8:1; 12:1). More specifically, the denial of the resurrection of the dead is attributed only to "some of you" (15:12). Hence, it is concluded that the matter is something of a detached problem (Perkins 2012, 172). Against this it is claimed that the chapter "forms not only the close and crown of the whole Epistle, but also provides the clue to its meaning" (Barth 1933, 11).

Similarly, M. J. Gorman sees ch 15 as "the foundation of the entire letter, and its most fundamental building block" (2017, 330). N. T. Wright, holding a kindred position, points to the implied references to resurrection throughout the epistle. The coming day of the Lord (1:8) when one's work will be tested to determine its durability and holiness (3:13-17); the futurity of judgment (4:5; 5:5; 6:14); the summons to live distanced from the world "for this world in its present form is passing away" (7:31); Paul's apostleship as grounded in his having seen the risen Lord (9:1), and his apostolic service having as its goal the wreath that is imperishable (9:25); the gifts to be coveted as those that will last (13:8, 13) rather than those that are passing (2003, 278-97): all are grounded in resurrection life as a reality after death, or, in Wright's preferred formulation, "life *after* 'life after death'" (31 and passim). Accordingly, Wright concludes that Paul regarded resurrection as "one of the keys to everything else he wanted to say" and kept it to the end because it was the unifying theme of the letter (278).

It seems fair to say that ch 15 has multiple concerns, many of which have appeared earlier in the letter. The first is the trustworthiness of the gospel he preached to them (vv 1-2). Cognate with this is his apostolic status, already under question in Corinth (9:1-2) but validated by his encounter with the resurrected Christ (15:8-11). If the dead are not raised, faith in Christ is futile (vv 14-17) as is Paul's suffering for the gospel (vv 30ff.). A further question apparently posed by some in Corinth concerned the nature of the resurrection body (v 35). The relation between the natural and the spiritual orders lay at the heart of it (vv 44-46): an apparent cause of confusion, not to say conflict in Corinth (v 50). It would seem, therefore, that many of the issues dealt with in the letter find their resolution in the proper understanding of the bodily resurrection of the dead. At the very least it made sense for Paul to have saved to the end of the letter the item that constituted the coping stone of the response to every issue of substance dealt with earlier.

2. Apparently, there had been unanimity of belief in the resurrection of Christ in response to Paul's preaching (vv 1, 11). However, a sea change of view—that the dead are not raised—had overtaken some of them (v 12), though not all (v 29). The heart of the problem appears to have consisted in the attempt of some to affirm the resurrection of Christ while denying the resurrection of anyone else (vv 12, 13). In Paul's mind this was tantamount to the denial of the resurrection in any meaningful sense. For Paul, the cross and the resurrection stood or fell together (vv 3, 17; compare Rom 4:30).

The resurrection of Christ not only validated the redemptive adequacy of his death but also created and embodied the resurrection life of those for whom he died. This indeed was the common Christian faith (1 Cor 15:11).

The precise reasoning by which the Corinthians—or some of them—came to reject this view can only be inferred. They probably saw Christ's resurrection as a singular symbolic happening, betokening a wholly spiritual redemption, emancipating them from the world of matter. Ideas of a bodiless spiritual existence after death were commonplace in Greek thought at that time. Paul feared that such a view could also have serious ethical consequences (vv 32-34). A further objection made by some was that, since bodily decay plainly followed death, resurrection was excluded (vv 35-38). Paul's reply is that the resurrection body is of a different character than the body of the present (vv 38-49). The change will take place in both the dead and the living at the end when the last trumpet sounds (vv 50-54).

3. There is widespread (Thiselton says "universal" [2000b, 1177]) agreement regarding the stages of the argument in this chapter. Paul begins with a demonstration of the resurrection as part of the apostolic gospel that he proclaimed and they believed (vv 1-11). He then proceeds to spell out the implications of denying the resurrection of the dead in general and of Christ in particular (vv 12-19). In contrast with this are the consequences of Christ's resurrection as the seal of God's ultimate victory in creation (vv 20-28). A short section then follows on the practical and ethical consequences in the here and now of denying the resurrection (vv 29-34). The nature of the resurrection body is then considered at length (vv 35-49). The chapter concludes with a description of the moment of final change (vv 50-58).

4. It is fair to say that interpretation of the chapter becomes more difficult as the chapter progresses. This is particularly the case with vv 20-28 and 35-57. N. T. Wright characterizes the chapter as "choppy exegetical waters" (2003, 317). I. Howard Marshall comments that what Paul says about the process of transformation is very difficult to interpret (2004, 460). A degree of tentativeness is therefore appropriate in any attempted exegesis.

A. The Resurrection of Christ as Central to the Gospel (15:1-34)

IN THE TEXT

1. The Resurrection as Central in the Apostolic Kerygma (15:1-11)

■ **1-2** The absence of the formula "now concerning" as found in 7:1, 25; 8:1; 12:1 suggests that the need of the Corinthians for instruction regarding the resurrection arose not from their inquiry but from a report received by Paul from someone with inside knowledge of the church (vv 12, 29). Since, however, the resurrection had been part of the gospel Paul had preached to them in the first place, anything he says about it now can only be by way of reminder. Hence **I want to remind you** (v 1). "Gospel" (*euangelion*) is a key term for Paul: sixty of the seventy-six instances in the NT are in writings that bear his name (Dunn 1998, 164 n. 2; Dunn suggests further that Paul may have coined the use of the term to denote his proclamation of the good news about Christ [168]).

The import of these verses is that what Paul is about to write is not anything new. This is true from two sides. From his side it is **the gospel I gospeled** [*euēngelisamēn*] **to you**. From their side it is the gospel that they received, in which they stand, through which they are saved if they hold firmly to the word he gospeled to them—unless, that is, they believed in vain. From the start, therefore, Paul indicates what is at stake. The Corinthians' questionings had to do with the resurrection. Paul's implied reply is that to deny the resurrection is to deny the gospel.

■ **3** Two fundamental tenets are affirmed in vv 3-5: the death of Christ for our sins and his bodily resurrection. The verses consist of four clauses each introduced by **that** (*hoti*) and may well have been an early creedal or confessional formulary. This is confirmed by the use of the terms **I passed on** (*paredōka*) and **I received** (*parelabon*), which are standard terms for the transmission of tradition (→ 11:2, 23, and Bruce 1977, 264-66).

The matter that Paul passed on was **of first importance**. It was not his invention: he himself had received it. The first clause makes three affirmations. First it was Christ who died. The use of **Christ** (rather than "Jesus") is typical of Paul's usage in referring to Christ's death and resurrection (e.g., Rom 5:6; 14:9; 1 Cor 1:23; Gal 2:21). It was Jesus as God's Anointed who died. Second, Christ's death was redemptive: his death was for us. What we could not do for ourselves because of what we are, he did for us because of who he is. He took our place, the innocent for the guilty. (A fuller statement of Paul's meaning is 2 Cor 5:21.) Third, Christ's death was in keeping with Scripture. Whether Paul had specific passages in mind is disputed (Thiselton 2000b, 1190). Isaiah 53:5-6, 11-12 are cited as possibilities, especially in view of allusions to them by Jesus at the Last Supper (Matt 26:28; Mark 14:24). More generally, Christ's ministry as the fulfillment of the saving purposes of God in the OT validate sufficiently the point made (Luke 24:44-47; Acts 3:17-26).

■ **4** The second clause contains the single statement **that he was buried**. The verb *etaphē*, like "died" (*apethanen*) in the first clause, expresses the actuality of the two events. The burial looks backward and forward, confirming the reality of both his death and his resurrection. The third clause asserts that **he was raised** (*egēgertai*): the perfect tense contrasting with the preceding aorists to denote the abiding character of the resurrection (Rom 6:10; 2 Cor 13:4).

The point is underscored by the use of the passive—**he was raised**—Paul's habitual usage, indicating that the resurrection was the work of God (Dunn 1998, 175 n. 72; the sole exception is 1 Thess 4:14).

The clause continues that the resurrection took place **on the third day according to the Scriptures**. This has usually been taken to be a strictly literal statement, echoing OT passages such as Hos 6:2; Jonah 1:17 (compare Matt 12:40). The expression may also reflect the Jewish view that the decomposition of a corpse begins after the third day of death (see John 11:17, 39). This can only mean that the resurrection in mind was the resurrection of his corpse: a point insisted on in Peter's Pentecostal sermon (Acts 2:24-31). (For a full exploration and examination of this point, see Martin Pickup 2013, 511-42.)

■ **5** The fourth clause of the creedal formulary records appearances of the risen Jesus. The verb *ōphthē* is to be taken as middle ("he appeared") rather than passive ("was seen"). The appearances were at the initiative of Jesus, stressing their objectivity. The mention of Peter and the Twelve follows Luke's account (24:34, 36) where the appearances to the women are not recorded (contrast Matt 28:1-10; Mark 16:1-8; John 20:1-10). Significantly, Peter is referred to as **Cephas**, the name given to him by Jesus (John 1:42), and the apostles are referred to as **the Twelve**, though only eleven survived (Matt 28:16) and only ten were present (John 20:24-25). These features confirm that a creedal form is being quoted.

■ **6** The listing of resurrection appearances continues. However, the word used for "that" (*hoti*) up to this point is replaced by "then" (*epeita*, which the NIV translates as **after that**). This may indicate that the creedal formulary in 1 Cor 15:3-5 is now ended. Paul now sets down additional traditions that not only confirm the fact of the resurrection but also include himself among the witnesses.

The large number who witnessed this appearance at the same time confirms its veracity. The same point is made by the statement that most were still alive and therefore could be questioned. The vivid observation that **some have fallen asleep** implies Paul's personal knowledge of at least a fair number of such witnesses.

■ **7** An appearance to James is mentioned only here. Like all of Jesus' family, his brother James did not believe in him during his lifetime (Mark 3:21, 31ff.; John 7:5). However, James quickly emerges as leader in the Jerusalem church (Acts 1:13-14; 15:13; Gal 1:18-19; 2:9-10). Paul may have learned of the appearance to James on his visit to Jerusalem (Gal 1:19). The appearance **to all the apostles** is apparently to be distinguished from the appearance to "the Twelve" (1 Cor 15:5). **All the apostles** were a larger number than the Twelve (Rom 16:7; 1 Cor 9:5; Gal 1:17, 19) though it included the Twelve (Gal 1:17-

19). The appearance was evidently to the entire group. (For a discussion of the possible options, see Fee 2014, 811-12.)

■ **8** Paul clearly regarded the appearance of Jesus on the Damascus Road (Acts 9:3-9; 22:6-11; 26:12-15) as being of the same character as the others he has just listed even if it was of different form. Not only so, but he regarded it as the last of the resurrection appearances of Jesus before his ascension. The implication of this is that Paul was thereby included among the apostles (1 Cor 9:1). Paul's description of the event **as to one abnormally born** has been variously understood, ranging all the way from premature birth (whether by abortion or miscarriage) to birth beyond term (*ektrōma* [BDAG]). N. T. Wright notes the definite article (*the* untimely birth), finding a reference to a specific example such as Job 3:16 or Num 12:12 describing someone as good as dead coming to life (2003, 328-29). However, due weight must be given to the expression **last of all** in defining the meaning of abnormal birth. The natural sense would seem to be not that Paul was born too early but too late: too late not merely to witness more of the resurrection appearances, but to have known Jesus during his earthly ministry of teaching, healing, and praying. It is seemingly not intended as a compliment and may have been used by his opponents in Corinth as a criticism of his ministry. The general drift of 1 Cor 15:9-11 may confirm this.

■ **9** The argument now moves on from the listing of the resurrection appearances to their application to the ministry of Paul. Though Paul may well have heard himself described by his Corinthian critics as **the least of the apostles** and **not** deserving **to be called an apostle**, there is no doubt that he would have said the same with perfect sincerity. The thought that he had **persecuted the church of God** was a source of abiding shame and regret (Gal 1:13, 22-23; Phil 3:6*a*).

■ **10** At the same time, the fact that he deserved nothing and had received so much could have only one result—namely, glorifying the grace and mercy of God (1 Tim 1:12-16). The word **grace** (*charis*) occurs three times in this verse. It is God's grace that has made him what he is. Moreover, the grace he received was not wasted on him. His record showed clearly that he had accomplished more than all of the apostles put together. (Two or three years later he would make the same point on an even wider scale: Rom 15:15-21.) Nevertheless, he repeats that his efforts were the product of the grace of God.

■ **11** Accordingly (therefore: *oun*), whether it was "the least of the apostles" (1 Cor 15:9) or the greatest apostles, the matter of moment was that the gospel was preached. The second half of the verse neatly combines the respective roles of all the apostles and of Paul himself. All of the apostles preach the same gospel; the Corinthians "have come to believe" (*episteusate* as in v 2 NRSV) through the ministry of Paul (despite his having been "abnormally born" [v 8]). The important thing in the end is not the messenger but the message.

FROM THE TEXT

1. The situation in the Corinthian church to which the whole of ch 15 is addressed is the possibility that the Corinthian believers—or at least some of them—have lost their faith (vv 2, 14). It is possible to receive the gospel and, indeed, to take one's stand on it, then to relapse, and so to have believed in vain. Paul has already had occasion to warn the Corinthians of that possibility (10:12). In 15:14 he repeats the idea that where the resurrection of Christ is denied, faith becomes futile and empty. Final salvation is dependent on continuance in faith. Accordingly, the whole chapter is not an abstract exercise in the theology of the resurrection. It is a pastoral attempt to salvage the faith of those who no longer believed in the resurrection and, consequently, had believed in vain. But this requires a theological argument. Theology is not a matter only for the classroom. It is a matter for the pulpit and the congregation.

2. The one gospel (vv 1, 2) has many facets (vv 3-5), all of which together are **of first importance** (v 3). They stand or fall together because they are interdependent. The fact that Christ's death was real and not simply a fainting fit is confirmed by the fact that he was buried. The reality of his resurrection is confirmed not only because he truly died and was buried but because he appeared to Cephas and the Twelve. Paul is thus able to attribute the forgiveness of sins to Christ's death (v 3) and his resurrection (v 17). To deny any one of these elements is to neutralize all. Paul proceeds to focus on the aspect of the resurrection because this was the focus of Corinthian skepticism. But the gospel is an integrated whole. To deny any one aspect is to undermine the whole edifice.

3. The encompassing character of the grace of God in life and ministry comes to vivid expression in vv 9-10. The term "grace" (*charis*) covers a wide area in Pauline thought, from the undeserved favor of salvation (Rom 3:24; 5:1-2) to specific spiritual gifts (1 Cor 1:4-7) to particular endowments for the service of God (3:10). All three are not far apart in 15:9-10, not least because Paul's conversion and appointment as an apostle were simultaneous (15:8; compare 9:1). Paul was enough of a realist to know—and say—that he had labored harder than all the apostles, but no sooner has he said it than he credits it all to the grace of God (15:10). His awareness of his past as a persecutor of the church never ceased to stir in him a sense of shame (v 9). It was divine grace that had made him what he had become—and that grace had been effectual (v 10). There can be no effective proclamation of grace where there has been no lively experience of it.

BEHIND THE TEXT

2. The Denial of the Resurrection as Fatal to the Gospel (15:12-19)

These verses consist of an exposé and rebuttal of the implications of denying the resurrection of the dead. The precise nature of the denial is not completely clear (Bruce 1976, 144; Soards 1999, 325). It is not certain whether the Corinthians were claiming that, while Christ had been raised, there was no resurrection for anyone else (15:13), but only bodiless immortality: survival of the spirit. On the other hand, the language could be taken as a blanket denial of resurrection for anyone—Christ included. The expression "from among dead people" or "corpses" defines clearly what Paul had in mind (vv 12, 13) and it expresses what Paul believed and the Corinthians denied. The drift of the argument, which affirms that the Christian dead share the same future as the living, resurrected Christ (vv 17-19), suggests that the second option is nearer the mark. The dominant motif in vv 12-19 is the correspondence between Christ and Christians.

IN THE TEXT

■ **12** The passive form of the verb (**is preached**) is used, building on the expression "whether . . . it is I or they" in v 11. It excludes the possibility that belief in the resurrection of the dead was a Pauline idiosyncrasy. Paul's Corinthian critics may have been making this claim. On the contrary, belief in Christ's resurrection was part of the gospel from the start, as Paul has just demonstrated (vv 3-8). Not only so, but the Corinthians themselves had believed it (v 11*b*). Faith in Christ's resurrection is nullified if it is now affirmed that there is no such thing as resurrection from the dead. This skepticism is attributed only to **some** of the Corinthians, but apparently to enough of them to cause Paul concern. Paul has referred already to his critics in Corinth (4:18; 9:3). They evidently were not slow to speak their minds. They were almost certainly Gentiles and therefore open to influence by Greek philosophy. The underlying assumptions of Paul and the Corinthians are thus made clear from the start. Paul believed there is no existence without bodily existence. The Corinthians believed that bodily existence was not necessary for personal survival. Precisely what Paul means by a resurrected body he will define later (15:35-54). It is sufficient for his argument at this point to cite the apostolic testimony to Christ's burial and resurrection on the third day (v 4) followed by multiple appearances to his followers, including Paul himself (vv 5-8). Paul now develops the case against Corinthian skepticism twice over. In vv 13-15 he expounds its destructive implications for Christ's resurrection (v 13), the gospel (v 14), and the apostolic witness (v 15). In vv 16-19 he expounds its nullifying impact on Christ's resurrection (v 16); faith in Christ, and the fate of the departed (vv 17-18); and any hope of life after death (v 19).

■ **13** Paul's first statement of the consequences of the denial of bodily resurrection focuses first on Christ, then on the gospel, and finally on his own integrity (vv 13-15). To rule out resurrection of the dead is to rule out Christ's resurrection. Whether the Corinthians regarded Christ as an exception (possibly by interpreting his resurrection as akin to the elevation of the deceased Roman emperors to divine status: Ciampa and Rosner 2010, 755), or simply flatly denied his resurrection, Paul begins with his fundamental affirmation that Christ's bodily resurrection is the foundation of every Christian claim. The entire Christian case rests on it.

■ **14** Two related consequences follow **if Christ has not been raised** (throughout the passage the passive voice is used to refer to Christ's resurrection, implying that it was the work of God). First, the gospel message is simply empty words; and second, the Corinthians' faith was equally empty. What this implies—as Robertson and Plummer point out (1914, 348)—is that the resurrection is not an isolated truth that can be accepted or rejected leaving other truths intact. Remove it and the whole edifice of the kerygma collapses.

■ **15** A further consequence is entailed if the resurrection was a non-event: Paul's character as a witness and that of his fellow apostles is fatally undermined. (The plural verbs are probably to be read in the light of v 11.) To claim that God raised Christ when resurrection does not happen is to bear false witness against God himself, an offense that the commandment does not even envisage (Exod 20:16).

■ **16-19** The seriousness of the issue is indicated in that Paul revisits the matter a second time, with a second series of conditional statements followed by a description of the consequences. There is partial repetition but also expansion of what has been said in the earlier sequence. Verse 16 is essentially a repetition of v 13.

■ **17-19** The futility of faith if Christ has not been raised is spelled out in two respects. First, his death loses its power to deal with sin. The kerygma declares that "Christ died for our sins" (1 Cor 15:3) but follows this up immediately with the declaration of his resurrection attested by the apostles and many others, including Paul himself (vv 4-5). The resurrection is the validation of the atoning significance of Christ's death (Rom 4:25). Without it the death has no particular meaning. It is assumed by Paul that, whatever other odd opinions the Corinthians might hold, deliverance from their sins was one truth that they would value. Second, those who have died (**fallen asleep**) in Christ have gone forever (1 Cor 15:18). To "fall asleep" was a common metaphor for death in Paul's world. Paul has already used it in this chapter (v 6), and the Corinthians apparently did not believe that death put an end to everything (v 29). But Paul says this is exactly what would happen to those who have died "in Christ" if he has not been raised. The experience of being "in Christ" is one of high potency (2 Cor 5:17; 1 Thess 4:16), but if he was not raised, it has been emptied of its power. Union with one who was defeated by death can only lead to the same fate.

The third conditional statement builds on the first two: that **Christ has not been raised** (1 Cor 15:16), and that therefore **faith is futile** and the departed **are lost** (vv 17-18). This leaves only one remaining option: that faith in Christ provides hope only for the present, but what is this worth if the reality of forgiveness and hope for the future have been demolished? (v 19).

FROM THE TEXT

1. For Paul, Christ's resurrection was an event after which history would never be the same. Christ's resurrection was not simply a wonder to strike amazement, like a horse with two heads. It was an event that brought the seemingly unstoppable onrush of death to a screeching halt. Until then, humanity lived under the curse: returning to the dust was the fate of all (Gen 3:19). If the only hope Christ brings is hope for the present life, then our case is pitiable indeed (1 Cor 15:19). The resurrection of Christ brings the guarantee of everlasting life, which was God's plan and purpose from the beginning (Gen 1:30; 2:7-8).

2. The assurance of deliverance from sin is guaranteed by Christ's resurrection (1 Cor 15:17). This apparently mattered to the Corinthians whatever other theological deficiencies they may have harbored. It is also named as the purpose of Christ's death (v 3). Its place should not be usurped by other emphases, which can happen very easily. The version of the gospel promising health, wealth, and happiness, which is fashionable in some quarters today, can very easily subvert the matter "of first importance: that Christ died for our sins" (v 3).

3. The Resurrection of the Dead as Fundamental to the Final Triumph of God (15:20-28)

BEHIND THE TEXT

These verses serve a double purpose. On the one hand, 15:20-23 is an emphatic assertion of the reality of the resurrection in response to Corinthian skepticism (vv 13-19). In particular they advance the argument by showing how the resurrection of Christ carries within itself the promise of the resurrection of others. On the other hand, vv 24-28 pick up the point made almost in passing in v 23 that the resurrection will take place at Christ's coming. This leads to an exposition of the end when death will be destroyed and God will reign supreme. Eschatological language—already found in 4:1-5, 6:1-11, and 7:29-31—comes into play with the mention of the end, the destruction of every dominion and power and the subjection of everything to God (15:24, 26, 28). The universal scope of the triumph first of Christ, then of God, is underlined by the repeated use of "all" (*pas*; variously translated as "all" or "everything" in the NIV) in vv 24-28. The overall pattern of Paul's teaching is thus that the resurrection of Christ has happened *already*; the resurrection of believers is *yet to come*. But as surely as the former has already happened, so surely will the latter follow in due time.

IN THE TEXT

■ **20** Christ's resurrection is affirmed emphatically. The beginning words "but now" (*nuni de*; rendered **indeed** in the NIV and "but in fact" in the NRSV) are logical, not temporal. Characteristically, the passive form of the verb is used—**has . . . been raised**. Resurrection is the work of God. It has been assumed in vv 12-19 that Christ's resurrection carried implications for those who believed in him. The nature of that connection is now stated explicitly: he was the firstfruits of those who have died. The image of the firstfruits—drawn from Lev 23:10-11—is used by Paul in a variety of ways (Rom 8:23; 11:16; 16:5). The common idea is that the first sheaf is the guarantee that the rest of the crop will follow. The resurrection of Christ is the guarantee that the resurrection of the Christian departed is secure. Their description as "those . . . who have fallen asleep" (compare 1 Cor 15:18) distinguishes them "from the dead" (v 20) and those who have died (v 22).

■ **21-22** The unique role of Christ as having been raised from the dead is now explained. The giver of resurrection life stands as the counterpart of the giver of death. Since death came **through a man** (v 21), its power could be broken only by one acting on the same plane—namely, by one who was also a man. But Christ is a man with a difference. In him the image of God was not defaced by disobedience as it was in Adam. Hence, just as Adam's disobedience brought death to all, the obedience of Christ brings life to all. (That this means "makes life available to all" is indicated immediately in the next verse. See also Rom 5:17.) The implication of this is that a new age has begun.

■ **23** The implementation of this new state of affairs is now spelled out. The question Paul essentially confronts is: when will death be reversed by resurrection? His answer is that everything will take place in due order. The term *tagma*—translated **turn** or "order" (NRSV)—is a military term denoting appropriate place or position. The appropriate order for resurrection is first Christ who, as the firstfruits, has already been raised, then at his coming (Parousia) those who belong to him. The term *parousia* was used in reference to the coming of personages of rank. Christ has the necessary rank to raise others because he himself has been raised. This resurrection will apply to **those who belong to him** (this qualifies the "all" of the previous verse). **Then** (*epeita*) clearly presupposes a time lapse between Christ's resurrection and Parousia. Presumably, this allows for the completion of the Gentile mission and the salvation of Israel (Rom 11:11-27). Paul's primary point is to affirm that the resurrection of those who belong to Christ will take place at Christ's Parousia.

■ **24-28** These verses have been interpreted in widely different ways, beginning with the opening phrase **then the end** (v 24). Some take the adverb *eita* **(then)** to mean the same as *epeita* ("then" [v 23]), which clearly denotes an interval between Christ's resurrection and the Parousia. F. F. Bruce takes the interval to be brief and to refer to the final phase of Christ's kingship when his people will rule and judge the world (4:8; 6:2; 1976, 146-47). Millennialist interpreters understand the adverbs in the same way but take the interval to be a thousand years, importing this feature from Rev 20:2-3. However, neither adverb in itself need denote length of time but simply succession (BDAG 295, 361). The context alone must decide. The end is apparently the event following the Parousia and is defined as the moment when Christ will return his kingly power to the Father. By then he will have subdued all of the hostile powers, the last of which will be death itself. That is to say, the kingly rule of Christ and the subjugation of the powers of darkness take place *before* and culminate in the Parousia. Immediately following the Parousia Christ yields his kingly power to the Father, since his task is now complete. Christ's lordship began with his resurrection and ascension when he was exalted to God's right hand (Rom 8:34; Eph 1:20-23; Col 1:13; 1 Pet 3:12; a parallel line of thought is Heb 2:5-9). The assumption on which Paul's argument is based is that Christ's lordship is a present reality. This is now worked out in detail in the succeeding verses.

The content of the end is indicated as the returning to God the Father of the power of kingly authority by Christ after he has destroyed every power hostile to God (1 Cor 15:24-27*a*). **Dominion, authority and power** (v 24) are standard apocalyptic terms denoting natural and supernatural powers that are opposed to God. Mark 13:22-27 is a typical example. (On the import of apocalyptic language, see Thiselton 2000b, 233-39; Wright 1996, 513-17.)

■ **25** The proof of the necessity and certainty of Christ's triumph is now given in citations from Pss 110:1 and 8:6 (7 LXX). Both are taken to find their fulfillment in Christ. There is debate as to whether the subject in **he has put**

(1 Cor 15:25) is the Lord God (as in Ps 110:1) or Christ. Since Christ is the doer of the actions in 1 Cor 15:24 and the same actions are in mind in v 25, it is probable that Christ is the subject in v 25.

■ 26 The **last enemy** is identified by name (v 26). The combined expression indicates both its power and its malevolence. It has been Paul's target from the beginning of the argument, as it has been humanity's foe from the beginning of creation (v 22). **Death** has resisted to the bitter end. In Christ it has met its match (Rom 5:17).

■ 27 Psalm 8:6 is now quoted as further scriptural support (in addition to Ps 110:1) of Christ's victory (**under his feet** [1 Cor 15:27a] is common to both quotations). Paul has added the conjunction **for** (*gar*) to the original text (Ps 8:6 [7 LXX]) immediately after the word **everything** (*panta*) for emphasis.

A possible misunderstanding is now addressed (1 Cor 15:27b-28). The subjection of everything to Christ might be taken to include God himself. This is a curious application of Ps 8:6. Was it favored by some Corinthians? Or did Paul fear they might relapse into polytheism (Ps 8:4-10)? His reply is strictly logical: that since Christ received the kingly power from the Father, God cannot be a subordinate figure in the kingdom.

■ 28 When Christ's kingly rule has subjugated every hostile power, he will return the kingly power to God the Father (1 Cor 15:24). The Son will thus acknowledge the Father as the source of the power he has exercised. The focus on the Father does not imply subordinationism as though the Son is an inferior being. It is entirely in harmony with Paul's teaching elsewhere (Rom 16:27; Gal 1:3-5; Phil 2:9-11). The reference throughout is to activity and agency rather than being and existence.

The verb translated **will be made subject** (*hupotagēsetai* [1 Cor 15:28]) should probably be taken as future middle (rather than passive): "will subject himself." This is in keeping with Christ's voluntary handing over of the kingdom to God the Father in v 24. In the end God will be directly involved in the work of restoring his creation as he was in its creation in the beginning. "From him and through him and for him are all things" (Rom 11:36).

FROM THE TEXT

1. Evil can assume a scale that gives it a superhuman, almost supernatural dimension. In oppressive societies where every movement is tracked and every word recorded, the power of evil seems omnipresent and almost tangible. Paul seems to have seen "spiritual power" as the inside of physical or social structures and systems (Wink 1984, 104-8; Reid 1993, 746-52). Ephesians 6:12 gives expression to this understanding. It is a sobering thought that human beings and institutions can become agencies of the powers of darkness.

2. Death is the ultimate contradiction of the deepest instincts of the human soul. What John Keats said poetically of the nightingale as he listened to its song—"Thou wast not born for death"—is true literally of creatures made in the image of God. Paul aptly names death "the last enemy" (1 Cor 15:26). Of all the powers of evil, it is the most resistant to the life-giving grace of Christ. But its doom is secure. Christ's resurrection broke its power not only for him but also for all those united to him. He was the firstfruits. In God's good time the rest of the harvest will be gathered in. Then will be celebrated the death of death.

3. Christ is already Lord. The lordship of the universe has already been entrusted to him by the Father. Already he is engaged in overthrowing the dominion, authority, and power of evil (Eph 1:19-22; Col 1:13; 1 Pet 3:21-22). Even—indeed especially—where evil is doing its worst its confidence is misplaced: blind to the realities of the power of God. We do not yet see everything subject to him, but with the eye of faith we see him enthroned in the place of authority until every usurper acknowledges his lordship (Heb 2:5-9).

> He sits at God's right hand
> Till all his foes submit
> And bow to his command
> And fall beneath his feet. (Charles Wesley)

The Lord reigns!

4. Some Personal Implications of the Denial of the Resurrection (15:29-34)

BEHIND THE TEXT

Paul has already drawn out several implications of the denial of the resurrection of the dead for himself (15:14, 15) and the Corinthians (vv 17, 18) as well as for both (v 19). He now returns to this aspect with examples that are evidently more sharply individualistic than those already named. Acute personal loss is apparently envisaged on the part of some of the Corinthians ("them" or "those" [v 29]), Paul himself ("us" or "I" [vv 30-32]), and others of the Corinthians addressed directly ("you" [vv 33-34]). (The distinction between those Corinthians who believed in the resurrection of the dead and those who did not is presupposed here.) The deprivation of gain of some sort to the active subjects seems to be implied where it is not explicitly stated.

IN THE TEXT

■ 29 The number of interpretations offered for this verse has been variously calculated at from forty (Fee 2014, 844) to two hundred (Conzelmann 1975,

276 n. 120), leading some to "exegetical agnosticism" (White 1997, 487). Any interpretation must be tentative. Two that have received a significant degree of support may be considered. The first argues that baptism **for** or "on behalf of" (*hyper* NRSV) the dead means vicarious baptism. Believers who had died without being baptized now had that omission made good by believers who were baptized in their name for their benefit. The background for such a mentality is sought in burial practices in pagan Corinth where the dead were believed to be assisted in their journey in the next world through aids and offerings placed in their graves (DeMaris 1995). This interpretation gives the natural sense of the Greek text. However, it assumes a sacramentalist and even superstitious understanding of baptism and does not sit comfortably with Paul's teaching on the need for personal faith. It has been replied that Paul expresses no opinion on the truth of the practice. He simply cites it as an illustration of belief in the resurrection of the dead on the part of some of the Corinthians (Bruce 1976, 148; Witherington 1995, 305-6).

A second interpretation takes the words **what will those do** to indicate that the effect of being baptized for the dead falls not on the dead but on those being baptized for them. The preposition *hyper* is taken in the sense of "on account of the dead." The thought is then that the faith of those being baptized has been inspired by the faith of those who have already died. What will become of such people if the resurrection of the dead is a fiction? (For fuller expositions of this line of interpretation, see Findlay 1912, 930-31; Robertson and Plummer 1914, 359-60; Thiselton 2000b, 1248-49.) What is clear on either of these interpretations is that the verse makes sense only on the assumption of the reality of the resurrection of the dead. This is precisely what Paul is contending for in this chapter.

■ **30-32** Those baptized on account of the dead were not alone in being exposed to loss if the resurrection of the dead was fictitious. Paul shared their experience in the danger to which his apostolic ministry exposed him **every hour** (v 30). Death was his daily companion—as certain as his boasting about them. His experience in Ephesus stood out in his mind as a time when death seemed a distinct possibility—like fighting with the wild beasts in the arena (Acts 19:23-41; 2 Cor 1:8-11). What would he have gained by it all if death were the end? The question in Paul's mind was rhetorical. If death is our final fate, the course to be followed is living it up while we are alive. The biblical quotation in 1 Cor 15:32 is from Isa 22:13. The idea is expressed even more flatly in Eccl 2:24-25. The description of Paul's experience serves as a further (though unspoken) defense of the character of Paul's apostolic ministry. He has already defended it against Corinthian contempt (4:8-13; 9:3-23). Here he implicitly defends it with the further argument that it is grounded in the fact of the resurrection.

■ **33-34** Paul now addresses the Corinthians directly: "Do not be deceived" (v 33 NRSV). His argument has seemingly led him to approve a life of unbridled indulgence. He repudiates this by quoting a line from Greek poet Menander: **Bad company corrupts good character.** While the dictum had probably become a popular proverb, its use here is carefully calculated. Some of the Corinthians had not been particularly discriminating in their choice of associates, whose influence on their lifestyle had not been altogether wholesome. The terms used in the quotation probably denote sexual misconduct. The earlier reference to the resurrection is in the context of his denunciation of fornication and prostitution (6:13-18). Paul's language is unsparing.

In three sharp statements Paul depicts their condition, explains how it has come about, and pronounces his verdict on it. First, they should **come . . . to their senses . . . and stop sinning** (15:34). Their judgment has lacked "rightness" (*dikaiōs*). Second, they should acknowledge that some people—presumably those with whom they have been associating—far from being fountainheads of wisdom, were ignorant of God. Third, rather than being a matter of congratulation as the Corinthians believed, their conduct has been shameful. Paul was not afraid to call a spade a spade—not even with his spiritual offspring (4:14-21).

FROM THE TEXT

A striking feature of these verses is the way in which an item of faith—namely, the resurrection of the body—is shown to be a determining factor in Christian life and practice. Several forms in which this emerges are spelled out.

1. The faith of the departed serves as a powerful stimulus to the faith of the living. For some the faith of those now gone was what brought them to faith in the first place. The classic expression of this idea is found in Heb 11 where the example of those who died before having received what was promised is cited as a spur to all believers (11:39—12:2).

2. The resurrection of the dead is a bulwark to those facing adversity and persecution. The point Paul makes is based on his own experience of adversity and the danger of death itself. The confidence that death does not have the last word is a strength to all believers caught in the stresses of life, and not least to those in the ranks of the persecuted church.

3. A direct link is drawn between belief in the resurrection and the moral life (1 Cor 15:32*b*-34). Paul has already made the connection between moral purity and the resurrection of the body (6:13-14). Once more he draws

a direct line between what one believes and how one behaves. If the Corinthians—"some" of them (15:12)—were thinking that the soul alone was immortal but the body was destined to destruction and therefore they could use it as they pleased, they were overlooking the truth of the resurrection of the body. If death involves the extinction of the body, there is no ultimate sanction against a life of immoral indulgence. The bodily resurrection of Christ is proof that the body has a future. It is not to be treated as dispensable.

B. The Nature of the Resurrection Body (15:35-58)

BEHIND THE TEXT

The argument thus far has concentrated on bodily resurrection as a fact: exhibited in the case of Jesus and holding out the promise of resurrection to those who are his (15:20-22). The focus now shifts to how such a resurrection takes place. In particular, the question arises as to how bodily resurrection is to be understood: indeed, how it is even possible.

Lurking behind this seems to have been an exaggerated understanding of the spirituality attainable in the present, offset by an underrated estimate of the character of life after death (vv 44, 46). What the Corinthians did not believe is clearer than what they did believe. The focal point of their problem was Paul's insistence that the life of the age to come was bodily (v 35). To the Corinthian objectors, as to Greeks generally, such a view was simply absurd. To them everything of spiritual value was attainable in the present. From one perspective this might be described as overrealized eschatology. But since what was driving the Corinthians was their Hellenistic mindset—which denied any form of bodily existence after death—it might also be seen as the Hellenization of eschatology: the interpretation of Paul's eschatological teaching in terms of prevailing Hellenistic notions about the afterlife. (Interpreters are divided in regard to the character of the eschatology favored by the Corinthians. Martin rejects the idea of overrealized eschatology, tracing the problems in Corinth to their viewing of the various gifts as indicators of status [1995, 86, 105-8].) Thiselton modifies his earlier view that overrealized eschatology was the unifying issue in 1 Corinthians. While not denying its presence, he now accepts that cultural attitudes from non-Christian Corinth also played a role (2000b, 40).

Paul's task in these verses is at least twofold (as v 35 implies). He is required to show (1) how bodily resurrection is a coherent concept (vv 35-49); and (2) how the bodily change he describes takes place (vv 50-58). Hence, the crucial term in these verses is "we will . . . be changed" (*allagēsometha* [v 51]).

IN THE TEXT

1. The Character of the Resurrection Body as Suggested by Nature (15:35-44)

■ **35** The argument now moves from Paul's side to that of the Corinthian skeptics. The question that Paul threw at them in v 12 he now allows them to throw at him. He casts their question: **But someone will ask** in a rhetorical form—the diatribe—well known at that time (Stowers 1992). It is taken by some to be two separate questions: the first querying the manner of the resurrection, to which Paul responds in vv 50-57; the second concerning the nature of the resurrection body, which he addresses in vv 36-49 (Ciampa and Rosner 2010, 799-800). More probably it is to be read as a single question, framed from the Corinthians' thoroughly skeptical point of view: "How can dead people be raised? What kind of body can they possibly have?" (Garland 2003, 727; Fee 2014, 862). Paul's response to how resurrection of dead persons is possible is given in his account of the resurrection body and the change involved in its realization.

■ **36** The rhetorical form continues with the exclamation "Fool!" (NRSV). Paul is not addressing any individual Corinthian but "someone" within the framework of the argument. He now introduces the analogy of the seed that controls the argument to the end of v 49. His thought is that of a layman, not a botanist (compare John 12:24). To all appearances, the seed that is sown returns to life only if it dies first.

■ **37** Further, the body (that is, the form) that is sown is not the body that it will become when it returns to life.

■ **38** This order of things is the work of God. It is God who is active in this process of bringing back to life (present tense) and God works **as he has determined** (*ēthelēsen*). Bringing dead things back to life and endowing them with new bodies has been God's work from the beginning. With the principle of resurrection from death and the consequent change in body thus established, Paul now proceeds to apply it directly to humanity.

■ **39-41** The analogy now shifts from "seed" to **flesh**. The key words in the argument are **flesh** (v 39), **bodies** (v 40), and "glory" (v 41 NRSV). Just as there are different kinds of flesh, there are different kinds of bodies, each glorious in its own way. The implied point is that since there is variety in God's world, there is no reason why only one kind of human body should be thought possible.

Flesh (*sarx* [v 39]) here refers to material substance. In God's creation there is more than one kind of flesh, hence variety in bodily composition is not surprising. It follows that there are **bodies** adapted to heaven and **bod-**

ies adapted to earth (v 40): each with its own kind of **splendor** or glory. The introduction of the term **heavenly** prompts the thought that, while there is a glory or **splendor** in the **earthly** body, the glory of the heavenly body is greater (a shaft possibly directed to Greek disparagement of the body).

■ **41** Each of the heavenly bodies possesses a real glory even if it differs from one body to another. In the same way (it is implied) God provides an equally real glory to the body of beings made in his own image, both on earth and in heaven.

■ **42-44** So far the answer to the question posed in v 35—"What kind of body can resurrected corpses have?" —has been indirect and analogical. Now it is addressed directly. The grammatical subject of the verses: **body** (*sōma*) does not appear until v 44 in the Greek. The general descriptions used in vv 36-38 and the categories employed in vv 39-41 are now supplemented by more concrete terms. The controlling image of seed sown is carried forward from vv 36-37. The formulaic expression **it is sown . . . it is raised**, expressive of the difference between the body of the present and the resurrection body, occurs four times in vv 42-44.

First, the body of the present is subject to decay; the resurrection body is **imperishable** (v 42). Second, the body of the present in its decay loses its dignity, but in its resurrected state is the embodiment of honor and **glory** (v 43). Third, the contrast between the body of the present and the future is the contrast between **weakness** and **power**. Fourth, the body that is buried belongs to the sphere of the human; the resurrection body belongs to the sphere of the Spirit (v 44).

The term here rendered **human** (*psuchē*) is variously translated as natural and "physical" (NRSV; BDAG [1100] prefers "physical"). The concluding statement affirms the reality of the **natural body** and the **spiritual body**. What this appears to mean is not that the natural body is composed of flesh while the spiritual body is composed of spirit. Rather, the physical body is animated by the natural power of life, while the spiritual body is animated by the power of the Spirit (Fee 2014, 869; Wright 2003, 348-52). Paul thus asserts the continuity between the two while also affirming their distinctness, particularly the superiority of the spiritual over the natural. This would almost certainly have caused raised eyebrows among the Corinthians who, on the one hand, could not envision bodily existence after death, but at the same time regarded themselves as being highly spiritual (14:37-38).

The overall thrust of 15:35-44 is that the resurrection of the body is not the reconstruction or reassembling of the body from the components of which it consisted before death. Change is involved (of which Paul will say more). This change is conveyed in part by the concept **glory** (*doxa* [vv 40 NRSV, 41 NRSV,

43]). Just as the glory of the heavenly bodies is greater than that of earthly bodies, so (it is implied) the glory of the resurrection body is greater than that of the earthly body. Just as there are differences between the glory of "heavenly bodies" and "earthly bodies" (v 40) there are also differences among heavenly bodies themselves (v 41). (The precise force of this last point is not clear. Perhaps it simply reinforces the idea of difference, which is Paul's chief concern in vv 39-41. He will make good use of it in the remainder of the chapter.)

2. The Character of the Resurrection Body as Indicated by the Contrast Between Adam and Christ (15:45-49)

The claim that there is such an entity as a spiritual body is now verified from Scripture. Adam and Christ are presented as two decisive figures, each begetting offspring after their kind.

■ **45** Genesis 2:7 (LXX) is quoted with the addition of the words **first** and **Adam**. This sets up the contrast between the **first Adam** who became a being endowed with natural life, and the **last Adam** who became **a life-giving spirit**. This confirms the distinction made in 1 Cor 15:44 between the "natural body" and the "spiritual body." It also sets the stage for the argument that the spiritual body comes *after* the natural, not before it.

■ **46-47** Verse 46 is probably directed against the view held by some Corinthians that they had already attained perfect spiritual existence and consequently needed no resurrection body. However, such a view was impossible, since **the first man** from whom they derived their existence belonged to **the dust** (v 47; Gen 2:7; 3:19). Hence, perishability and decay were part of their inheritance. **The second man** is of heavenly origin: the giver of life that lasts (1 Cor 15:47). The expression "from heaven" (NRSV) refers not to Christ's preexistence in heaven but to his resurrection life (Bruce 1976, 153). This will be made available to his people when he returns from heaven at his Parousia (v 23).

■ **48-49** The thought expressed in theoretical terms in vv 46-47 is now applied in personal terms to the Corinthians. Just as there are two ancestors: one the source of dust and decay, the other the source of the life of heaven (v 47), so the descendants of each exhibit the corresponding characteristics (v 48). Personal verbs are now used. The meaning of v 49 is debated because the manuscript evidence heavily favors reading the second verb as subjunctive ("let us bear" [*phoresōmen*]) rather than future ("we shall bear" [*phoresomen*]). Most scholars opt for the future (see the note in Thiselton 2000b, 1288-89) as do the NIV, NJB, and NRSV, on the grounds that vv 35-44 point that way. Others see the note of exhortation as preferable, not only because of the manuscript evidence, but also because it fits the need of the Corinthian situation. They believed all spirituality was theirs already. They needed to conform to the life of the man from heaven here and now (Fee 2014, 880). The Corinthians were not wrong in believing that the life of heaven was already available and being reproduced in them here and now. But this did not cancel out the truth that the fullness of the life of heaven awaits the coming of the man from heaven.

3. The Necessity for the Transformation of the Earthly Body (15:50-58)

The implied argument in vv 35-49 now reaches its conclusion. It began with questions about how the resurrection of the dead will take place and what will be the nature of their body. Both issues have been addressed, though analogically rather than directly. The illustration of the seed not only shows the reality of death but also the fact of the new body (vv 37-38). Similarly, the resurrected body exhibits a series of sharp contrasts with the body of the dead (vv 42-44). The idea of change has been present throughout, though in implicit rather than explicit form. It now comes to explicit expression in v 51.

■ **50** The opening phrase, "What I am saying . . . is this" (NRSV), indicates that Paul is about to summarize the argument he has been developing. Its essence is that what is corruptible (a body of **flesh and blood**) cannot find a place in what is incorruptible (**the kingdom of God**). The latter is enduring; the former is **perishable**. Just as there are moral barriers to be removed if one is to enter the kingdom (6:9-10), there is also a physical barrier common to all.

■ **51** The Corinthians could have readily agreed with Paul's conclusion in 15:50. They evidently believed that immaterial life after death was inevitable. Paul's conclusion was different—and stunning. He had news for them: "Look—I will **tell you a mystery**." For Paul **mystery** denoted not something that was unknown and unknowable, but that which had been unknown but was now revealed (2:1; Col 2:2). Part of his apostolic mission was to explain these mysteries (1 Cor 4:1; Rom 16:25-26; BDAG 662). His explanation was addressed in directly personal terms—**you** and, including himself, **we**.

There were two aspects. First, Paul and his readers would not all die before the coming of the eternal kingdom. Second, however, **all** (*pantes*) those who had died and those surviving till the Parousia would **be changed**. The living were as much in need of being changed as the dead. It would be God's doing (as the passive verb *allagēsometha* implies). At that moment, the living as well as the dead will exchange a natural body for a spiritual body, by which Paul means (as he will proceed to say) a body fashioned for eternity, removed from the ravages of time (Phil 3:20; see Flemming 2009, 201-3).

■ **52** Figurative language is now supplemented with the language of apocalyptic. The trumpet blast was a standard feature of apocalyptic description

(Isa 27:13; Zech 9:14; Rev 8:2, 6, 13). This trumpet would be **the last**. At its sounding, the dead will be raised, never to be touched by death again. The living will **be changed**. The verbs are divine passives: the twin actions are God's.

■ **53-54** The twin actions of resurrection and change are now defined more precisely. The image of clothing (NIV) was common in Jewish apocalyptic tradition (*1 En.* 62:15-16; 1QS 4:7-8) and is used widely in the NT in various ways (BDAG 333-34). Paul uses it to denote the new life of believers in Christ (Rom 13:12-14; Gal 3:27-28). Here the metaphor indicates that the life of the age to come will be bodily. To attain this end two actions are indispensable. If the dual focus of 1 Cor 15:51 and 52 is continued, then the **perishable** body that puts on imperishability refers to the dead; and the **mortal** that puts on **immortality** refers to the living. That is to say, the dead will be raised in bodies that are immune to corruption; and the living will exchange mortality for immortality. The effective result is the same for both.

This change is stated emphatically to be necessary (*dei*): it is something that **must** happen (NIV, NRSV). This emphasis is continued in v 54 in two ways. First, what is necessary must become a fact: "but when" (*hotan de* [NASB]). Second, the exact language of v 53 is repeated, leaving no doubt. Note particularly the fourfold repetition of "this" (*touto* [omitted in the NIV but present in the NRSV]); it is "*this* perishable body" and "*this* mortal body" that are in mind in both verses. This indicates clearly that Paul's focus in this context is on the body, as indeed it has been since v 35 (note the frequency of the term in vv 35, 37, 38 [2x], 40 [2x], 44 [3x]; compare "flesh and blood" [v 50] and **perishable** and **imperishable** in vv 52-54). This will happen as the fulfillment of Scripture. The passage in mind is Isa 25:8, which proclaims the overthrow of death. The past tense is used, indicating that death has already suffered defeat, even if its overthrow has not yet been completed. This will happen at the resurrection. The word "forever" in Isaiah is replaced by the phrase **in victory**, which expresses the import, even if not the words, of the original. (For discussion of Paul's use of the passage, see Beale and Carson 2007, 747-48; Fee 2014, 888-89.)

■ **55** The word **victory** is carried forward into the (partial) quotation of Hos 13:14. (On Paul's use of the passage, see Beale and Carson 2007, 748.) While the term does not appear in the original, the idea of victory over death is present. This is especially expressed in the taunt flung at death and the grave, asking **where** is death's **sting**. The image is that of the deadly bite of a viper (Rev 9:10)—which has been neutralized.

■ **56** Death's **sting** is now identified as **sin**, and what gives sin its **power** is **the law**. Sin is meaningful only because the law condemns it (Rom 5:13; 7:7-13). The language of sin and the condemnation it brings has not been prominent in 1 Corinthians, but its reality was clearly something to which Paul could make reference and expect to be understood (1 Cor 6:18; 7:28, 36; 8:12; 15:3, 17, 34). Sin brings condemnation because the law exposes it for the evil it is. Apart from sin, death would have no sting. Dying would merely be the mode of transition from this life to the next. But since sin, empowered by the law, gives death its character as the penalty of sin, death becomes the termination of life (vv 19, 21, 22) and hence the ultimate enemy (v 26). When death is defeated, sin is defeated; and when sin is defeated, the law has lost its sphere of operation.

■ **57** In contrast with the bleak picture painted in v 56, Paul now sounds the note of **victory**: bringing that term forward from vv 54-55. Several ideas are compressed within a few words. First, the victory is the gift of God. It is not a human accomplishment. Second, it is an ongoing, enduring victory. Death, the enemy, has lost its power to terrorize. Third, this victory has been accomplished **through our Lord Jesus Christ**. The victory was Christ's in the first place. It is he who drew the sting of death by absorbing and neutralizing it in his own sacrificial death (15:3; Rom 8:1-4; Gal 3:13). He shares that victory with us: now in expectation and at the Parousia in fulfillment when the life of resurrection fullness will be ours.

■ **58** The practical conclusion now follows. The connecting conjunction (*hōste*) is more precisely inferential than **therefore** (*oun*), carrying the sense "so then" and appealing to the possession of victory as a fact in 1 Cor 15:57. The chapter ends on a note of affection as it began (v 1): Paul's love for them remains deep and unshaken. Three responses are enjoined on the Corinthians. First, firmness or steadfastness. The term translated **stand firm** ("steadfast" [NRSV]; *hedraios*) denotes being solidly in place. In Col 1:23 it is used of not shifting from the hope promised in the gospel. Second, immovability. This is the only example of the term in the NT. The verbal form is used in harness with *hedraios* in Col 1:23. Third, involvement in the work of the Lord. This is expressed in terms of constant, unlimited involvement. What makes such labor sustainable is the confidence that it is not in vain. That fact that it is **in the Lord** guarantees this. Paul has described his own labor in these terms (1 Cor 15:10). To have seen his labor produce similar results in the lives of his converts has been confirmation of his own calling as well as theirs (1 Thess 1:2-5).

FROM THE TEXT

1. The reality of a body that suffers from progressive weakness and eventual dissolution—"a natural body" (v 44)—is an indisputable fact of life. The prospect of a body freed from decay and dissolution—"a spiritual body"—is

envisioned in the world of nature (vv 35-44) and realized in the risen Christ (vv 20-27). At the Parousia it will be realized in all believers (vv 51-54).

2. The body is not to be despised despite its weakness. Since it is to be raised and redeemed, it is to be treated as a gift of God. The doctrine of the resurrection implies that life in the body has moral significance (2 Cor 5:7-10). Hence, the body is not to be disdained or treated with contempt. At the same time, neither is it to be idolized. Despite its worth, our fallen body is the instrumental cause of our being distanced from Christ (2 Cor 5:16) as well as the requirement that we walk "by faith, not by sight" (2 Cor 5:7). Accordingly, it must be kept under control (1 Cor 9:24-27).

3. Death is not to be feared. It has already been defeated (15:55-57). The experience of dying becomes the means of transition from a life where perishability is inevitable to a life where it is impossible. Rather than being the path to extinction it becomes the door to immortality. At the same time, since it is an experience wholly unknown to us and involving separation from all that is known to us, it is understandable that the prospect and experience of dying should occasion apprehensiveness. Paul seems to have known both sides of the experience. On the one hand, he shrank from dying and wished he could pass directly to being with Christ (2 Cor 5:2-4). At the same time, his knowledge of the house prepared for him and the assurance of the Spirit made him confident in the midst of his apprehensiveness (2 Cor 5:1, 5-9).

4. Personal identity is not lost in the act of transformation of the living or resurrection of the dead. The resurrected Jesus was identifiably the same as the Jesus of the ministry. In the same way the "we who are alive" (2 Cor 4:11) are the same as the "we" who believe (v 13) and will be raised (v 14). The language used denotes relationships. At the same time, the life of the age to come is embodied life (2 Cor 5:1), and body is the guarantor because it is the bearer of continued identity.

5. We are to live now in faith in the reality of Christ's victory over death (1 Cor 15:57-58). The victory declared to have been won (vv 54-55) is now traced to its source: the Lord Jesus Christ. The power of his sacrificial death (1:17-18; 2:2-4) and mighty resurrection (15:20-22) are the twin guarantees of victory over death to those who trust him. On this secure foundation believers may engage confidently and continuously in the Lord's work. Christ's victory over death and sin assures us that our labor, performed in his name, will not go for nothing.

Paul's Understanding of the Resurrection Body

1. The guideline for Paul's understanding of the resurrection body was the risen body of Jesus. This is clear from the proportionate amount of space he

gives in 1 Cor 15:1-11 to Christ's death and burial on the one hand (vv 3-4a) and his resurrection on the other (vv 4b-8). Not least significant is the fact that the two individuals he mentions by name as witnesses of the resurrection—Cephas (Peter [v 5]) and James (v 7)—are the two whom he saw on his visit to Jerusalem following his conversion (Gal 1:18-19). Both were singularly well placed to bear witness to the physicality of Christ's risen form. Peter is reported as having witnessed several of the appearances of the risen Jesus in which his physicality is particularly noted (Luke 24:33-43; John 20:6-7, 19-20, 24-28). James, likewise, was uniquely well placed to bear witness to the bodily character of the risen Jesus, by virtue of having grown up with Jesus as his brother. Like his other brothers, James did not believe in him (Mark 3:21; John 7:5). Apparently, it took a special appearance of the risen Jesus to bring him to faith (1 Cor 15:7; compare Acts 1:14). It is not surprising, therefore, that, when Paul visited Jerusalem following his conversion, he should have spent all his time there with Peter and James. This is not to say that the resurrection of Jesus was the sole topic of their conversations. However, it was a very probable topic in the light of the evidence listed (Bruce 1982, 98-100; Fung 1988, 74).

2. The body of the resurrection differs from the natural body in that it is animated by spirit. It is therefore described as a spiritual body (1 Cor 15:42-44). (It is described more explicitly in Phil 3:20-21. See Fee 1995, 375-84; Flemming 2009, 79-80, 201-3.) This is the destiny of those who have put their faith in the risen Christ (1 Cor 15:48-49). Just as the body of the risen Christ was subject to the spirit and therefore not bound by the limitations of space and time, so it will be with believers at the Parousia.

3. The resurrection body is the work of a creative change or transformation wrought by God (vv 51-52). It is not the reconstitution of the body from the materials of the natural body. It is rather the re-creation of the natural body into a form that is identifiably the same while free from the confines imposed by time and space. Hence, this transformed body will be free from the corruptibility that involves bodily change, but it does not involve loss of identity. While there is an element of change, there is also an element of continuity (Green 2008, 173-78).

4. In 1 Cor 15 Paul does not address the question of what happens at death to believers who die before the Parousia. However, he takes up the issue in 2 Cor 5. There is much debate as to what Paul means by the "eternal house" referred to in 2 Cor 5:1. Some claim the passage is too obscure for any plain conclusion to be drawn (Dunn 1998, 61; Schreiner 2001, 855-56). Two things seem to be reasonably clear. First, Paul makes plain that he views with distaste any kind of bodiless existence such as is involved in physical death (vv 2-3). Second, he appears to envisage the swallowing up of mortality by life as God's gift guaranteed by the Spirit (vv 4-5). This appears to mean that, while the perishable body suffers decay and will not be restored imperishably until the Parousia, yet fellowship with God will not be broken. If anything, it will be greater since it will mean being at home with the Lord despite being away from the body (vv 6-9; Lincoln 1991, 59-71). At death there is no break in communion with God for the believer. (For reviews of the range of more specific options, see R. P. Martin 2014, 252-72; Harris 2005, 375-80; Carver 2009, 168-82.)

VII. REMAINING ISSUES AND FINAL GREETINGS: I CORINTHIANS 16:1-24

Overview

Chapter 16 stands apart from the rest of the letter. The main arguments are over. The comprehensive exhortation has been given (15:58; Mitchell 1992, 291 n. 596). At the same time, chs 1—15 have not dropped out of Paul's mind, even less the situation that evoked them. The chapter has been understood in a variety of ways. On the one hand, it has been seen as a random collection of exhortations and greetings (Garland 2003, 750, 764; Ciampa and Rosner 2010, 839). On the other hand, it has been read as containing final matters of concern (Thiselton 2000b, 1315). There is truth in both views. The items drawn together belong here because they relate to the movements of Paul, Timothy, and others as these will have bearings on the church in Corinth.

The chapter is freighted with travel language: coming (*erchomai* [vv 2, 5, 10, 11, 12]); sending (*pempō* [vv 3, 6, 11]); passing through (*dierchomai* [v 5]); remaining (*epimenō* [vv 7, 8]). However, it is the aims and accomplishments of these comings and goings that concerned Paul. It is difficult not to see the conflicts in Corinth (3:3-9; 4:6-7, 17-20) with their specific references to Timothy, Apollos, and Paul's declared intention to visit Corinth as being picked up in the closing verses. The same may apply to the references to other churches (16:1, 19, 20) whose existence the Corinthians were apparently in danger of overlooking (14:33-36). The repeated exhortations to love (16:14, 19, 20, 22, 24) inevitably recall 4:21; 8:1; and ch 13. What this amounts to is that it is a mistake to read the chapter merely as a collection of afterthoughts: unless, that is, one sees the afterthoughts as being rooted in the forethoughts. If any difference of tone is discernible between the two, it may reveal something of the state of the relationship between Paul and his readers, as well as among the Corinthians themselves. Mitchell is almost certainly correct in seeing the danger of factionalism as lying behind many of Paul's specific suggestions and observations in the chapter (1992, 177-79). Accordingly, his language is carefully guarded.

A. The Collection for the Church in Jerusalem (16:1-4)

BEHIND THE TEXT

The collection for believers in Jerusalem was a matter of prime importance to Paul. The fact that he had given instructions to the Galatian churches on the subject (16:1) is sufficient evidence of this. That the Corinthians knew of it is clearly implied. If Paul was the source of their information, he evidently did not give them directions as to how they should collect it. Had he avoided doing so out of fear of being accused of money-grabbing (9:3-15)?

The whole idea of the collection comes to light more clearly in Paul's second visit to Jerusalem (Gal 2:1-2) when James, Cephas, and John recognized the validity of his mission to the Gentiles (vv 7-9). The one thing they requested was that he should "continue to remember the poor" (v 10). This is best understood as referring to financial help for the materially poor. If Acts 11:27-30 and Rom 15:25-28 refer to this same issue, as is widely agreed, then this is clearly the meaning. However, for Paul it carried the further significance that the Gentiles were also incorporated into the people of God (Longenecker 1998b, 55-61; Lyons 2012, 121-22; S. McKnight 1993, 143-47).

IN THE TEXT

■ 1 The expression **now about** (*peri de*) has already appeared in the letter to mark the transition to a new topic (7:1, 25; 8:1; 12:1). It may also denote a topic raised by the recipients (compare 7:1, 25). The issue here is **the collection**: a term used only here in the NT (BDAG 597), referring to a monetary gift. It is designated "for the saints" (*tous hagious*, lit. "the holy ones"; "the saints" [NASB, NRSV]; **the Lord's people** [NIV]). The Corinthians have already been described as saints (1:2); they also are part of the holy people of God. It is assumed that the Corinthians had contact with the churches in Galatia, which were within Paul's apostolic care and direction, just as the church in Corinth. Accordingly, the Corinthians should handle the collection as the Galatians were doing.

■ 2 Even so, Paul now spells out in detail how the collection should be gathered. (*a*) It should be given regularly. **On the first day of every week** is a clear reference to Sunday as a worship day, while avoiding the pagan name "Sunday" (Fee 2014, 899-900; Laansma in *DLNT*, 879-86). (*b*) It should be given by everyone. (*c*) It should be given generously, based on "whatever extra you earn" (NRSV). The purpose of this planned giving was that there would be no need for taking a collection when Paul came. This would have a twofold advantage. First, it would guarantee a larger total than a one-time offering. Second, it would spare Paul from having to be a fundraiser, which had been a cause of gossip during his previous ministry in Corinth (9:18).

■ 3-4 It appears that Paul had two parties to satisfy when it came to the delivery of the collection. First, the Corinthians. Since they had given the money, they would expect that some of their own number would be involved in presenting it to the Jerusalem church. Since the offering would be in metal currency, a sufficient number of bodies would be needed to transport it physically as well as safely. Paul recognizes this and promises letters introducing the Corinthians to the Jerusalem church. The second interested party was Paul himself. He also wanted to go to Jerusalem, but there was doubt about the advisability of this. The uncertainty probably refers to his reception in Jerusalem (Rom 15:25-26, 30-31; compare Acts 20:22-23; 21:10-13). If he did go, it would be as leader: **they will accompany me** (1 Cor 16:4). Whether by letter or personal presence, he would be seen to be the ultimate author of the collection and more importantly—of the Gentile mission. As F. F. Bruce puts it: "The Gentile delegates themselves were Paul's own offering, presented not so much to the mother-church as to the Lord who, many years before, had called Paul to be his apostle to the Gentiles" (1977, 323).

B. Paul's Forthcoming Travel Plans (16:5-9)

The mention of his intention to visit Corinth in vv 2-3 leads naturally to a discussion of his travel plans. He evidently had particular reasons for the route he proposed to follow, though they remain unstated, except in regard to his time for setting out.

■ **5** He planned to follow the land route through Macedonia rather than the faster and shorter sea route from Ephesus. The presumptive points of interest in Macedonia were the churches in Philippi and Thessalonica. The church in Philippi had experienced conflict stirred up by Judaizers (Phil 3:2—4:1; Flemming 2009, 155-62). The church in Thessalonica had been born in trouble emanating from the same source, though not confined to it (Paige 2017, 32-35). Paul thus had good reasons for "passing through Macedonia," as the repetition of that phrase suggests.

■ **6** In contrast to "passing through Macedonia" (v 5) he is planning to stay (*parameno*; compare Phil 1:25) with the Corinthians through the winter. They would then be able to help him on his way. The verb translated **help** (*propempō*: "send forward") is a technical term for providing food and other resources (MM 544). However, this plan was only a possibility (*tuchon*: **perhaps** [NIV and NRSV]).

■ **7** The alternatives Paul faced were seeing the Corinthians sooner for a short period of time or later for a long period. There was evidently something in the Macedonian situation that required his attention before too long, if not immediately. By the same token, there was something in the Corinthian situation that called for an extended stay.

■ **8-9** A factor that took precedence over all others was his current ministry in Ephesus. Pentecost was the Greek name for the Festival of Weeks, which fell on the fiftieth day after Passover. The reason for Paul's delay in leaving Ephesus was the prospect of his ministry there. Remarkably, he describes this in terms of the greatness of both the opportunity and the opposition. (That ministry is recounted in Acts 19:21—20:3.)

There is necessarily no indication in 1 Corinthians of how or whether these plans worked out. That it became an occasion of conflict between the Corinthians and Paul is evident from 2 Cor 1:8—2:13. (For discussion, see Carver 2009, 95-113; Ralph Martin 2014, 157-80.)

C. Two Other Visitors to Corinth: Timothy and Apollos (16:10-12)

Paul now names two others, a visit from whom would be profitable to the Corinthians. Timothy had joined Paul during his mission to Greece (Acts 16:1-3) and become a trusted colleague. Paul refers to him three times as a co-worker who does the Lord's work as he does himself (Rom 16:21; 1 Cor 16:10; 1 Thess 3:2; Ellis 1993, 183-89). Apollos and Paul also seem to have crossed paths first during Paul's mission to Greece (Acts 18:24—19:7). Unlike Timothy, Apollos never seems to have maintained an ongoing involvement in Paul's ministry, though their personal relationship apparently remained unbroken (Blue 1993, 37-39).

■ 10 Timothy had already left for Corinth (4:17) but had not yet arrived. The opening clause is best translated "whenever Timothy comes." The following words sound a peremptory note prompted less by Timothy's fragility than by the Corinthians' capacity for bellicosity, which Paul knew only too well (4:19-20). Paul's purpose in sending Timothy was to give the Corinthians a refresher course in Paul's teaching (4:17). The double implication of these travel data is that Timothy was not the bearer of 1 Corinthians and that it might reach Corinth before he did.

■ 11 The Corinthian reaction to Timothy that Paul feared was that he might be treated with contempt. What they should rather do is facilitate (the same word, *propempo*, used in v 6) his return to Paul, who was waiting for him. It is not clear whether **the brothers** were Timothy's traveling companions whom Paul awaited, or Paul's companions in Ephesus who awaited Timothy's return there.

■ 12 The expression **now about** (*peri de*) appears for the last time and denotes, as previously, a matter raised by the Corinthians. Apollos, referred to as **our brother** and earlier as a co-worker (3:5-9), had made a profoundly favorable impression on the Corinthians as elsewhere (Acts 18:24-28). His earlier imperfect understanding of Jesus, which nonetheless involved ministering in the power of the preresurrection Spirit (Luke 10:1-2, 10-11, 16-24; Acts 18:25) was made good through the instruction of Priscilla and Aquila (Acts 18:24-28; compare 19:1-6). Allied with his Alexandrian eloquence, this made him a great favorite among those Corinthians who placed a high value on rhetoric (1 Cor 1:17, 20; 2:1, 4). He was at least a factor in the emergence of parties in the Corinthian church: no doubt as unwillingly as Paul (1:12; 3:4-9). The Corinthians very much wished Apollos to return, and Paul urged him to do so in company with **the brothers**. The firm refusal of Apollos to do so at this time most probably indicates that the danger of party strife remained. This may be confirmed by his readiness to return when the time was right (*eukairēsē*: a term that could have more than one shade of meaning [BDAG 406-7]).

D. The Need for Stability in the Corinthian Church and the Role of Stephanas (16:13-18)

It is debated whether these verses are merely casual concluding thoughts or carry echoes of earlier issues. Witherington sees 16:13-14 as a recapitulation of the basic purpose of the letter as stated in 1:10; and 16:15-18 as a practical strategy for achieving it (1995, 318-19). This is probably correct.

■ **13-14** The four verbs in v 13 are present imperatives and therefore enjoin an ongoing mindset and attitude. Constancy and commitment—features not common among the Corinthians—are prescribed. The one area in which this is specified is **the faith** (*tei pistei* [v 13]), the definite article denoting not the act of believing or trust but the thing believed: the gospel (Thiselton 2000b, 1336; Garland 2003, 766). Above all is the comprehensive solution: doing everything in love. Paul has not changed his mind since ch 13.

■ **15-18** The inclusion of this material about **Stephanas** here seems odd at first sight. There is the further feature that 16:15 begins with a strong expression of concern: **I urge you**, which is then interrupted by a description of Stephanas and his ministry. The original introductory statement is not picked up until v 16. (The KJV and NASB preserve the order of the Greek text. The NIV and NRSV delay the introductory statement till the beginning of v 16.)

■ **15-16** Stephanas and his household have appeared already in the letter as one of two households in Corinth baptized by Paul (1:16). Here two further data are given: first, Stephanas and his household were Paul's first converts in Achaia (the area of southern Greece of which Corinth was the capital); and second, they took upon themselves ministry to the saints. The form of this ministry is not spelled out. The evidence indicates that it involved the use of their resources for the Lord's people. This was the reverse of the prevailing pattern in Greek society in which the lower orders were regarded as existing to support the lifestyles of their social superiors (Winter 2001, ch 9). Paul's message to the Corinthians was that, if they were to submit to anyone, let it be to such as Stephanas.

■ **17-18** Paul himself was the recipient of the ministry of Stephanas and his companions who had arrived recently in Ephesus from Corinth. They probably brought the Corinthians' letter to Paul (7:1). **Fortunatus and Achaicus** were probably freedmen (16:17; for a discussion of possibilities, see Garland 2003, 770-71). Their names meaning "lucky one" and "man of Achaia" suggest as much. Together with Stephanas they represented opposite ends of the social scale, a phenomenon that some in the Corinthian church found difficult to digest. For Paul it was exactly the opposite. Together their presence made up for the absence of the Corinthians. They brought refreshment and renewal to Paul's spirit, just as they had done in their home church (if only the Corinthians had eyes to see it!). The closing word is not a statement (as in the NIV) but an order: "So give recognition to such persons" (v 18 NRSV).

E. Final Greetings (16:19-24)

For all their casual appearance, these are at the same time carefully calculated and considered. The way in which Paul says farewell conveys his special message to the Corinthians.

■ 19 The greetings from the **churches** in **Asia** where Paul was then ministering (v 8) served also to remind the Corinthians that they were not the only believers on earth (14:33, 36). Greetings came also from **Aquila and Priscilla** and the church in their house (compare Rom 16:3-5). Earlier they had been in Corinth when Paul arrived. He stayed with them and worked with them, for they shared the same trade (Acts 18:1-4). The order of their names is usually reversed and the form "Prisca" is used by Paul (Rom 16:3; 1 Cor 16:19; 2 Tim 4:19 [all NRSV]) rather than **Priscilla** (a diminutive form), which is favored by Luke (Acts 18:2, 18, 26). It may be that Aquila is named here first because he came from Pontus (Acts 18:2), a region commonly dismissed as uncultured and ignorant. His prominence in the church in Ephesus illustrates again Paul's insistence that the social distinctions that divided the Corinthian church had no place in the church of God (den Dulk 2020, 177-89).

■ 20 **Brothers and sisters** can refer either to Christians generally or Christian workers. Since they are apparently distinguished from "the church" (1 Cor 16:19), the latter is probably their meaning here (Ellis 1993, 183-85). The **kiss** was a common social greeting within families and beyond. In the churches it was an expression of mutual fellowship among those of very different levels of society, hence its designation as **holy** (Rom 16:16; 2 Cor 13:12; 1 Thess 5:26; Keener 2000a, 628-29).

■ 21 Paul regularly used an amanuensis in writing his letters (Rom 16:22). This was common practice in the world of his day. Equally common was an entry in the hand of the author authenticating the letter as his (Deissmann 1978, 166-67). This was Paul's habit (Gal 6:11; Col 4:18; 2 Thess 3:17).

■ 22 The wording of the verse is unusual in several respects. First, the word for **love** (*philei*) is not used elsewhere by Paul except for Titus 3:15, where it occurs also in a word of greeting. Second, the language of anathema (**be cursed**) and invocation (**Come, Lord**) is formal and may be liturgical in origin (Bruce 1976, 162). The language of anathema is found in Gal 1:8-9, where it is pronounced against those who reject Paul's gospel (compare 2 Thess 3:14-15). This would appear to be its import here: it is a final warning to those in Corinth who oppose the gospel. *Marana tha* can be taken either as a prayer (**Come, Lord**, as in the NIV and NRSV) or a declaration ("our Lord is coming" or "has come"). On any understanding it speaks against the ideas and conduct found among the Corinthians and contested by Paul (Wu 1993, 559-60). Let them love the Lord rather than their own opinions!

■ **23** The letter ends as it began (1 Cor 1:3): with the invocation of God's grace. Paul saw his entire life as being held in the embrace of God's grace (Gal 1:15-16). Many of his letters begin with it; all of them end with it. It is both a greeting and a benediction. There is no greater gift.

■ **24** An additional statement of Paul's personal affection following the invocation of God's grace is unique to 1 Corinthians. While it has been disputed (Garland 2003, 774-75) it seems likely that Paul's corrective treatment of Corinthians—which has continued into the final chapter (including the Final Greetings [v 22])—has prompted this expression of his deeply felt affection. It is emphatically personal. He sends **his** love to **all** of them in the covenant fellowship of **Christ Jesus**.

FROM THE TEXT

In ch 16 Paul is clearly addressing a local situation that dictated the particular issues he treats. At the same time these issues embody principles relevant in other times and places. Among these the following are given particular notice.

Support for the needy (16:1-4). In the Corinthian situation this meant monetary support for the poor in Jerusalem, where it had the further meaning of expressing the unity of Jews and Gentiles in Christ. It will assume different meanings in different settings. Even so, the need for it remains as the differences between classes, nationalities, and races demonstrate. The engine that drives it is grace. Freely you have received, freely give (Matt 10:8). Just as Paul gave directions regarding the giving of the collection, so the showing of grace should be intentional. It is more than what is commonly meant by "being charitable." It is the spontaneous expression to others of the grace that believers themselves have received. Paul will develop and apply this argument more fully in 2 Cor 8. There he cites the generosity of the Macedonian churches (1 Cor 16:1-7) as being grounded, not in any order from him, but in the surpassing grace of Christ (vv 8-9).

All members of the community can be of service irrespective of social status. The Greco-Roman world was highly structured socially. The socially advantaged expected recognition of their superior status, not least when they gave gifts or benefits to their inferiors. Such gifts were expected to be received with public acclaim. Paul explodes this rigid stratification by naming Fortunatus and Achaicus, who at the very least were freedmen, in the same breath as Stephanas as together a means of grace to himself. This was and is a mark of authentic Christian community.

There is a clear place in the Christian life for watchfulness. Verse 13 has the appearance of marking a change from consideration of how the Corinthians should act in regard to issues involving or affecting others to a focus on how they should safeguard themselves. It is not an unknown idea in Pauline thought (see 10:12; Gal 5:1; Eph 6:11, 13, 14; Phil 1:27; Col 4:12; 2 Thess 2:15). Significantly the verbs in 1 Cor 16:13 are all present imperatives—constant watchfulness is called for. It is instructive that when Paul speaks in this vein he can either express his thought absolutely: **Be on your guard; . . . be courageous; be strong**; or he can express it with an indirect object: **stand firm in the faith**. In 10:12-13 he intermingles the need for watchfulness with the faithfulness of God. The Christian life is not a matter of being put on automatic pilot. But neither is it a matter of being left to our own devices. The armor of God is available. It is for us to gird it on (Eph 6:13; 2 Thess 2:15).

The comprehensive grace is love. That, indeed, is the dominant theme of the letter: either deploring its absence (1 Cor 1:10; 8:1) or extolling its presence (13:1—14:1). In the concluding ten verses it is the theme of Paul's final exhortation: everything should be done in love (16:14). It is exemplified in Stephanas and his household who had **devoted themselves to the service of the Lord's people** (v 15). Not to "love the Lord" is the ultimate condemnation (v 22). Paul could not conclude without adding a conclusion to the "official" conclusion (v 23), assuring the Corinthians of his deeply affectionate love for them (v 24). In these uncalculated expressions we see into the heart of the apostle who can instruct, commend, remonstrate, and rebuke, and yet do all under the motivation of the love he had come to know in Christ Jesus.

www.ingramcontent.com/pod-product-compliance
Lightning Source LLC
Chambersburg PA
CBHW070759230426
43665CB00017B/2419